First published and distributed by
viction workshop ltd

viction:ary™

viction workshop ltd
Unit C, 7/F,
Seabright Plaza, 9-23 Shell Street,
North Point, Hong Kong
Url: www.victionary.com
Email: we@victionary.com

@victionworkshop
@victionworkshop
@victionary
@victionary

Edited and produced by viction:ary
Creative Direction: Victor Cheung
Design: Leanne Lee
Editorial: YL Lim, Ynes Filleul
Coordination: Leanne Lee, Katherine Wong
Production: Bryan Leung

ISBN 9789887684558
Printed and bound in China

CODE CRAFTED

PREFACE

Design is in a state of perpetual evolution. With every technological leap, the boundaries of creativity expand, as the tools at our disposal grow more sophisticated than ever. While it was often seen as a static endeavour in the past—with fixed logos, rigid guidelines, and immovable templates—it now reflects the state of the world around us and the dynamic, ever-changing nature of the accelerating digital age.

As the interconnectedness of technology, culture, and society continues to shape our experiences and redefine the way we live, work, and communicate, design must reflect and respond to this fluidity. By highlighting an increasingly integrated approach that merges creativity and coding in the following pages, we hope to pave the way for a future where generative branding and adaptive design become the new norm.

At its core, CODECRAFTED represents a paradigm shift. Traditional ways of thinking are giving way to a mindset that embraces creative coding as an integral part of the design process. This approach is not about replacing designers with algorithms or automating creativity; rather, it is about empowering them with what they need to elevate their work for modern audiences. By harnessing the potential of code, they can craft visual systems that adapt in real time, unlocking possibilities that were once unimaginable.

PREFACE

One of the most exciting aspects of this emerging field is its profound impact on branding. Historically, brands have been defined by visual identities that remain constant across platforms; however, in today's fast-paced digital landscape, they risk feeling outdated and unresponsive. Creative coding offers a solution in this regard by introducing agility and adaptability into brand design, enabling visual identities that can shift and transform according to the context while staying true to their essence.

The rise of creative coding is also part of a larger trend influencing different industries, from fashion and architecture to entertainment and product design. Designers are increasingly adopting interdisciplinary approaches, blending art, technology, and science to create experiences that break boundaries. Driven by advancements in programming languages, machine learning, and real-time rendering software, they are able to bring fresh concepts to life that prioritise systems over outcomes, process over product, and motion over permanence.

In creating this book, we were fortunate to consult leading experts Patrik Hübner and Tim Rodenbröker, whose work and insights have been invaluable in shaping our understanding of this new frontier. Patrik, through his expertise in generative branding, continues to demonstrate how this approach can revolutionise identity systems, while Tim, a pioneer in creative coding and education, inspires a new

PREFACE

generation of designers to embrace code as a creative tool. Together, their contributions highlight the transformative potential of their approaches for the design industry as a whole.

CODECRAFTED is also more than a theoretical exploration; it is a showcase of compelling projects from around the world that stand as testament to the impact that creative coding can have to inspire, innovate, and challenge conventions. Each project tells a story of experimentation, discovery, and the blending of human creativity with computational logic – demonstrating how generative or adaptive identity systems and design can respond to shifting frameworks while pushing the boundaries of what branding can achieve in the digital age.

Looking ahead, we can expect creative coding to play an even greater role in shaping the visual landscape. Artificial intelligence, for instance, is already starting to influence design practices, and while it cannot replace the intuition, vision, and human touch of a designer, it can augment creative processes – helping generate ideas, test variations, and optimise workflows. Similarly, real-time data integration will enable designs that respond dynamically to user behaviour, environmental conditions, or even global events for visually striking outcomes that are also deeply connected to their context.

Another exciting development is the integration of virtual and augmented reality into generative branding. As immersive technologies become more accessible, designers will be inspired to think beyond traditional screens and explore new dimensions of interaction, where a brand's identity could be experienced as a living, breathing environment – an experience that blends storytelling, technology, and emotion in unprecedented ways.

Whether you are a seasoned designer, a curious coder, or someone entirely new to the field, we hope that this book will spark your imagination and motivate you to look into new possibilities, collaborate across disciplines, and constantly rethink what design can be. This is not just about learning a new skill or mastering a tool; it is about embracing a mindset that encourages exploration, adaptability, and a willingness to question what you once knew. As you read, we hope you will view these pages not just as a guide, but as a springboard for your own journey into uncharted territory – so dive in, experiment boldly, and let your creativity lead the way!

CREATIVE HIGHLIGHT

Photography: Bob Sala

PATRIK HÜBNER

As a programming designer and creative director, Patrik Hübner has been working at the intersection of design and technology for over 15 years. With a rich background in communication and brand design, he discovered the potential of generative systems in 2014 and quickly became one of the few individuals to successfully establish this seamless blend of algorithmic creativity, data and storytelling into dynamic branding frameworks on a global scale. Today, he works as a generative designer and consultant with brands, agencies and cultural institutions to help them craft meaningful and engaging experiences across a multitude of touchpoints. As a lecturer at universities, he teaches on the topic of generative design, is a regular keynote speaker, gives workshops and shares his expertise through his books.

Patrik's clients include Landor, Interbrand, VML, Publicis, FutureBrand, The New York Times, Evian, Petronas and Lexus. He has also given talks at Deutsche Telekom, IBM, Columbia University, Carnegie Mellon University, The Atlantic as well as events such as re:publica Berlin and Dutch Design Week.

Since 2018, his generative work has won over 30 design and brand awards, including the ADC Award, the European Design Award, the German Design Award, the D&AD Award, the Red Dot Award, the World Brand Design Award and many more.

Find out more at www.patrik-huebner.com.

FROM FIXED TO FLUID: A SHIFT IN PERSPECTIVE

I didn't come into design through a traditional path. My gateway was code. For as long as I can remember, I've been drawn to this peculiar space between design and technology—a space where logic meets creativity, where structure and expression collide in unexpected ways. In this space, code never felt like just a tool to develop applications or solve problems, it always felt like an empowering extension of my curious mind.

Long before I had the words to describe it, I was captivated by the idea that the results of my creative explorations didn't have to be confined to a singular fixed outcome—that with code, my work could be something fluid and emergent. In my early days, this meant spending caffeine-fuelled nights tirelessly building small experiments—interactive visuals that responded to sound, kinetic sculptures that responded to human motion, systems that transformed aspects of their environment into unexpected visual expressions. Throughout hundreds of experiments, I discovered that with code, I wasn't limited to just determining what something looked like—I could dictate how it behaved, transformed and interacted in real time. I could set a stage of possibilities and watch excitedly as new opportunities unfolded before my very eyes, often in ways I couldn't have predicted. This discovery—that design could be adaptive, interactive and continuously unfolding—actively shaped and influenced by systems, data, people and our very environment, challenged what I had learned about traditional creative work. And it didn't take long for my mind to wander beyond the scope of my explorations. After all, I thought, if my experiments could be dynamic, why couldn't a brand?

THAT CHANGED EVERYTHING FOR ME.

I became fascinated by the idea that a brand's expression didn't have to be limited to a fixed set of assets—that it could instead function as a dynamic framework, capable of generating endless variations while remaining unmistakably itself. If I could create dynamic identities that weren't just expressed as static fragments, but as living frameworks that adapted to their environment, what new forms of brand expression would emerge?

This perspective inspired me to merge my work as a creative director in communication and brand design with my newly acquired generative mindset. At first, these ideas existed at the fringes of my mainstream design practice. But when I saw an opportunity to break beyond rigid structures and embrace this approach fully, I jumped on it and never looked back. Ever since then, this way of thinking has shaped my approach to how I work with international brands, agencies and cultural institutions around the world. It has allowed me to collaborate with some of the brightest minds in the industry on projects where design is not just about execution, but about building meaningful connections that empower brands to evolve and tell their stories in impactful new ways.

What started as a personal journey soon revealed itself as a fundamental shift happening across the industry. The more I worked with forward-thinking brands and institutions, the clearer it became: the traditional rules of branding were no longer enough—a new approach was needed. And as the diverse selection of projects and examples in this book from all over the world so powerfully illustrates, the real challenge in today's industry is no longer to simply define what a brand is. The challenge is to design how a brand becomes.

A NEW AGE OF BRANDING

The act of branding has always been a process of distillation—taking something vast and complex and turning it into something simple, recognisable and consistent. For decades, designers have refined and perfected this process, aiming to craft brand identities that are intentional, cohesive and timeless. For the most part, a brand was a fixed presence, executed consistently across print, packaging, advertising and digital channels.

BUT SOMETHING FUNDAMENTAL HAS CHANGED.

The world that brands exist in today is one of constant acceleration—where culture seems to move at the speed of algorithms, where brands live in a thousand contexts simultaneously, where engagement happens in real time across devices, platforms and networks that never stop shifting. A modern brand can't afford to be a singular entity anymore. It has to exist in a network of interactions, constantly shaping and reshaping itself through a series of dynamic moments that unfold across an ever-expanding landscape.

This is where Generative Branding is at home, and where it matters most. As a necessary response to a new reality—one in which branding can no longer be a fixed act but must become a fluid system. A good generative brand does not solely rely on mechanical repetition however; it thrives on variation within a set of guiding principles. It is not controlled in the traditional sense but orchestrated—designed to shift and respond while staying true to its core identity. In a modern world where everything static and rigid is bound to break down, flexible and dynamic generative brands thrive.

THE DESIGNER'S ROLE IS EVOLVING

As the many examples in this book illustrate, branding is undergoing a fundamental transformation. The challenge is no longer *how do we design a brand?* but rather *how do we design a brand that continuously designs itself?*

For many, this transition feels uncomfortable. Design, at its core, has always been about intentionality—about making precise choices, refining details, shaping experiences with clarity. But in a world that refuses to stand still, the most empowering thing a designer can do is let go of control and embrace emergence. This is not about surrendering authorship; it is about redefining it. A generative mindset invites creatives to leverage both human intuition and computational power—curating systems where machines generate possibilities and designers bring meaning, direction and refinement to what unfolds.

I want to emphasise that I wholeheartedly believe that the true power of this approach isn't found in the automation of design. Nor is it found in removing the designer's hand from the process. If anything, a generative approach demands even deeper curiosity, sharper vision and more strategic thinking than ever before.

The true power of generative creativity is in how it shifts the designer's role from crafting individual visual artifacts to designing the conditions for an entire identity to emerge from its interaction with the world.

Generative Branding is not a rejection of traditional design; it is an expansion of it. It retains the core principles of craftsmanship, intuition and storytelling but extends them through systems-thinking, data, interaction and real-time adaptability. This transformation is not just about how brands behave but about how designers think and act. To design for the future, creatives will have to move beyond the idea of branding as a fixed act and recognise it as an ongoing dialogue—one that continuously unfolds between brand, audience and context. The challenge ahead is not simply to navigate complexity: it is to create with it.

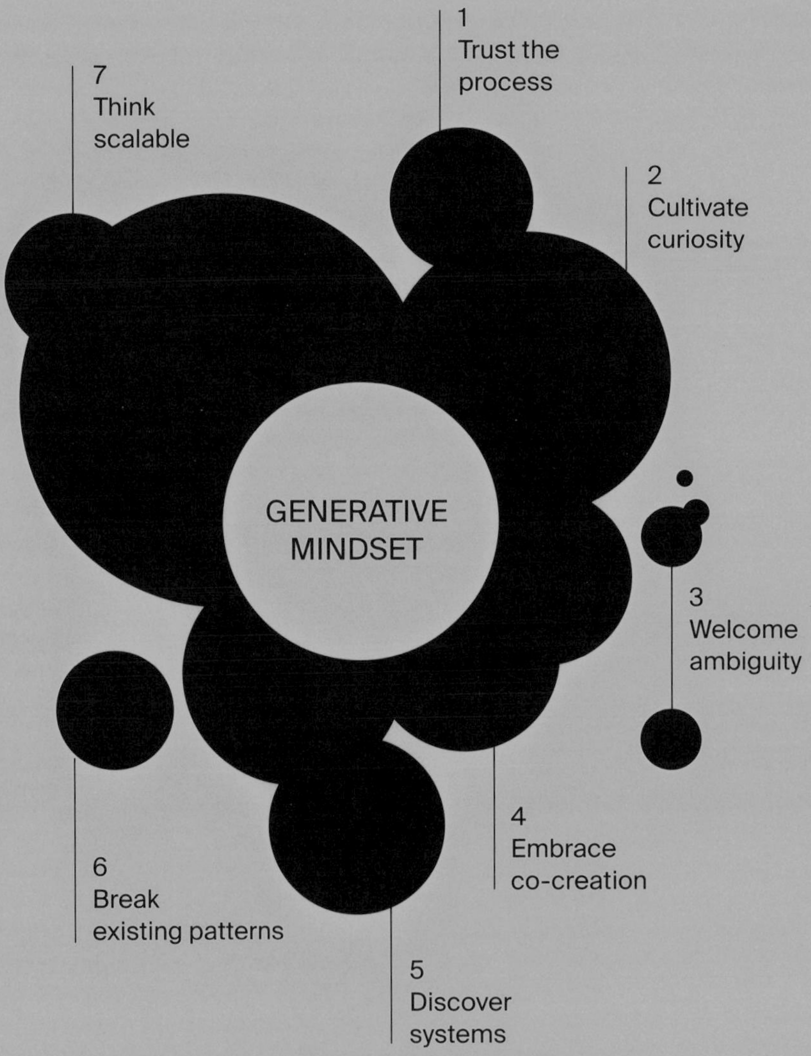

The core principles of a generative mind. Design is a conversation—a space where ideas emerge through connection, interaction and co-creative exploration, delivering lasting and meaningful impact in motion.

CREATIVE CODING AND GENERATIVE BRAND DESIGN

Before getting into this section, I want to point out and acknowledge that there are almost as many definitions of the terms Creative Coding and Generative Design as there are practitioners in the field, each bringing their valid perspectives and approaches to the table. What follows are my personal findings based on years of experience. My goal in making a clear distinction between Creative Coding and Generative Brand Design is not to claim a singular, absolute definition nor is it to exclude anyone's practice or perspective, but rather to provide you with a useful way of understanding their unique strengths and where I believe they best fit in the creative process. By drawing this line, I aim to highlight how each approach serves a different purpose so that you can better appreciate their roles and harness their full potential on your creative journey. I encourage you to share your thoughts and ideas—the beauty of this space is that it is unfolding before our very eyes, shaped by the perspectives and contributions of those who engage with it.

As we shift from static brand identities to fluid, adaptive systems, it's easy to assume that Generative Brand Design is an extension of the field of Creative Coding. After all, both involve computation, both rely on algorithmic thinking and both deal with systems rather than static compositions. But beneath the surface, their mindsets are fundamentally different—one is an open-ended playground of creative exploration, driven by curiosity and experimentation; the other is a structured approach to create functional, goal-oriented solutions with clear intent.

CREATIVE CODING: A PLAYFUL SYSTEM OF DISCOVERY

Creative Coding is where art, design and computation collide in an open-ended dance. It is unbound by commercial constraints, fuelled by curiosity and driven by an iterative process of experimentation, failure, feedback and unexpected discovery. Unlike traditional programming, which often seeks efficiency and predictability, Creative Coding thrives on the unpredictable, the emergent, the unknown.

It is about creative exploration in conversation with technology—a process where the designer sets initial rules and then lets the machine surprise them. Mistakes are not failures but pathways to new possibilities. A slight tweak in an algorithm can generate an entirely new visual universe. A misplaced decimal point can create unexpected beauty. Creative Coding is a deliberate act of letting go and seeing where the process takes you.

In this way, it almost serves as a commentary on technology itself. It invites designers to reflect on the tools they use, to play with the logic of computation and to push digital aesthetics into territories traditional design software wasn't built to explore. Some of the Generative Branding systems that shape this book's plethora of cases and examples have their roots in this experimental world—born not from a need to create deliverables, but from the sheer joy of seeing what happens when you embrace technology in the creative act and, at least partially, let the machine take the lead.

At its core, Creative Coding is an act of curiosity—an ongoing conversation with the unknown that begins with a simple question: *what if?* It is this spirit of inquiry that fuels the creativity of a new generation of designers, showing a pathway to move beyond a static way of thinking and instead create ideas that breathe, adapt and unfold in ways we can't always predict. It is a gateway to understanding that a generative mindset is not merely about integrating computational techniques into the design process; it's about cultivating a sense of exploration, this willingness to let go of fixed outcomes, while developing a comfort with uncertainty and embracing a deep curiosity for how design can exist as something alive.

For many designers, the world of generative design can feel like a locked room—full of dazzling outputs, yet lacking transparency around how they come to be. Creative Coding is one of the most powerful keys to unlock that door. It offers a hands-on, empowering entry point into creative technology: one that lets you not only understand and experiment with its possibilities, but also anticipate where it's heading and actively shape its trajectory. If you're ready to take the next step and engage more deeply with this mindset, I highly recommend diving into the insights of designer, educator, and critical thinker Tim Rodenbröker, whose reflections on Creative Coding begin on page 258 of this book. Tim's work stands out for his commitment to making this field accessible to creative minds, while bringing a much-needed sense of reflection and criticality to the conversation around technology and its impact on us—not just as designers, but as human beings.

GENERATIVE BRAND DESIGN: DESIGNING FOR PURPOSEFUL EVOLUTION

While Generative Brand Design shares the same toolkit as Creative Coding—algorithmic rules, procedural generation and real-time adaptation, to name a few—it applies these principles with a distinct and intentional purpose: to build a brand identity that is not just visually consistent but structurally adaptive. And more importantly, it always does so in service of storytelling, emotional connection and the deeper resonance that makes a brand truly matter.

This means that at its core, a successful generative brand isn't just a collection of visual assets; it's a living system of perception, a continuous exchange between brand and audience. The brands that endure (generative or not) don't just stick in our minds because they are recognisable; they resonate because they make us feel something. They create moments of connection—whether through emotion, perspective, or a sense of belonging. And the most powerful brands don't just represent something; they invite us into something bigger than ourselves.

Generative Branding embraces this by designing not just how a brand looks, but how it behaves—how it responds to context, evolves alongside culture and continuously reinvents the ways it expresses its story while remaining unmistakably itself. This isn't about relentless novelty for the sake of change; it's about deepening connections. A generative brand has the power to make the familiar feel new again—to reveal unexpected facets of its identity, to open fresh perspectives that challenge assumptions, to create moments of rediscovery that make people see, feel and engage in ways they hadn't before. It doesn't just communicate—it invites, it surprises, it reveals. This leads to a clear insight: a generative brand cannot afford to be random. It cannot be an endless playground of disconnected possibilities. It needs coherence, recognisability and meaning—even and especially as it continuously transforms. The challenge of Generative Branding is to design a system where every iteration reinforces the brand's character while allowing for variation and evolution in a style that is distinct and ownable.

This means that Generative Branding operates at the intersection of adaptability and intention, constantly balancing flexibility and structure. The focus is not on limitless variation but on designing a system where every transformation reinforces the brand's core identity rather than diluting it. At the core of it are these questions:

- How can a brand remain flexible without losing coherence?
- How does a brand invite participation rather than simply broadcast its identity?
- What parameters and datasets shape a brand's evolution without descending into randomness?
- How can a brand's shifting expressions create new layers of meaning, deepening its connection with its audience?

What I want you to take away from this is that the final visual outcome of a Creative Coding or Generative Design process can, at times, look identical. The distinction between these two approaches is not found in their aesthetics—it lies in their underlying processes, intent and methodology. Just as two paintings might depict the same subject yet stem from entirely different artistic philosophies, Creative Coding and Generative Design may produce similar visual results but serve fundamentally different purposes.

The cases, experiments and interviews in this book show us what is possible when we stop to see branding as an endpoint and start seeing it as a beginning. Some of these works are actually much more than pure branding projects; they are design provocations. They challenge the assumption that a brand must be a single, fixed idea. They prove that a brand's greatest strength is not in how well it repeats itself, but in how well it transforms while staying unmistakably itself. To start with, you can refer to the following projects in the Showcase section, through which I have sought to exemplify this approach in action:

BRUTE – Crafted by the Elements
PP 080-081

Polkadot
PP 100-101

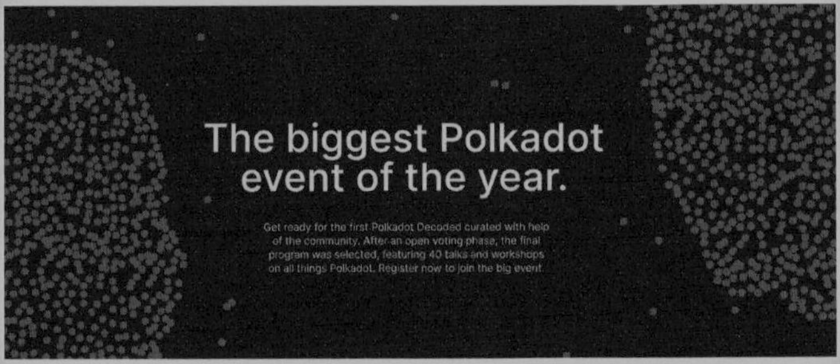

Philharmonie Luxembourg
PP 140-143

Munken Creator
PP 244-245

THE POWER OF GENERATIVE BRANDING IN A CHANGING WORLD

FROM RANDOMNESS TO RELEVANCE

Now that we have briefly discussed the differences between exploratory Creative Coding and purpose-driven Generative Brand Design, I feel it is important to address one of the most prevalent misconceptions about Generative Branding: the notion that its value lies in sheer volume—that if a system can generate infinite variations of a brand's identity, it should. To me, the most compelling generative identities are neither defined by randomness nor endless iteration; rather, they are defined by purposeful transformation. Their variations are not arbitrary but intentional—each shift reinforcing, deepening and evolving a brand's narrative in ways that feel organic rather than mechanical. Generative Branding is not about difference for difference's sake; it's about creating meaningful expressions that adapt with context while remaining unmistakably true to their core essence.

This is where data becomes essential. Instead of generating arbitrary visual expressions, a well-designed generative system establishes a clear relationship between the real-world phenomena that shape a brand and the way it expresses itself.

Whether it's a dynamic identity that shifts in response to cultural trends, a typographic system that adapts to a product's properties, or a campaign that morphs based on real-time environmental data, the strongest generative expressions are those that tie their adaptability to something concrete.

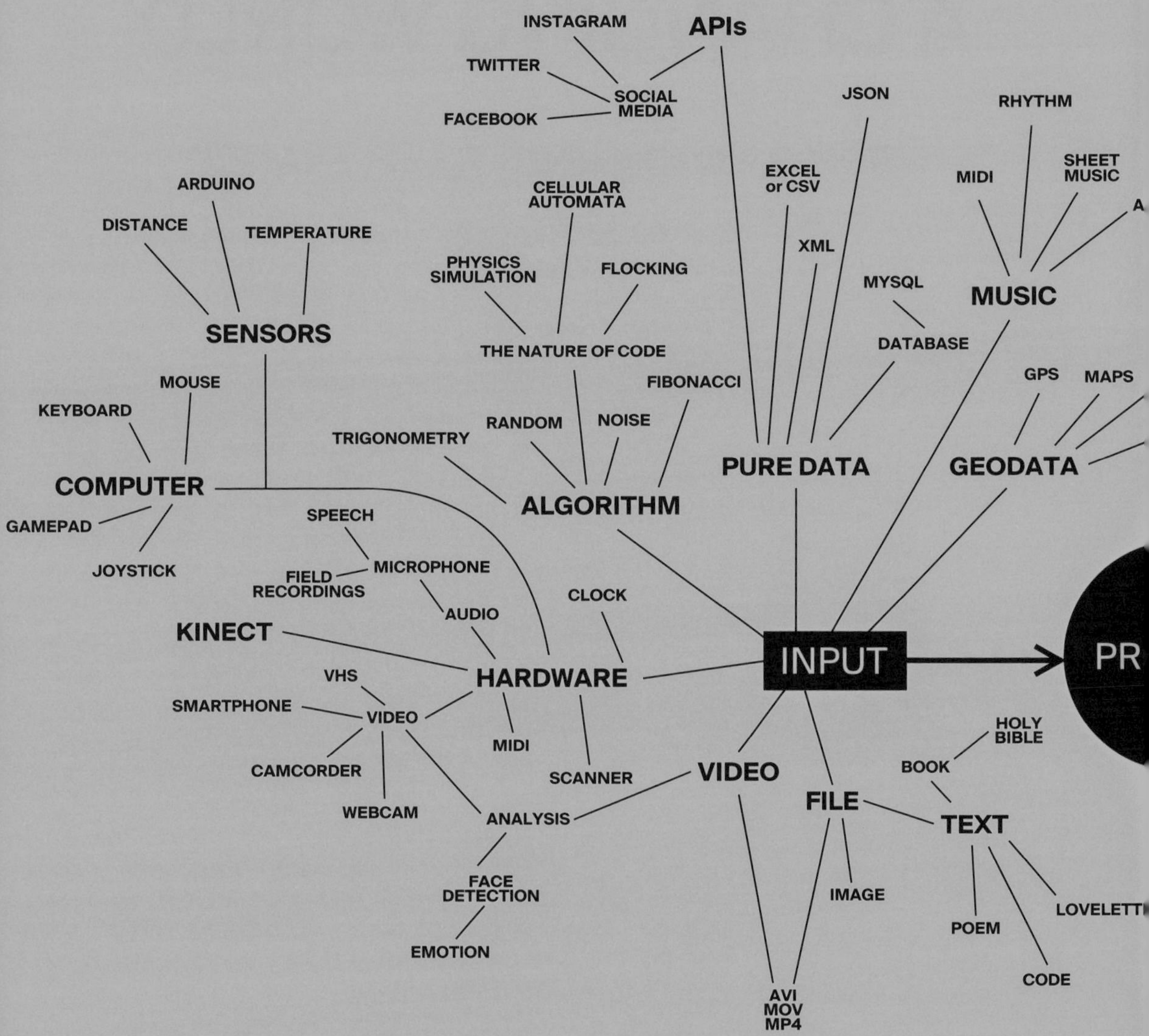

A mindmap of possible inputs and outputs to be used within a data-driven transformation.
Created by Tim Rodenbröker and Patrik Hübner

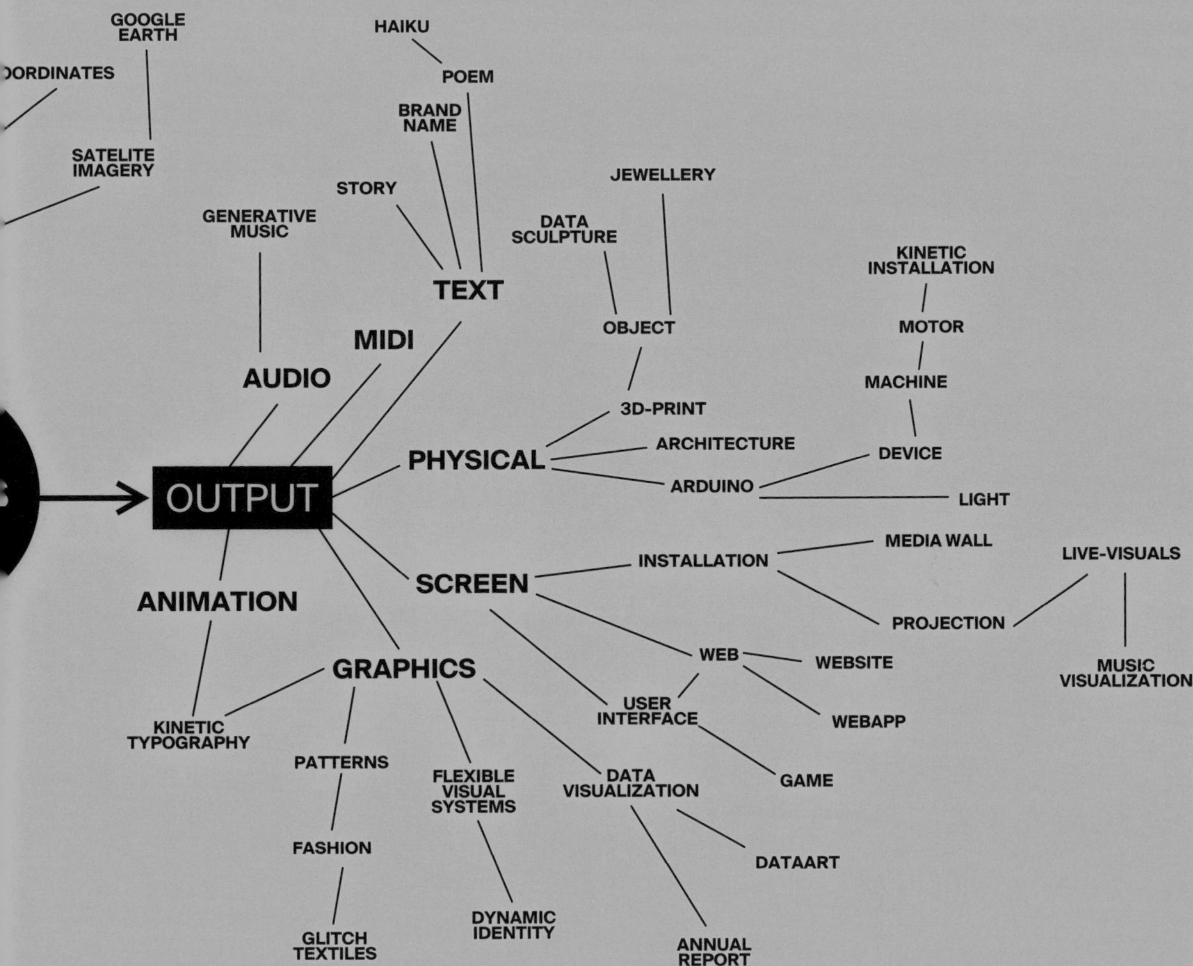
GOOGLE EARTH
ORDINATES
SATELITE IMAGERY
HAIKU
POEM
BRAND NAME
STORY
GENERATIVE MUSIC
TEXT
MIDI
AUDIO
JEWELLERY
DATA SCULPTURE
OBJECT
3D-PRINT
KINETIC INSTALLATION
MOTOR
MACHINE
PHYSICAL
ARCHITECTURE
ARDUINO
DEVICE
LIGHT
OUTPUT
MEDIA WALL
INSTALLATION
LIVE-VISUALS
SCREEN
PROJECTION
ANIMATION
WEB
WEBSITE
MUSIC VISUALIZATION
GRAPHICS
USER INTERFACE
WEBAPP
KINETIC TYPOGRAPHY
PATTERNS
FLEXIBLE VISUAL SYSTEMS
DATA VISUALIZATION
GAME
FASHION
DATAART
GLITCH TEXTILES
DYNAMIC IDENTITY
ANNUAL REPORT

Consider the case studies I have contributed to this book—brands that don't just exist in a space but engage with it: a visual identity that responds to sound waves at a live event. An identity that shifts its tone and imagery in real-time based on unfolding conversations and collaborations. A wine packaging system that evolves with the weather, reflecting the changing seasons and conditions that have influenced each unique vintage. These are not arbitrary expressions; they are manifestations of a deeper connection between a brand and the world it inhabits. All of this reinforces the idea that brands are not static emblems but living, breathing entities shaped by the realities around them.

The paradox of Generative Branding is that, despite being data-driven, its success isn't based purely on the fact that is uses data. Data is merely the means by which brands can create deeper resonance, more personal connections, more meaningful experiences. A generative brand that adapts in real time is not compelling because it is technologically advanced. It is compelling because it creates a sense of personal immediacy, emotional presence and human connection. It mirrors the way people engage with the world.

The best generative identities do not just change; they create moments of recognition, surprise and wonder.

A NOTE ON THE ROLE OF ARTIFICIAL INTELLIGENCE

I want you to take a moment and think about this thesis: for too long, creativity has been constrained by nostalgia. Why do I bring this up? Because I believe that we live in an era of remakes, sequels and endless iterations of what's already been done. Branding, too, has often followed this pattern—reinforcing what audiences already expect, anchoring itself in past successes rather than stepping into uncharted territory. In branding, as in culture, we are often guided by what has already been proven. The familiar is safe. We look to past successes to define future strategies, measuring new ideas against the templates of what has worked before.

But true creative evolution doesn't come from repeating what we know; it comes from asking what's next.

Given what times we live in and the subject we are covering, it's impossible to ignore the elephant in the room: Artificial Intelligence (AI). In the context of this book, I believe it's crucial to at least briefly point out that I personally have found that AI accelerates what already exists, but it cannot imagine what doesn't. It refines, optimises and scales creative execution. Yet, without direction, it risks turning design into an exercise in polished predictability. The generative mindset that I've outlined in my words to this point ensures that AI serves creativity, not the other way around. Without this critical mindset, we risk an era where design is not shaped by human vision and creativity, but by algorithms trained on the past—repeating, refining, but never truly reimagining.

Modern algorithms thrive on patterns, feeding us variations of what has already worked. Left unchecked, they create loops of familiarity, reinforcing the expected and suffocating creative risk. As designers, I believe, it is in our best interest to break free from this cycle—to push beyond pure efficiency and seek out unpredictability. When used with intent, AI doesn't replace imagination—it extends it. It can help surface hidden connections, unlock richer layers of meaning and bring dynamic and responsive intelligence to Generative Branding systems. But make no mistake: the future of design isn't really about AI. It's about the mindset we bring to it—the questions we ask, the ideas we pursue and the relationships we enable. AI is just another (albeit very powerful) tool in an ever-expanding creative toolkit, capable of amplifying our work but not replacing the intuition, curiosity and critical thinking that drive true innovation.

This is where Creative Coding and Generative Design emerge as two powerful approaches to gain more agency and independence in a design landscape where designers must navigate a growing array of commercial tools, unclear workflows and the constant push and pull between innovation and skepticism. In this space, true innovation and agency doesn't come from simply adopting new commercial tools built by corporate entities. To truly expand our creative horizons, we must go beyond passive adoption, ideally developing our own tools or at least influencing their evolution by actively shaping how they are built and used. Otherwise, we risk being locked in to an ever-growing list of subscription services, each offering only a fragment of creative possibility at a time. You don't need to actively write code to gain agency, but understanding the concepts of these fields will give you the words to articulate your vision, challenge limitations and guide others in pushing creativity forward in meaningful ways.

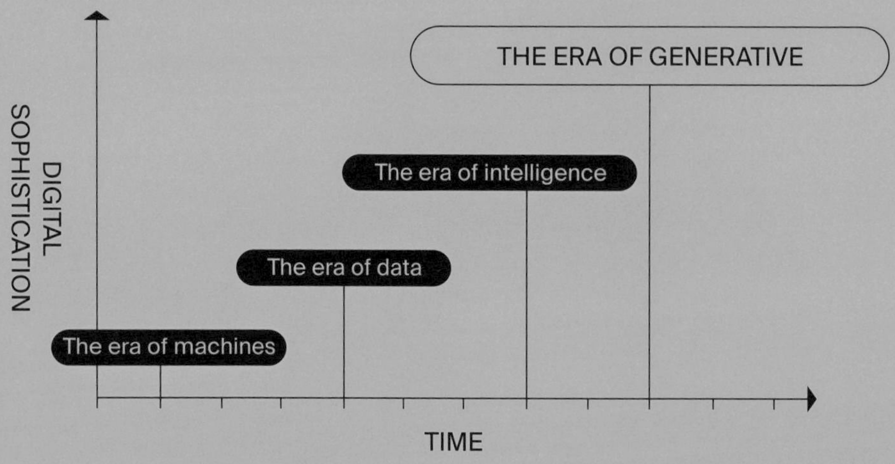

THREE FUNDAMENTAL PRINCIPLES OF GENERATIVE BRAND DESIGN TO EXPLORE IN YOUR WORK TODAY

I have dedicated an entire book, seminars and talks to help students and seasoned creative professionals unlock their generative mind. And while I can't do the same in the amount of pages I have been given to share my ideas with you in this book, my hope is that I can offer you a starting point: three fundamental principles of Generative Branding. Three key ideas that can help you begin to question, ideate and integrate this approach into your own creative practice. Each of these steps is an invitation to experiment. My tip: start small. Choose one principle and apply it to your work today. Generative Branding isn't a formula; it's a mindset—one that welcomes change, embraces experimentation and continuously finds new ways to connect.

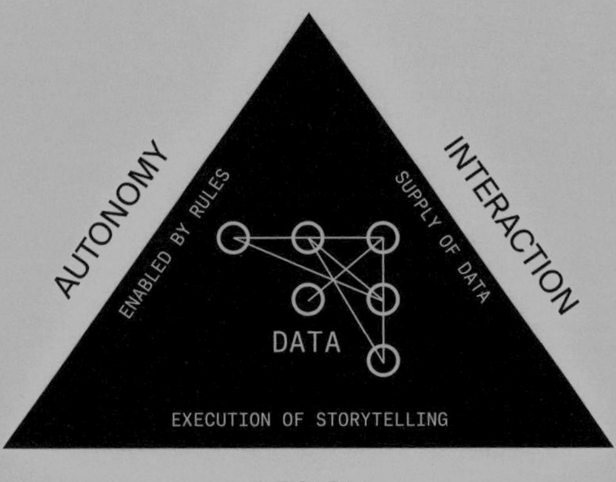

Above: Generative Brand Design, at its most powerful, is not a static act—it is an orchestration of relationships between autonomy, interaction and execution. The data at its core does not exist in isolation; it is shaped by the systems that supply it and the rules that enable it, powering the narratives that emerge from it. Autonomy ensures that a system is not micromanaged but guided—its behaviours shaped by rules rather than rigid constraints.

1 DESIGN BRANDS AS SYSTEMS

Challenge yourself to move beyond fixed assets. Instead of designing a logo, a colour palette, or a single composition, think about what it takes to create a design system—one that is flexible, responsive and capable of adapting without losing its identity. Look at your current branding projects: can they exist beyond a single format or execution? Experiment with visual ideas that allow for variation while maintaining a clear sense of recognition. Deconstruct your current work into its smallest entities and reconstruct it so that each element is assigned a place and task based on a specific rule. Ask yourself: *how can I design rules instead of just outputs? How can this brand continuously express itself rather than be locked into a single form?*

Practical Exercise #1

Assign the different design elements you identified—such as colour, shape, size, or texture—to each number on a dice. At key moments, roll the dice and apply the result to your system, letting randomness (as one of the simplest forms of machine co-creation) influence the process instead of deciding everything yourself.

2 CREATE MEANINGFUL EXPRESSIONS

Resist the temptation of endless variation for its own sake. A successful generative brand is not about producing countless random outputs; it's about crafting meaningful connections that deepen engagement and storytelling. Analyse the ways your brand could evolve with purpose. What properties make your brand fundamentally tick and evolve? Are there real-world phenomena or data-points that you can use to make your brand respond to those properties? Audit your brand's current assets and ask: *how can variation enhance meaning rather than dilute it? How can each iteration tell a deeper story? What data is tied to the brand, product or identity and how can it meaningfully help communicate and express that story?*

Practical Exercise #2

Take a dataset related to your daily life—your screen time, step count or sleep patterns—and represent it visually in a way that makes it feel alive. Avoid traditional graphs and charts; instead, experiment with sketches, organic shapes or even physical materials to express its meaning in a more intuitive way. Try to create something that evokes emotion and connects your real-world experience to an expressive design.

3 TURN YOUR BRAND INTO AN INTERACTIVE EXPERIENCE

Think beyond static and passive visuals. Generative Branding thrives on participation—on creating moments where users can engage, play and shape a brand in real time. Consider how your brand might invite interaction: can your audience influence its form? Can it change in response to their behavior? Prototype a small-scale thought-experiment where a branding element shifts dynamically based on external inputs, whether that's user input, time of day, or location. Ask: *how can I transform my brand from something to be seen into something to be experienced?*

Practical Exercise #3

Spend a morning noticing and taking notes on how systems around you interact—how traffic flows, how animals move in flocks, or how people interact in a space—and reflect on how these patterns emerge from simple rules rather than rigid control. Ask yourself how you can use these patterns as an interactive influence and force in your own creative and design work and have the system react to these external influences.

WHAT COMES NEXT?

We are no longer designing just for today. Every decision we make as designers, strategists and storytellers shapes the fabric of the world we will live in tomorrow. To embrace this role is to understand that our work is not just about aesthetics or technical capability anymore. It is about responsibility. We are designing the systems that will define the future of human connection.

The next challenge of our industry isn't about making more, faster—it's about making things that matter. As AI, generative systems and automation continue to reshape the creative landscape, efficiency alone will not define the future of design. I believe the real frontier is emotional intelligence: the most impactful brands of tomorrow won't just be visually responsive—they'll be emotionally aware. They'll sense shifts in culture, adapt to the moods of their audiences and react in real-time to unfolding events. Impactful generative brands do not just communicate—they influence behaviour, shape perceptions and resonate with the infrastructures of culture. If we reduce our work to automation and optimisation, we strip it of its power to move people.

If we treat Generative Brand Design as a novelty rather than a fundamental shift in how we tell stories, we miss the deeper opportunity: to design brands that are not just efficient, but deeply resonant.

The future of branding will not be dictated by those who wait for permission. It will be built by those who are willing to experiment, to disrupt and to question.

SPOTLIGHT 01

Studio Dumbar/DEPT®
Liza Enebeis

JULI
202

"The NN North Sea Jazz Festival, one of the largest and most beloved jazz events globally, attracts over 90,000 fans each July to the Ahoy venue in Rotterdam, showcasing 1,300 artists across fifteen stages. The festival's new visual identity embodies rhythm and movement, celebrating the vibrant energy of live music performances.

To achieve this, we developed a custom coding tool that allows for the animation of text in both motion and still applications, resulting in a dynamic, type-led aesthetic. This tool featured an interactive interface where users could input text and manipulate its dynamic flow—primarily for creating printed materials—as traditional design software proved challenging for this purpose. Through this project, we learned that to effectively creative a lively, moving identity inspired by the pulsating rhythm and energy of jazz, we needed tools that facilitated experimentation and dynamic adjustments, rather than relying solely on static design software. It also reinforced our belief in the necessity of playful exploration in the design process to truly capture the essence of a live performance."

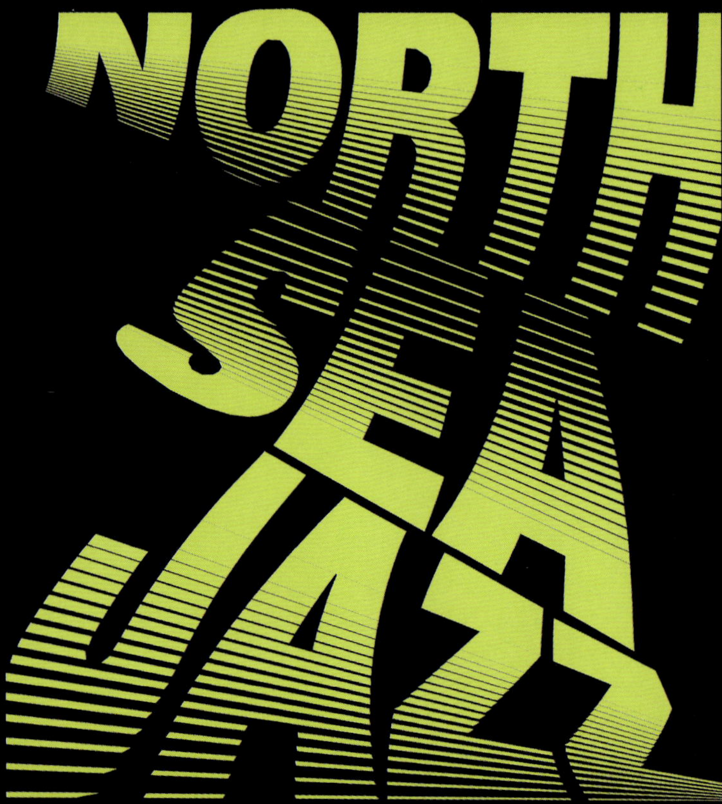

FRIDAY
8 JULY
2022
north sea Jazz
FESTIVAL PROGRAM

NN
north
sea Jazz

Cumulus Park

programming languages
Processing, p5.js

client
Cumulus Park

project year
2019

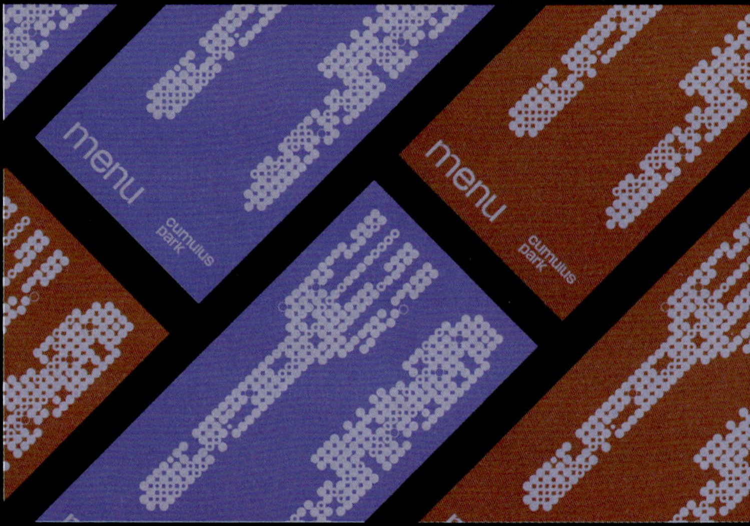

"Cumulus Park is an innovative hub in Amsterdam Zuid-Oost for fostering collaboration among diverse talents and disciplines. The vibrant development aims to enhance business, residential, and leisure opportunities while attracting bright minds eager to share ideas and skills. We were tasked with crafting a visual identity that encapsulates this spirit of community and cooperation.

To achieve this, we developed a sophisticated tool in Processing, featuring an extensive UI that allows for precise control over various elements, including the speed and movement of particle chains, their length and momentum, and visual design options such as colours, text input, and particle types. The creative concept was inspired by the exchange of knowledge among individuals from varied backgrounds, which fuels the generation of new ideas and outcomes."

cumulus
park
17.02.2020
09.30 - 17.30
more info:
cumuluspark.com
masterclass
data value
talk

adapt

JCDecaux
cumulus
park
urbanization
and digital
identity
talk

hello
hello
hello
hello
hello

JCDecaux
cumulus park
17.02.2020
09.30 - 17.30
more info:
cumuluspark.com
masterclass
data value
talk

16:59

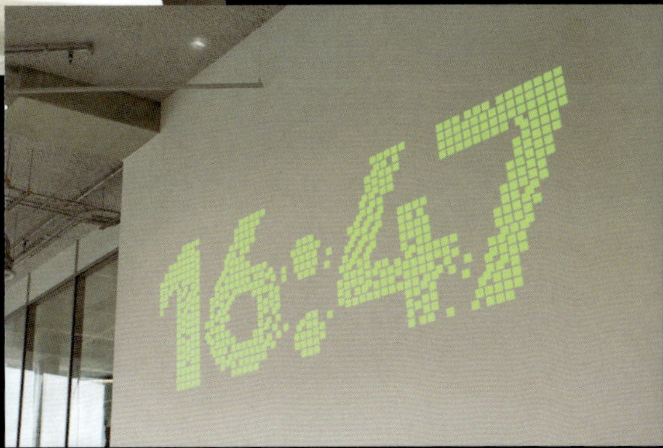
16:47

share
ideas

cumulus
park
meetup
9.10.2019

042

Amsterdam Sinfonietta

programming languages
Processing, p5.js

client
Amsterdam Sinfonietta

project year
2025

“Amsterdam Sinfonietta, a renowned string orchestra in Amsterdam, has been a long-time collaborator of ours, particularly in creating their poster series. Their commitment to experimentation and innovative collaborations among diverse artists inspired the development of a new visual identity that reflects these values.

This project marked a significant milestone for us, as it was our first attempt to actively integrate coding into a visual identity. We designed a dynamic grid of letters that flowed with the music, capturing its emotion while allowing for versatile design options. Initially, we faced challenges using After Effects due to the complexity of rendering numerous variations, which hindered our ability to experiment swiftly. To overcome this, we created a custom tool in Processing, enabling live iterations and adjustments to details and visuals. This experience not only enhanced our design process but also deepened our appreciation for generative design, reinforcing our belief in maintaining designer control while leveraging the strengths of code. Through this project, we learned the importance of creating our own tools, making thoughtful decisions about the balance of control between designers and code, as well as the value of frequent iteration and sharing throughout the creative process.”

Amsterdam
Sinfonietta
Piet Heinkade 5
1019 BR Amsterdam
The Netherlands
+31 20 52 70 770
info@sinfonietta.nl
www.sinfonietta.nl
Amsterdam
Sinfonietta
Chris Meeuwissen
marketing en communicatie
06 457 114 59
chrismeeuwissen@sinfonietta.nl
Amsterdam
Sinfonietta
Amsterdam Sinfonietta
Piet Heinkade 5
1019 BR Amsterdam
The Netherlands
+31 20 52 70 770
info@sinfonietta.nl
www.sinfonietta.nl
KvK 41208445

Amsterdam
Sinfonietta
club
van 100

Programma
Amsterdam
Sinfonietta

Amsterdam Sinfonietta
Nacht
muziek
Candida Thompson,
leiding & viool
Beatrice Rana,
piano
za 30 maart
Muziekgebouw
zo 6 april
Het Concertgebouw

Amsterdam Sinfonietta
Ferschtmans
Fratres
Candida Thompson, leiding & viool
Liza Ferschtman, viool
vr 5 en di 9 oktober
Muziekgebouw

Amsterdam Sinfonietta
Andriessen
& Moore
Daniel Bard, leiding & viool
Harriet Krijgh, cello
Claron McFadden, sopraan
Tim Persent, dans
za 3 november
Muziekgebouw

Amsterdam Sinfonietta
Quartetto
Serioso
Candida Thompson, leiding & viool
Marc-André Hamelin piano
do 6 & za 8 december
Muziekgebouw

Amsterdam Sinfonietta
Duivels-
kunstenaar
RayChen
vr 15 februari
Muziekgebouw
zo 17 februari
Het Concertgebouw
Candida Thompson, leiding & viool
Ray Chen, viool

"Designed to challenge and enhance the existing landscape of digital finance, Entropy empowers users to interact seamlessly with their cryptocurrencies and digital assets across various blockchains. Its groundbreaking protocol enables users to set their own rules and conditions, ensuring that custody services are accessible to everyone, regardless of their background or net worth. To reflect its ethos of open source for open minds, this project uniquely called for a generative approach from the outset, inspired by Entropy's dynamic security code and its expanding community.

To that end, we developed custom code that produces evolving, free-moving visual elements, symbolising the creation of limitless, borderless worlds. Using Processing, P5, and WebGL, we generated distinct logos—both static and animated—as well as background elements that allowed for an infinite variety of unique visuals. The primary outcome was dynamic, responsive, and one-of-a-kind, embodying the same principles as its predecessor while retaining its exclusivity.

Central to the visual identity is Entropy's guiding principle of 'radically open', with generative elements fostering new interactions and spaces. Through this project, we (re)discovered the joy of crafting generative identities and showcasing potential for creativity in the digital realm."

TRUSTLESS AND
SECURE CRYPTO
CUSTODY
FOR EVERYONE

HOW DO YOU THINK CREATIVE CODING/GENERATIVE DESIGN HAS CHANGED THE BRANDING WORLD AS A WHOLE?

Creative coding opens up a new way of working in design. It's interesting to see how it not only focuses on the visual result, but is more about designing a way to get there. It empowers designers to create beyond the limits of the design software they know – a way of creating custom tools where the concept and idea genuinely come first.

However, when considering how it has changed the branding world, the impact has not been enough, to be honest. We have barely scratched the surface of how we can implement creative coding and generative design in branding. While there are many exciting concepts and tech demos out there, applying these in actual design and branding projects remain challenging.

FOR OUR READERS WHO ARE UNAWARE, WHAT IS THE CREATIVE/DESIGN ETHOS THAT DRIVES STUDIO DUMBAR/DEPT®? HOW HAS THIS ETHOS SHAPED YOUR WORK OVER THE YEARS?

Keeping an open mind is crucial, and we trust that one more solution/idea is always hiding around the corner. It's about pushing the concept you're working on as far as possible and always taking one more step.

We heavily encourage using whatever tool you see fit in the design process. Going wide in our concept phase is essential – you always want to know if you can make something new and unexpected. Making the same thing twice is not fun for anyone. In that regard, creative coding is a powerful practice: it offers surprise and ultra-quick iterations and changes how you interact with your design.

This ethos hasn't changed over the years, but we just have many more tools and ways to see this in practice – 3D, motion, code, sound, and all the new things in our design arsenal that help us build things we never could before. Or we make our own tools, of course!

WHAT ARE SOME KEY CODING/DESIGN PRINCIPLES YOU ADHERE TO WHEN IT COMES TO THE DIFFERENT PROJECTS YOU WORK ON?

It's good to remember we often make something for someone else. The best projects are the ones where our interests and excitement align with the client's needs.

We fully believe in sharing and collaboration; sharing what you're working on with each other even if you're unsure about it yourself, is important. There is always something to take away from it.

This also applies to code. We like to share the code as quickly as possible with the designers and let them mess around with it. Providing them with a finished code immediately is inefficient and takes too much time. It's better to work with a quick coded sketch and see where it breaks to know where we want to go next. It's far more interesting to dive in together, break things, push things, and look at new possibilities from different angles.

WHICH IS MORE IMPORTANT TO THE PROCESS: THE CONCEPTUALISATION STAGE OR EXPERIMENTING? AND WHY?

These go hand in hand. We leave ample room for experimentation both in and outside the conceptualsation stage. It's like asking which of your kids is your favourite (hint: they're all equally your favourite!).

Experimenting keeps us engaged and excited and lets us find new things. But this all has to be grounded in an actual concept that makes sense for us, the design, and most of all, the client. Experimentation opens up more possibilities to get to the best concept and design possible. The more different ways we try to get somewhere, the greater the chance we discover something good along the way.

YOUR TEAM COMPRISES A DIVERSE GROUP OF NATIONALITIES, PERSONALITIES, AND SPECIALISTS. WHAT IS YOUR STUDIO STRUCTURE LIKE AND HOW DOES EVERYBODY WORK TOGETHER, INCLUDING WITH THE CLIENTS?

Our team consists of a diverse group of people coming from all over the world with different backgrounds, talents and approaches to how they design. It feeds into our way of working, where we want to converge on a project from as many different perspectives as possible. This diversity is found in the tools/software we use - even more so in the people we work with. We always want to add someone to the team who does things differently than we already do, knows things we don't know yet, and looks at things from a new angle.

The most essential thing in our studio is collaboration. We all share one space and sit together when designing; no one is larger than the concept or design we're working on. We believe in sharing all ideas early on, are open to feedback, and are not afraid to "steal" from each other or change ownership of an idea if that helps the project.

This also goes for sharing with the client. It is important to show things early on and get feedback on things they might not like and, more importantly, why they do or don't like something. Getting a client on board with your train of thought and getting them excited about what you're excited about is essential, since we make something they have to live with in the end. We have to see from their perspective as well.

WHAT LED YOU TO INITIATE THE DEMO DESIGN IN MOTION FESTIVAL? WHAT DO YOU HOPE TO ACHIEVE THROUGH IT, AND HOW HAS THE FESTIVAL EVOLVED OVER THE YEARS?

In the studio, we are very focused on motion design. A lot of the work that inspires us daily is usually shared on Instagram and is limited to the eyes of designers. As early as 2017, we already had the idea to share the beautiful work we saw with a broader audience and create an accessible exhibition for the wider public. We were lucky enough to be introduced to Global (formerly known as Exterion Media), the largest outdoor media owners in the Netherlands, who shared our ambition and became our partners in this project. In 2019, Global offered all their screens located in Amsterdam Central station for 24 hours to showcase all the beautiful motion designs from designers all around the world.

In 2022, we organised DEMO again – this time at a slightly larger scale. We took over 5,000 screens in the Netherlands, spanning all the screens on the Dutch Train railway network, the three major airports, petrol stations, highways, shopping malls, and streets for 24 hours. Both events were magical. Just seeing passers-by and visitors staring at the screens, mesmerised by the motion, felt like the whole station was at a standstill.

Of course, we could not stop here. In 2025, we are organising an International edition – connecting 16 cities all around the world!

WHAT ARE SOME OF THE KEY LESSONS YOU LEARNED FROM ORGANISING DEMO? WHAT WERE SOME OF THE CHALLENGES THAT YOU HAD TO OVERCOME OVER THE YEARS AND HOW DID YOU FACE THEM?

We definitely learned that organising a festival is a lot of work, and that there are a lot of great designers all over the world. This third time around, for 2025, we've become much more streamlined, especially in receiving and reviewing all the work – we're talking about hours and hours of motion here! (Although people could only submit videos with a maximum length of 10 seconds, they all add up when you receive thousands of entries.)

Getting everything connected and responded to at the correct time is a logistical nightmare, but we're working with great people and partners to get everything done on time.

WHAT FUTURE TRENDS DO YOU SEE EMERGING IN CREATIVE CODING/GENERATIVE DESIGN?

Obviously, we see AI on the rise. Although AI image and video generation share a lot of similarities with creative coding and generative design (letting a computer do the work for you), they are also entirely different in some ways. With creative coding, we aim to keep as much control over what the computer creates for us. We decide on the rules, exceptions, and environment – shaping them to let the code generate things we like. There is still much room for unexpected results and random outcomes by tweaking the numbers and using mathematical functions like randomness and noise, but the creator always decides the where and the how. With generative AI, you give a lot of that control away – the black box is much larger. This is not necessarily a bad thing, but a different way of working.

AI does speed up the process of writing code a lot. It has replaced googling and going through old abandoned forum posts, becoming a helpful assistant and rubber duck for the coder. While 10% of being a creative coder is writing the actual code, it's more about knowing how to chop a larger problem into smaller sections and seeing the opportunities and possibilities where you can take things next. The code is just the means to get this done. Before, you had to be good at googling how to do this. Now, the AI assistants of this world help you do this quickly and efficiently.

Another thing we see is that design software, especially newer tools (think Cavalry, Modyfi, etc., as well as geometry nodes in Blender), share the same design approach that made creative coding so attractive to us. Often, these UIs are node-based and make for quick iterations, loops, and non-destructive tweaking by creating connections between smaller subparts of your design. The work created with these tools significantly overlaps with work we could only have done in code before. It may sound counter-intuitive, but the fact that we have to write less code improves the creative coding process.

WHAT ADVICE SHOULD UPCOMING DESIGNERS KEEP IN MIND AS THEY EXPLORE OR PURSUE CREATIVE CODING/ GENERATIVE DESIGN IN BRANDING?

Learning about coding and generative design is always valuable, even if you find out it's not for you. The technical part has to suit you, and it's a different approach to design altogether. However, it is super helpful to be able to think in terms of generative design and see the possibilities and opportunities of creating your own tools instead of relying on the tools you have available. It makes you think outside the box and allows you to see opportunities you otherwise might not have considered.

If coding does end up resonating with you, keep going. Don't get discouraged if you see other projects and have no idea how to make something like that. I often compare coding to LEGO bricks, where people can create wildly different things with the same bricks as someone else. While you'll learn about the bricks themselves rather quickly in your coding journey, you'll also find more interesting and exciting ways to put them together as you keep at it. Enjoy the process!

WHAT'S NEXT FOR STUDIO DUMBAR/DEPT® AS A WHOLE? ANY DREAM PROJECT(S) IN MIND?

We always have dream projects in our minds, but lately, it feels like we're already going from dream project to dream project. Our favourite ones happen when our excitement aligns with the client's needs and wants. We love pushing the boundaries of motion design, sound, and coding – projects where all this comes together are perfect for us. This will sound cheesy, but the next dream project is always the one that hasn't begun yet and where everything is still possible!

052

Vilnius TechFusion Brand Identity

Vilnius TechFusion positions the city as a tech hub by engaging its local tech community and attracting talent and investment. The project's visual identity is flexible, featuring dynamic elements like shapes, colours, and illustrations, all driven by a custom generative tool. This approach ensures consistency while allowing for endless visual interpretations, reflecting the vibrant, ever-evolving nature of both Vilnius and its tech scene.

Programming Tools/Languages:
p5.js, Processing, Three.js, Paper.js

Client:
Go Vilnius

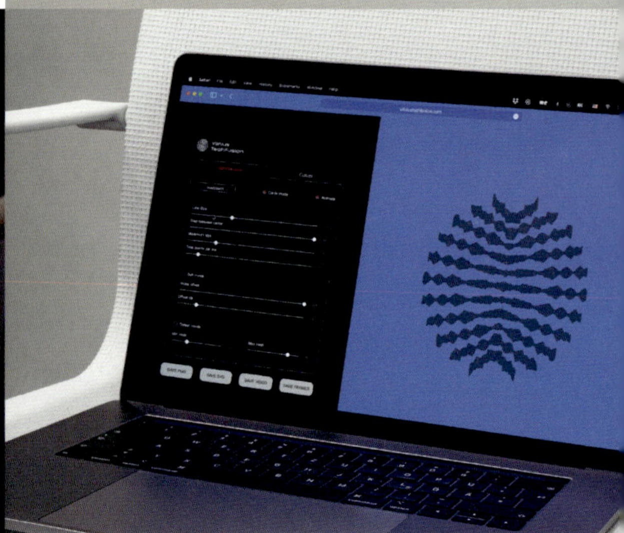

Tech moves in mysterious ways
Vilnius TechFusion
Surprising combinations, big results.
Vilnius TechFusion
Vilnius TechFu
Disco the "hc side of V

cohere
import cohere
co = cohere.Client('{apiKey}'
response = co.generate(
prompt = 'Write a beautiful
NEW
NATURE

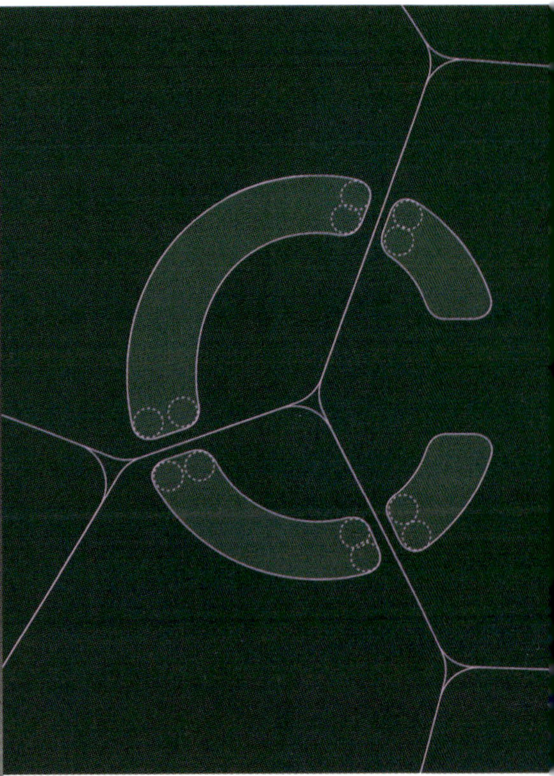

Pentagram developed a visual identity for Cohere to make language AI more accessible. Inspired by "new nature", the system features Voronoi patterns, rooted in mathematics and seen throughout the identity. Custom tools, including a Figma plug-in and Cinema 4D tool, enable Cohere to generate unique layouts, reinforcing its dynamic and innovative brand presence.

Programming Tools/Languages:
Custom Cinema 4D tool built with Python,
bespoke Figma plug-in

Client:
Cohere

Find in playlist
Sort
ATMOS-PHERES VOL 40
Cohere Atmospheres VOL 40
Nick Frosst
1,629,592 likes • 6h 48m
Alchemist
Good Kid
chance with you
mehro
Nirvana
Alchemist • Good Kid
Home
Search
Your Library

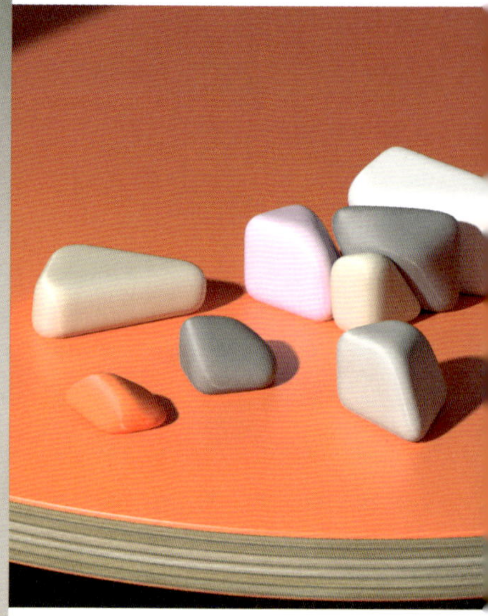

XYZINE
VOL 001
URZA

COHERE TALKS
2023
LANGUAGE AS SOFTWARE
14.00 – 15.00
AIDAN GOMEZ
CO-FOUNDER & CEO

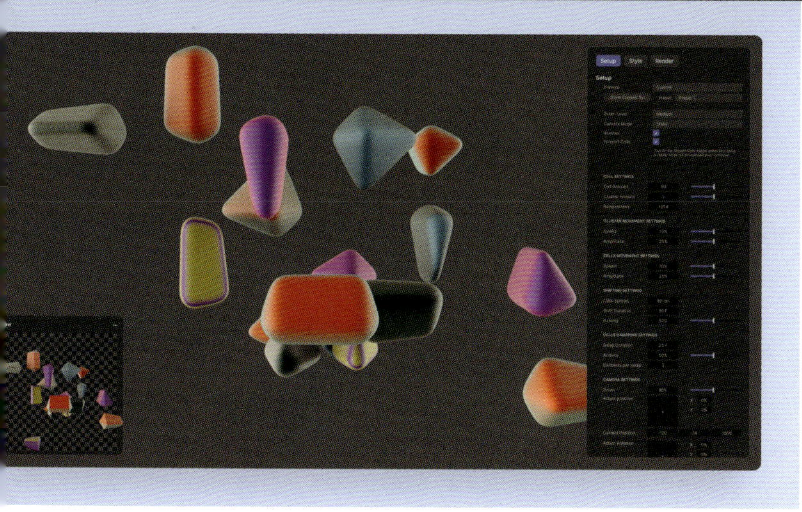

ARTERY
Charge yourself up
The place there sharp minds

ARTERY
Synergy

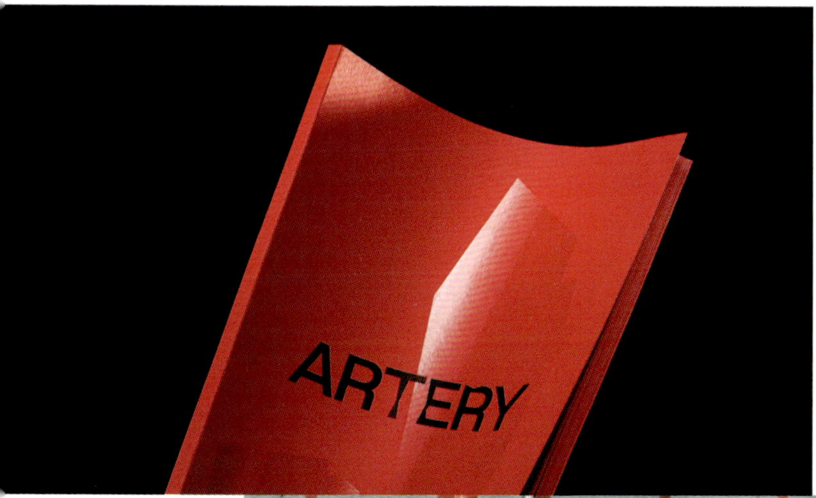

Artery is a dynamic business centre in Vilnius, designed by Daniel Libeskind. The brand's identity incorporates generative elements, evolving throughout the day to reflect the city's rhythm. The logo adjusts its form from morning to evening, mirroring the activity levels of the bustling city. This adaptive approach highlights the bold, ever-changing nature of both the space and the brand itself.

Programming Tools/Languages:
p5.js, Processing, Three.js, Paper.js

Client:
Lords LB Asset Management

inion
inion

inion

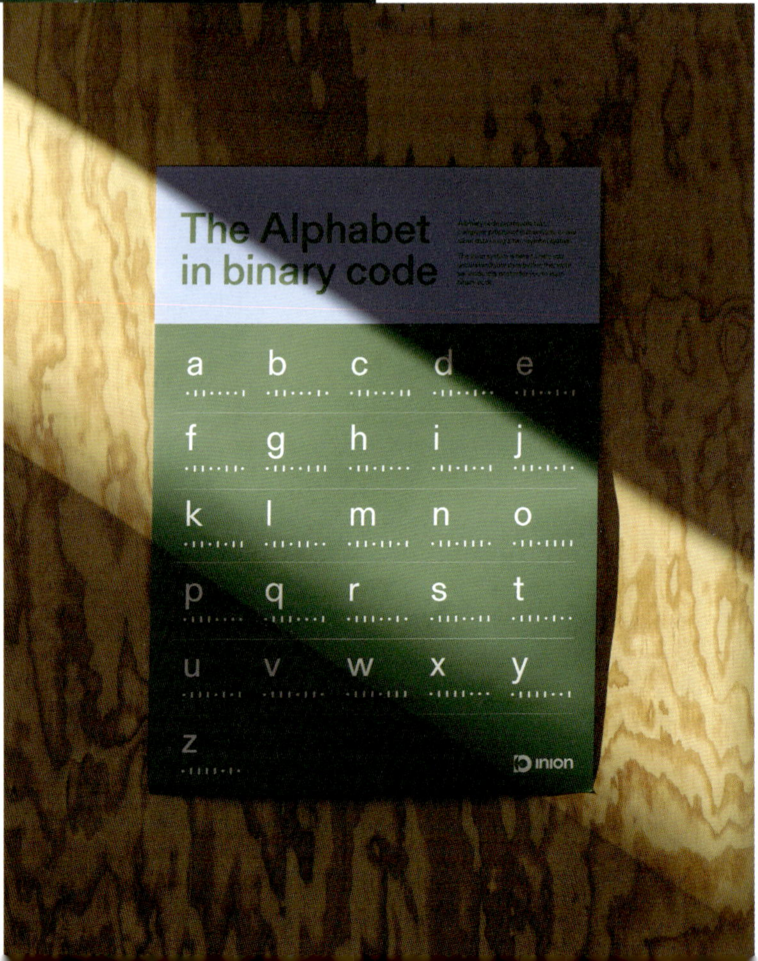
The Alphabet in binary code
a b c d e
f g h i j
k l m n o
p q r s t
u v w x y
z
inion

Inion develops software and hardware for PV plants, focusing on maximising electricity production efficiency through user-friendly code. Binary code is key to their design language, reflecting the digital precision of their work. A custom generative tool was created to transform any word into a unique Inion pattern, where zeros and ones embody a true form of beauty, encapsulating the brand's commitment to innovation.

Programming Tools/Languages:
p5.js, Processing, Three.js, Paper.js

Client:
Inion Software

SMALL EXHIBITION
2024 12 05
Šonta.
The Archives.

From Within

Mo, a modern art museum in Vilnius, Lithuania, embraces the concept of "shifts" in its identity to reflect both societal evolution and the museum's physical space. The logo and design incorporate angled planes that mirror the letter "M" and complement its sharp architecture. A generative tool was created for the museum team to ensure brand consistency.

Programming Tools/Languages:
p5.js, Processing, Three.js, Paper.js

Client:
Mo Museum

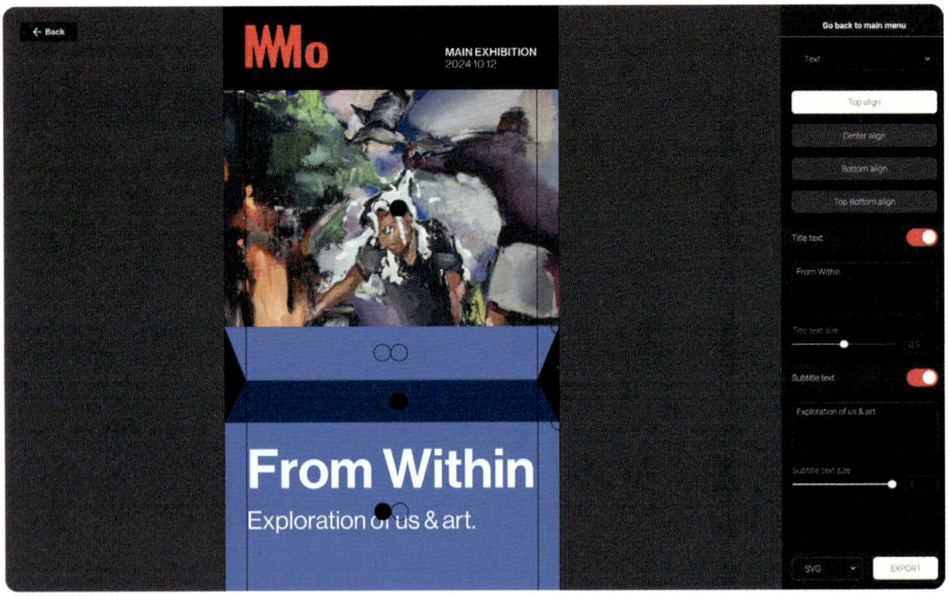
Back
MAIN EXHIBITION
2024 10 12
From Within
Exploration of us & art.
Go back to main menu
Text
Top align
Center align
Bottom align
Top Bottom align
Title text
From Within
Subtitle text
Exploration of us & art
SVG
EXPORT

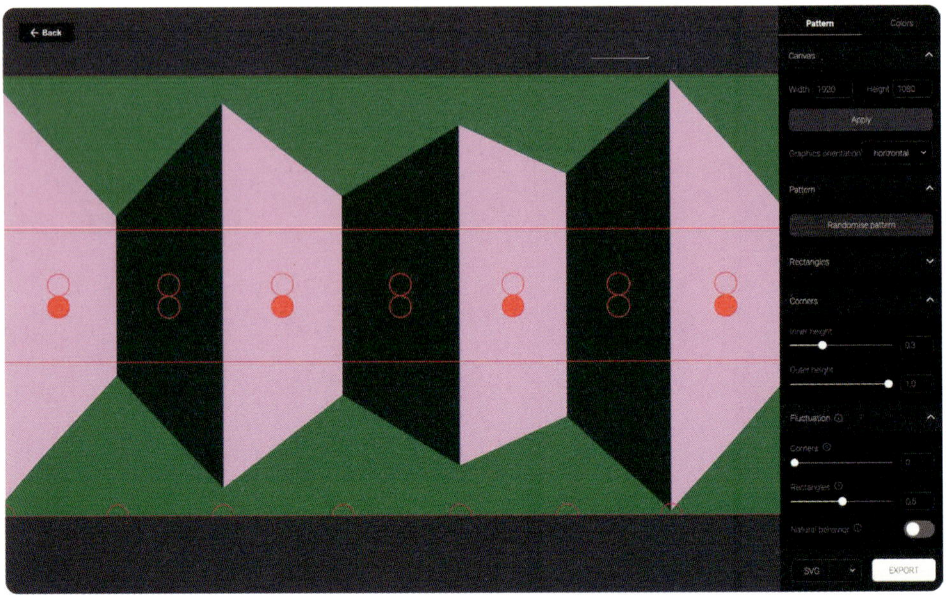
Back
Pattern
Colors
Canvas
Width 1920
Height 1080
Apply
Graphics orientation horizontal
Pattern
Randomise pattern
Rectangles
Corners
SVG
EXPORT

Apsilankymas
muziejuje šeima
Apsilankymas
muziejuje

WEEKLY EVENT
Family
Sunday

Apskriti potepiai
Tyla XIV

Boundary Analytics

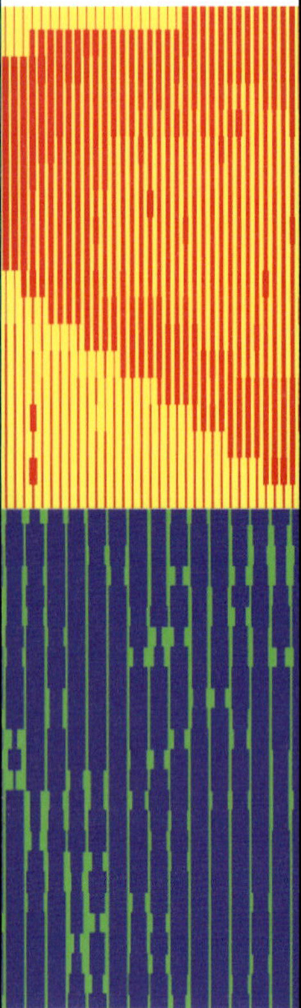

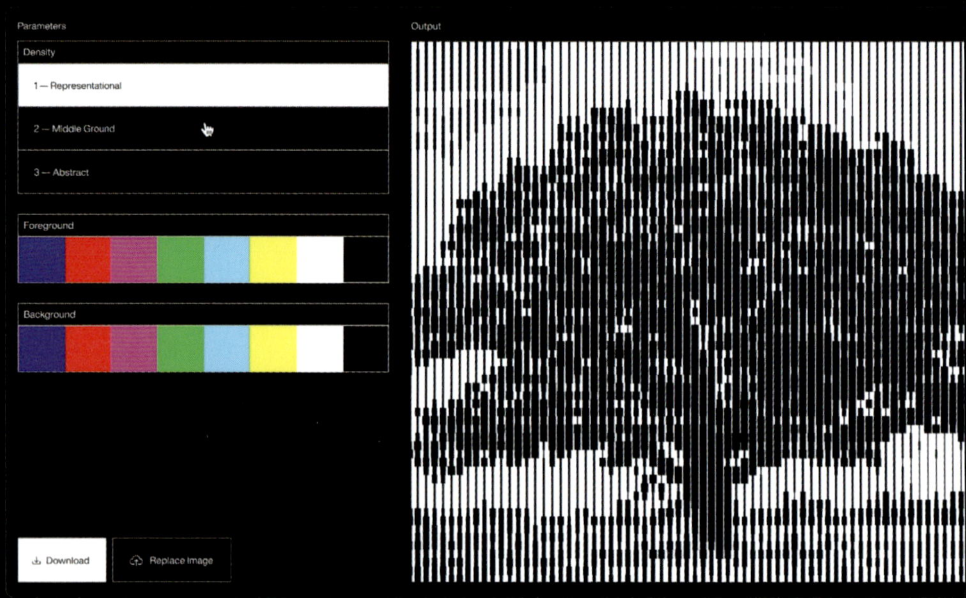

Abstraction Level 1

Abstraction Level 2

Abstraction Level 3

Boundary Analytics

Boundary Analytics

Boundary Analytics

Boundary Analytics is a B2B marketing analytics platform that leverages correlation modelling and time lag analysis to pinpoint activities driving pipeline impact. Cotton's design for Boundary reflects the team's faith in data's explanatory power, its potential to bridge marketers and analysts—rooted in co-founder Jeff Sirkin's dual expertise—and a bold departure from typical SaaS branding, embodying a mindset shift as co-founder Victoria Gamlen envisioned.

Programming Tool/Language:
p5.js

Client:
Boundary Analytics

All the insights attribution never promised you.
Directional insights for intelligent marketers.
Boundary Analytics

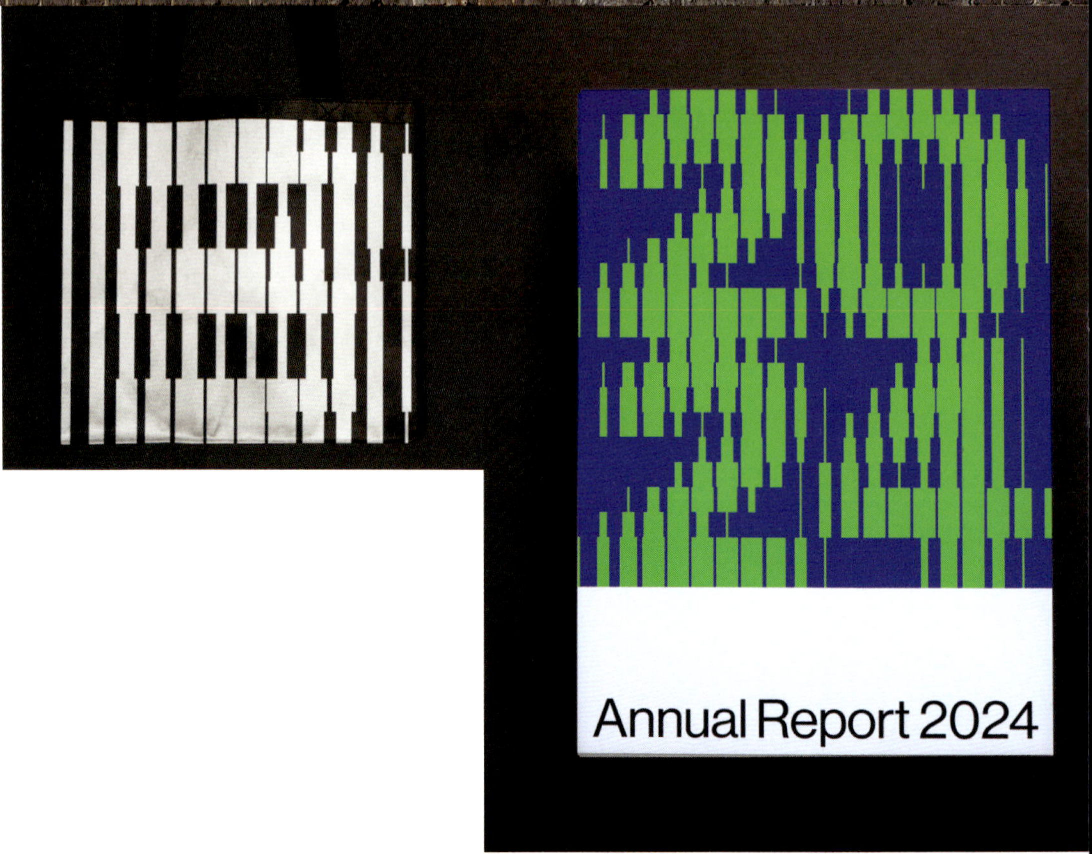
Annual Report 2024

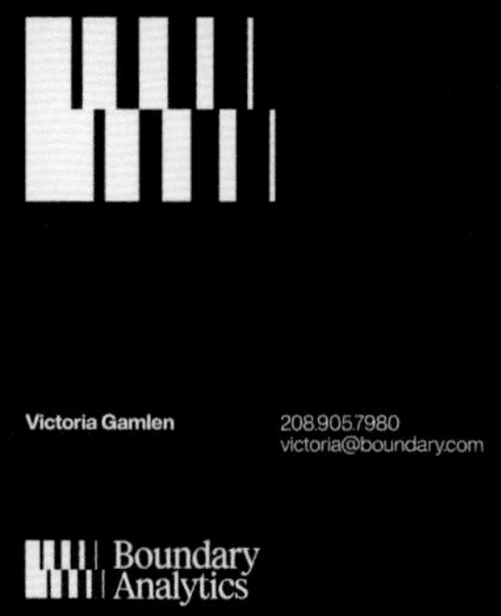

BOUNDARY DISPLAY REGULAR

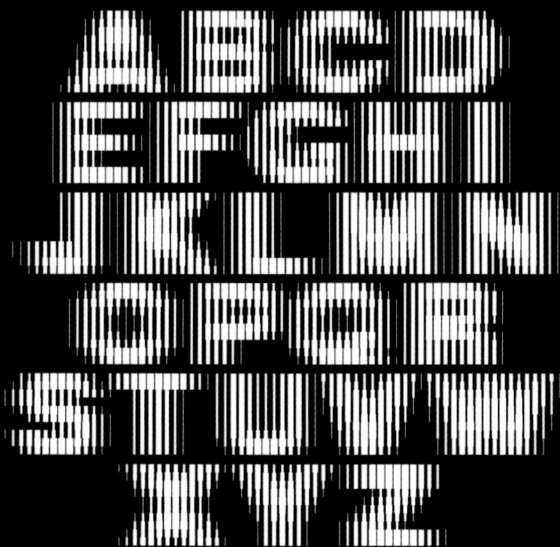

BOUNDARY DISPLAY EXPANDED

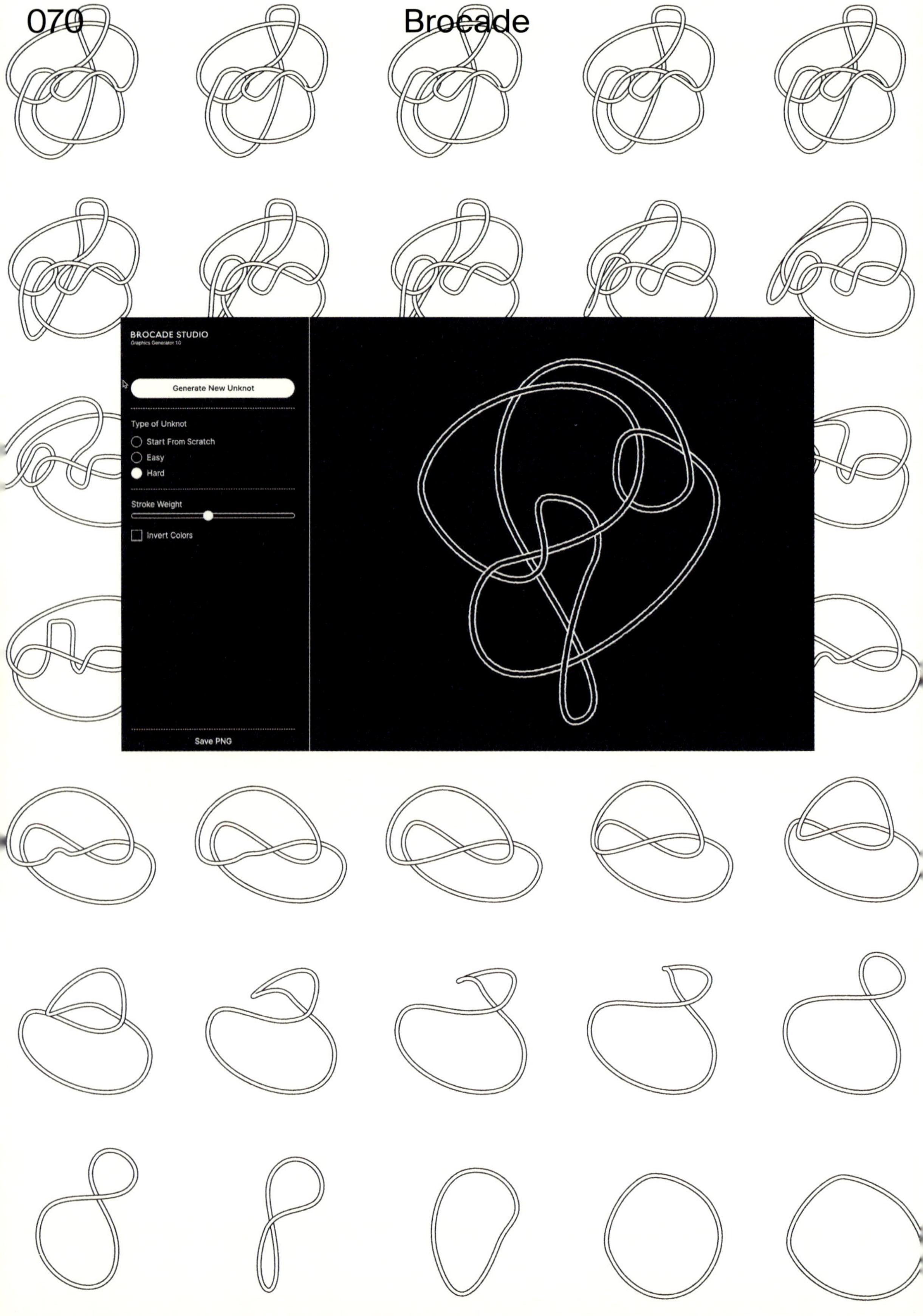
BROCADE STUDIO
Graphics Generator 1.0
Generate New Unknot
Type of Unknot
Start From Scratch
Easy
Hard
Stroke Weight
Invert Colors
Save PNG

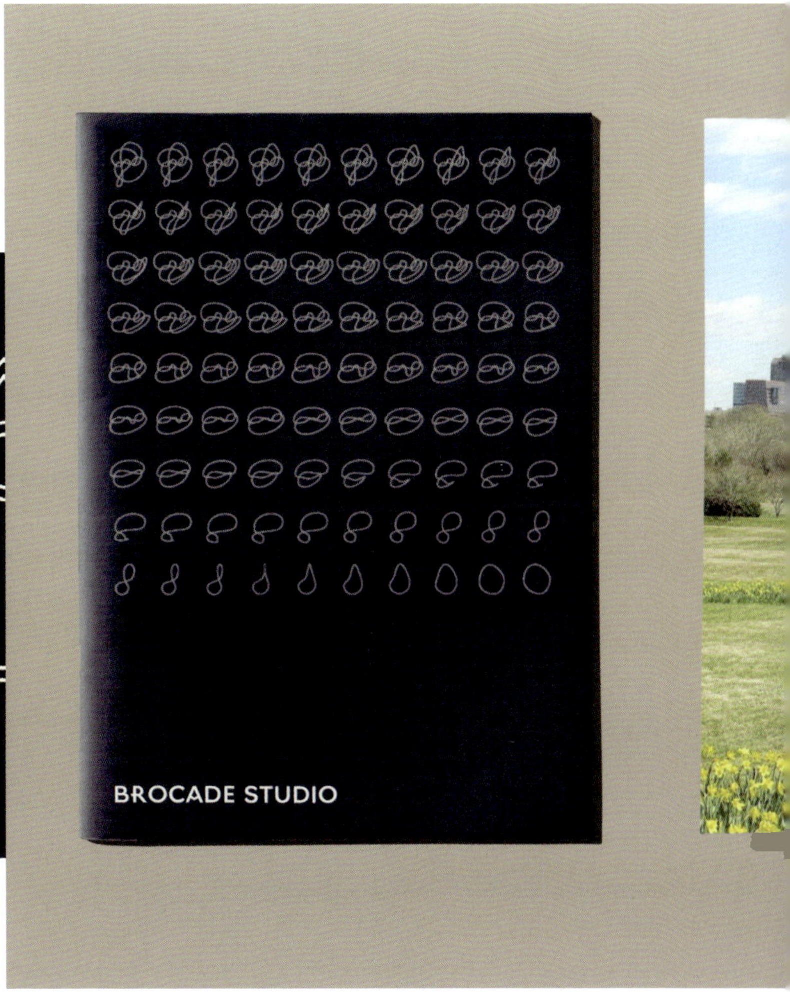

Brocade, a multidisciplinary consultancy, partners with purpose-driven organisations to address complex challenges using strategic facilitation, data science, and interpretive planning. Inspired by the term "unknot" in knot theory, which refers to a simple, untangled loop, Cotton crafted a generative web-based graphic. This elegant, ever-unique unknot, coded in Javascript, defies typical blocky web visuals, serving as Brocade's distinctive brand motif across various touchpoints.

Programming Tool/Language:
p5.js

Client:
Brocade

Isomorphic Labs

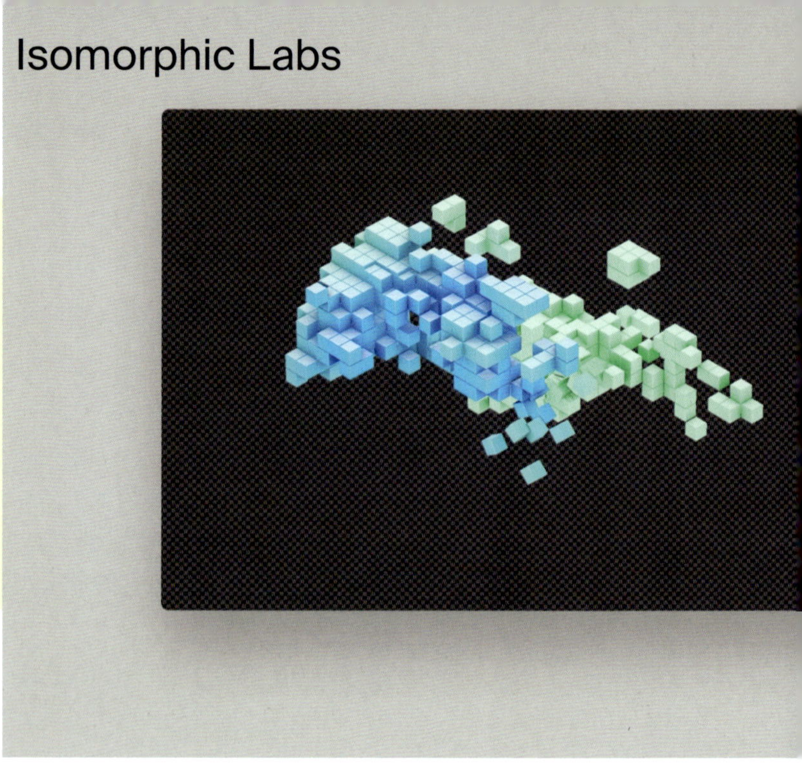

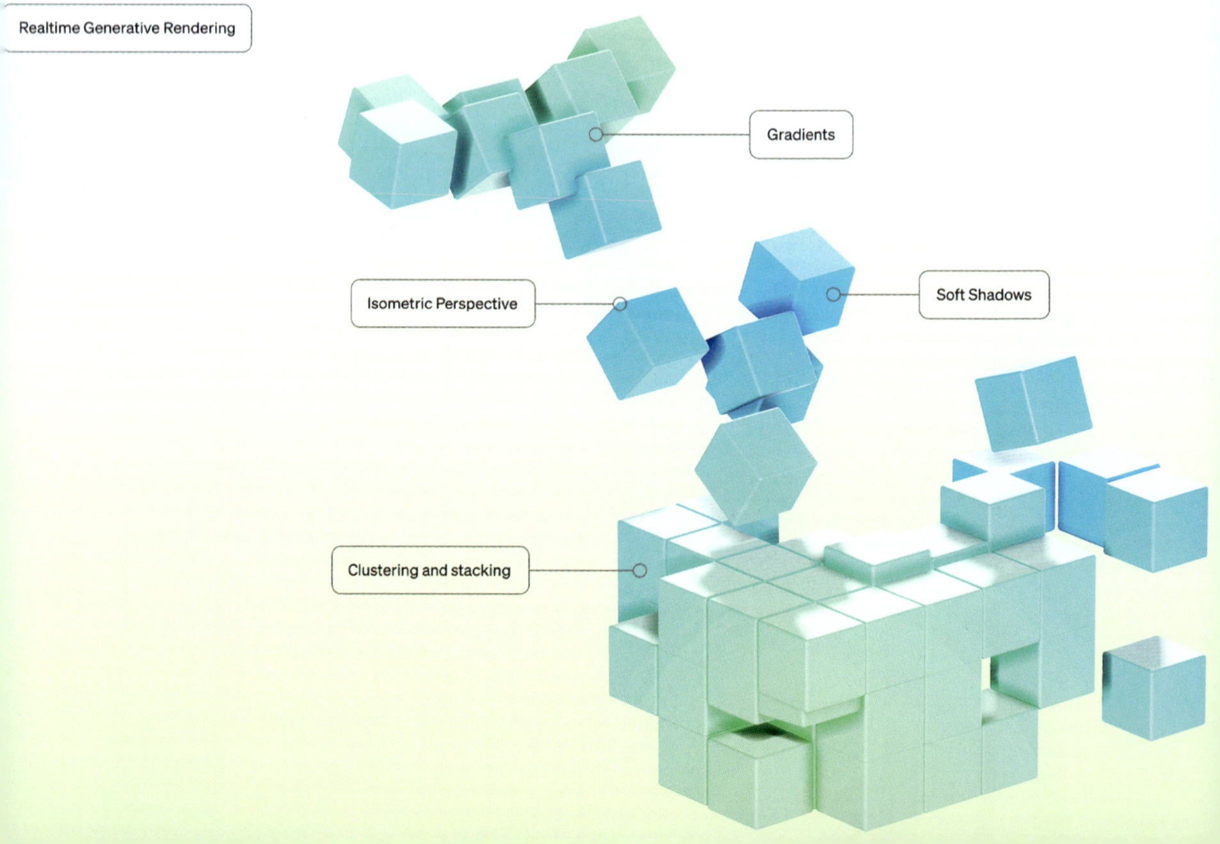

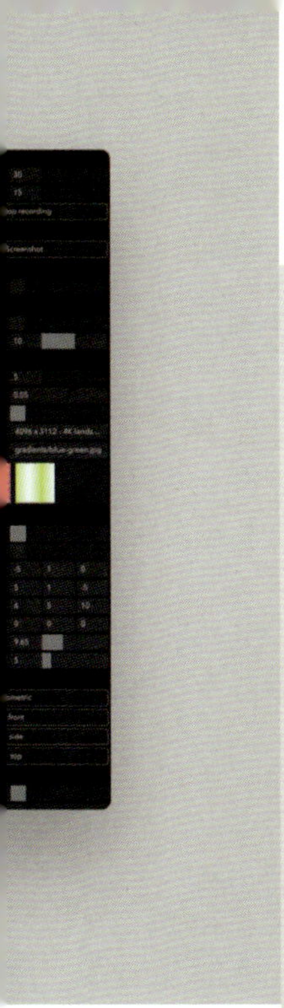

Isomorphic Labs, founded by Demis Hassabis, leverages AI to transform drug discovery. Its 3D visual language merges biology and technology, using dynamic colour expressions and fluid motion to depict AI's role in modelling biological processes. A bespoke 3D tool, developed with Marcin Ignac, was created to enable real-time visuals, offering high-resolution outputs and customisable parameters for diverse scene compositions.

Programming Tools/Languages:
JavaScript, WebGL

Client:
Isomorphic Labs

Isomorphic Labs
Reimagining drug discovery
Isomorphic Labs

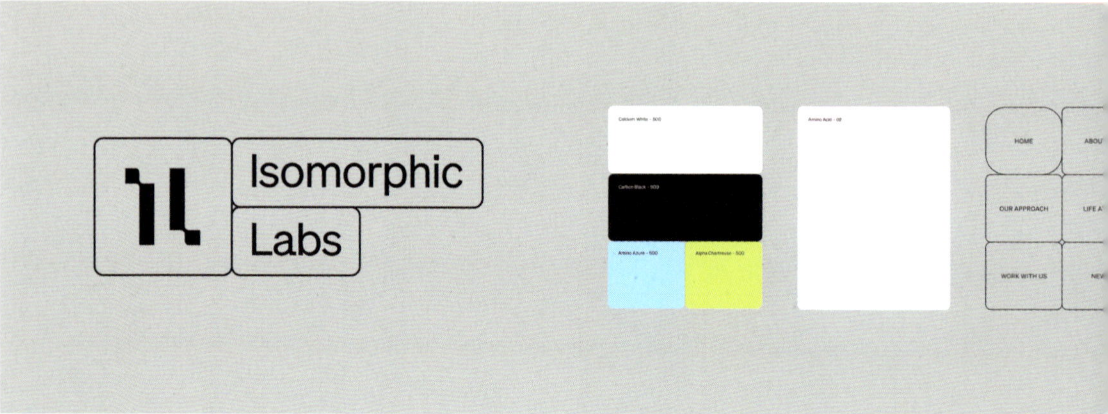
Isomorphic Labs
HOME
OUR APPROACH
WORK WITH US

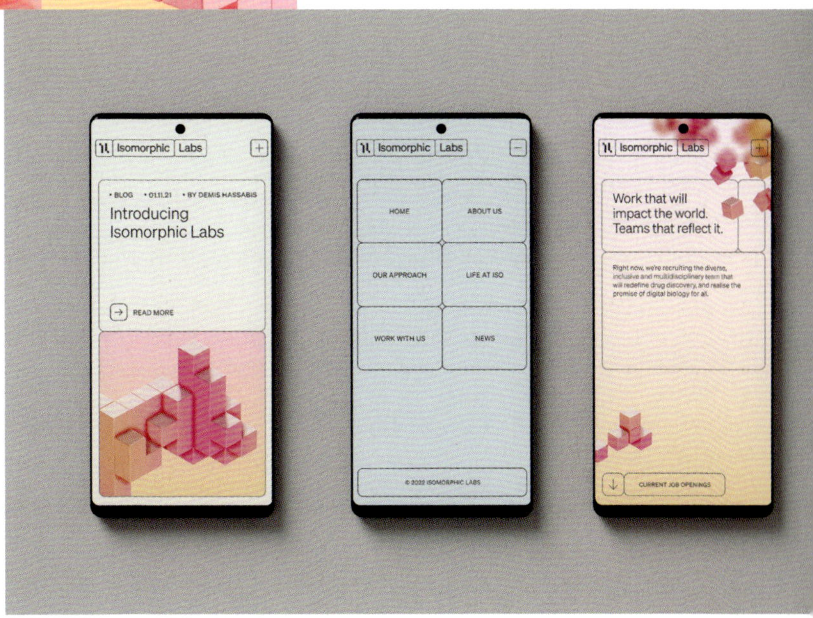
Isomorphic Labs
• BLOG • 01.11.21 • BY DEMIS HASSABIS
Introducing Isomorphic Labs
READ MORE
Isomorphic Labs
HOME
ABOUT US
OUR APPROACH
LIFE AT ISO
WORK WITH US
NEWS
© 2022 ISOMORPHIC LABS
Isomorphic Labs
Work that will impact the world. Teams that reflect it.
Right now, we're recruiting the diverse, inclusive and multidisciplinary team that will redefine drug discovery, and realise the promise of digital biology for all.
CURRENT JOB OPENINGS

Finiam

Finiam sought a refreshed identity to highlight its expertise and attract talent. The updated brand emphasises warmth and approachability through an expanded colour palette, motion elements, and illustrations. Earth tones replaced traditional tech blues, while custom typography and interactive animations added personality. A strategic social media plan reinforced engagement, making complex crypto concepts more visually compelling and accessible.

Programming Tools/Languages:
Webflow, p5.js

Client:
Finiam

We make
it easy.
About
Work
Blog
Contact
We're hiring
We make
it happen.
Work
Blog
Contact
We're hiring
finiam
make

Crypto
madness?
We make
it easy.
Unexpected
chaos?

078

Aura

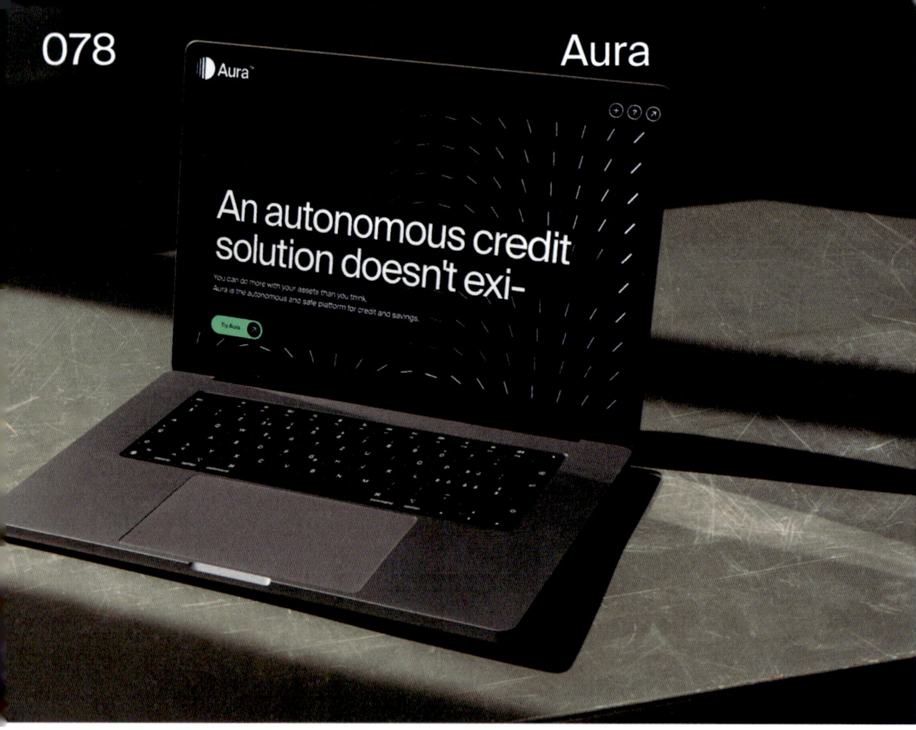

Aura
An autonomous credit solution doesn't exi-

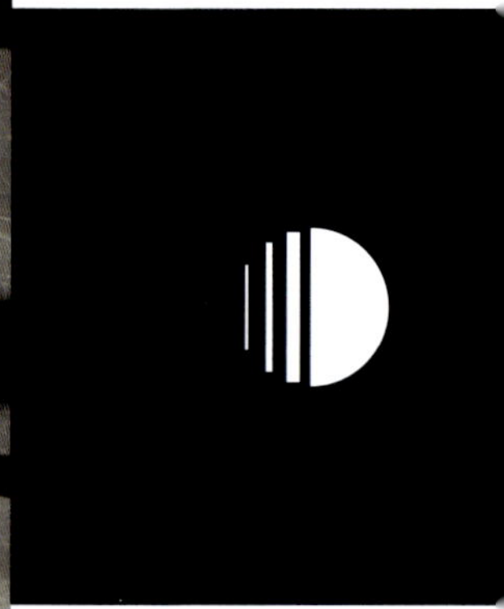

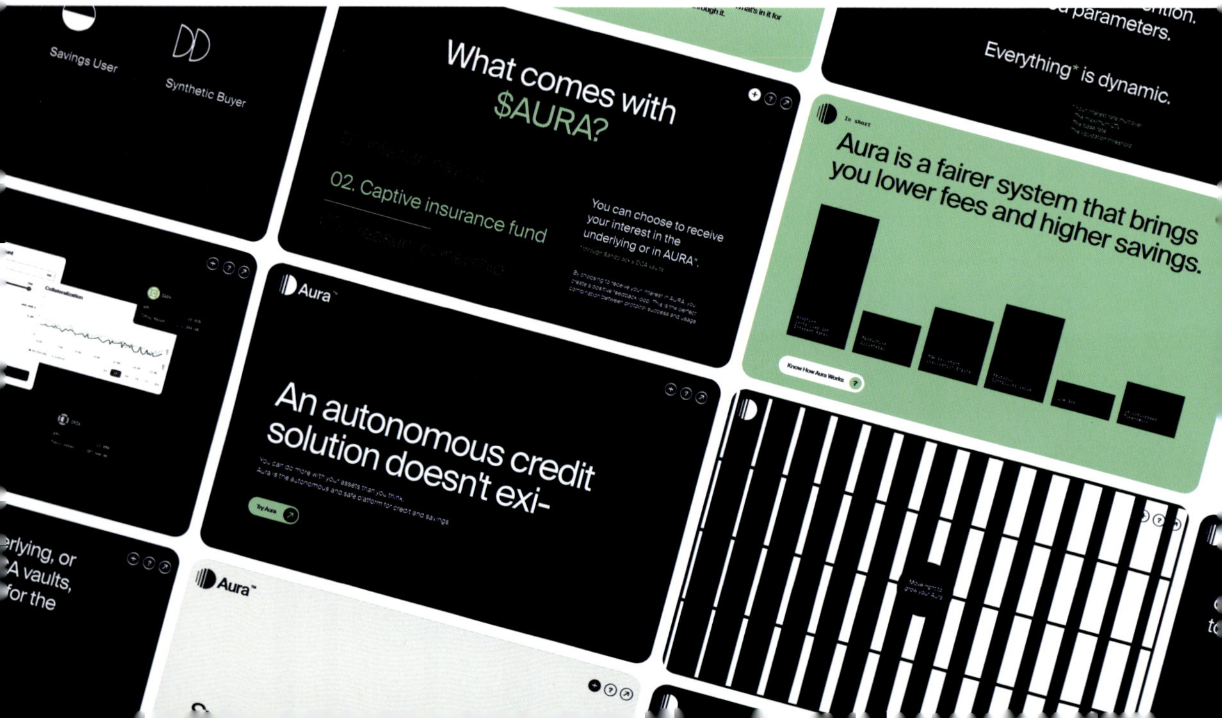

Savings User
Synthetic Buyer
What comes with $AURA?
02. Captive insurance fund
You can choose to receive your interest in the underlying or in AURA*.
Everything* is dynamic.
Aura is a fairer system that brings you lower fees and higher savings.
Aura
An autonomous credit solution doesn't exi-

Aura, a complex DeFi product, needed an accessible and engaging visual identity. The solution used transformation and motion to symbolise energy transfer and growth. Optical illusions, interactive p5.js elements, and Webflow development created an immersive experience, simplifying complex content with animations and intuitive charts to make Aura's depth more engaging and visually compelling.

Programming Tools/Languages:
Webflow, p5.js

Client:
Sandclock Holdings

BRUTE is a Hamburg-born wine brand that challenges traditional notions of winemaking by embracing the city's harsh climate. Created by Landor Hamburg and Patrik Hübner, it uses real-time and historical weather data to generate dynamic label designs reflecting wind, rain, and sun patterns. More than just wine, BRUTE tells a story of nature's raw, untamed beauty.

Programming Tools/Languages:
JavaScript, WebGL, GLSL

Client:
Schatoh Feldmark GmbH

BRUTE
Crafted by the elements

BRUTE
Wine crafted by the elements
Some grapes are nurtured. Ours are tortured.

Lobe

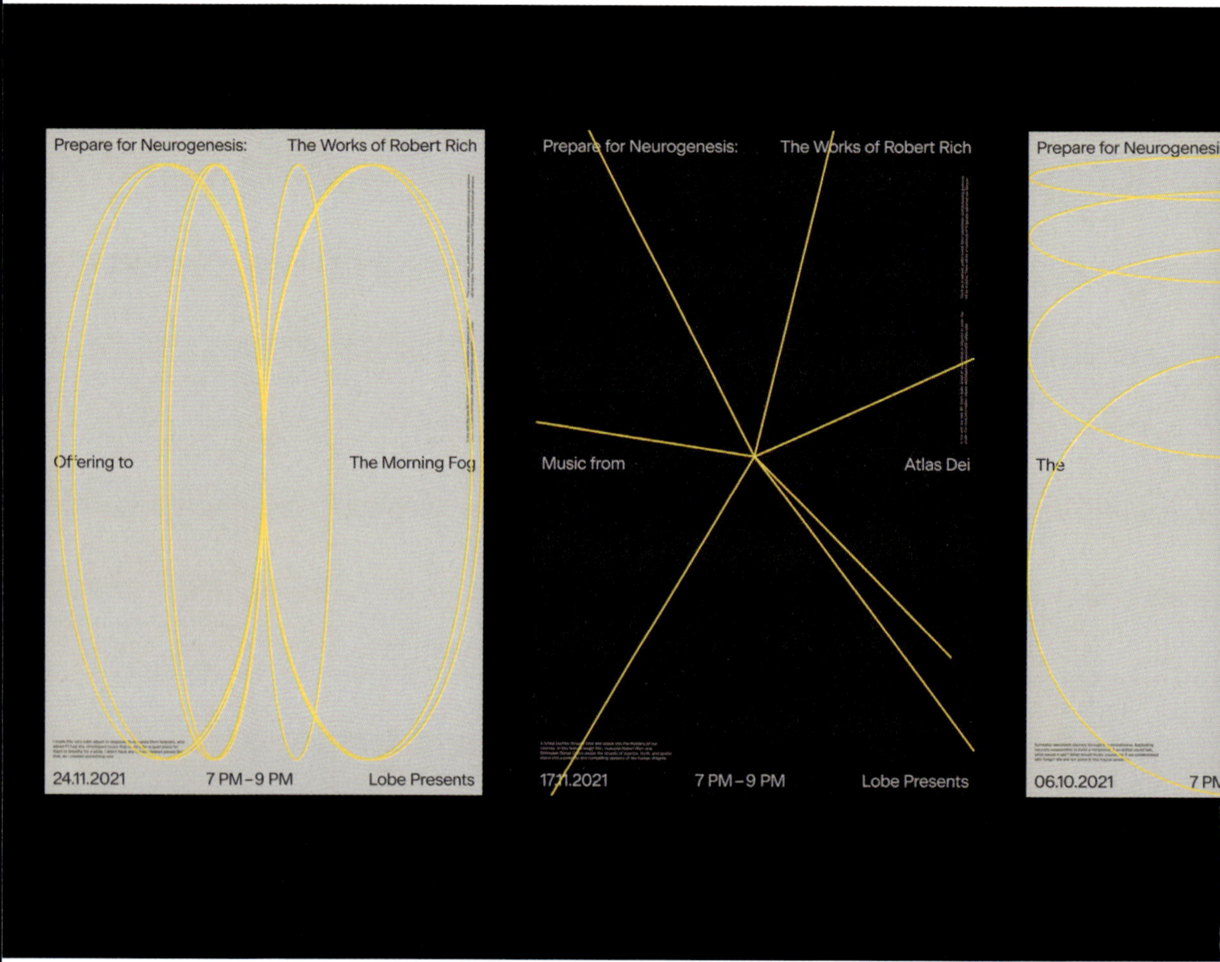

FAY designed a brand identity for Lobe, the first North American spatial sound studio to use 4DSOUND technology. The visual system includes custom generative software that animates the letters of "Lobe", reflecting the movement of spatial sound through their space. This tool allows the studio to generate their own event-specific assets and sync the logo's motion to live sound during studio sessions.

Programming Tools/Languages:
Processing, Java

Client:
Lobe

s of Robert Rich
Lobe Presents
LOBE
BY INSCAPES
SPATIAL SOUND
LOBESTUDIO.CA
EXPERIENCE
4D SOUND
LOBE
STUDIO
4D
SOUND
Lobe is the first spatial sound studio in the western hemisphere using 4DSOUND technology.

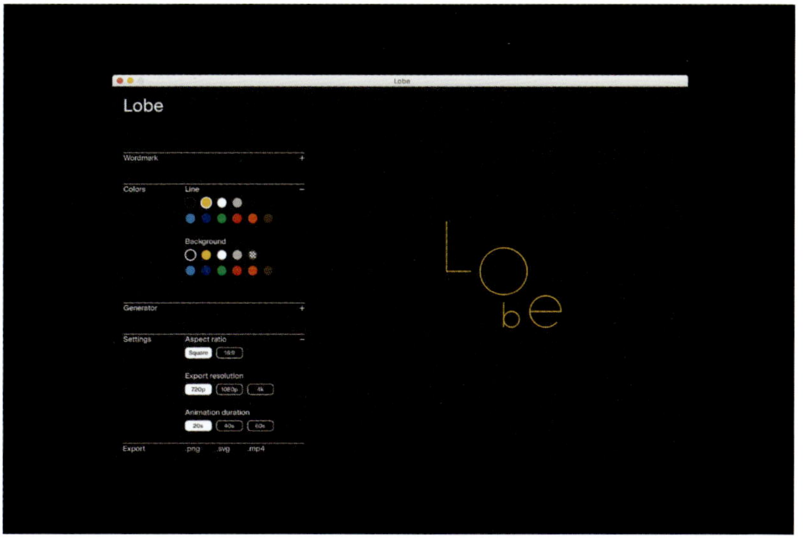
Lobe
Wordmark
Colors
Line
Background
Generator
Settings
Aspect ratio
Square
16:9
Export resolution
720p
1080p
4k
Animation duration
20s
40s
60s
Export
.png
.svg
.mp4
Lobe

Lobe

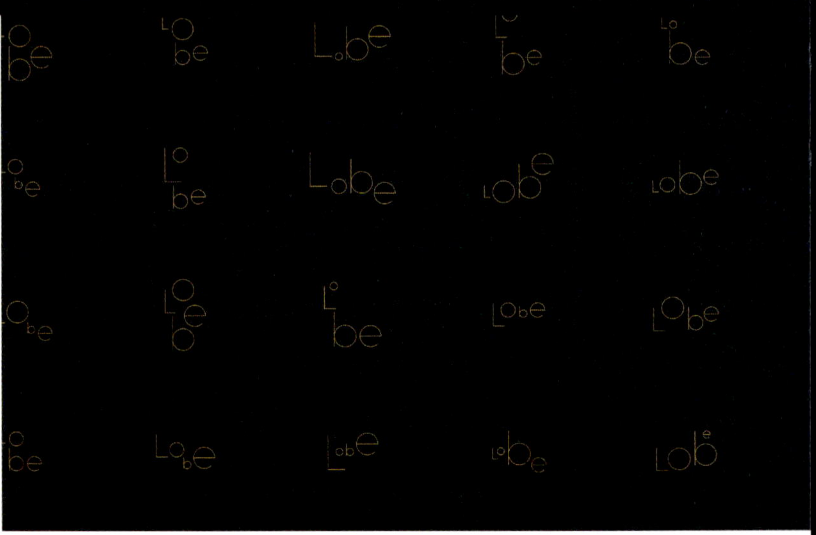

Lobe

Lobe

↙ Eén

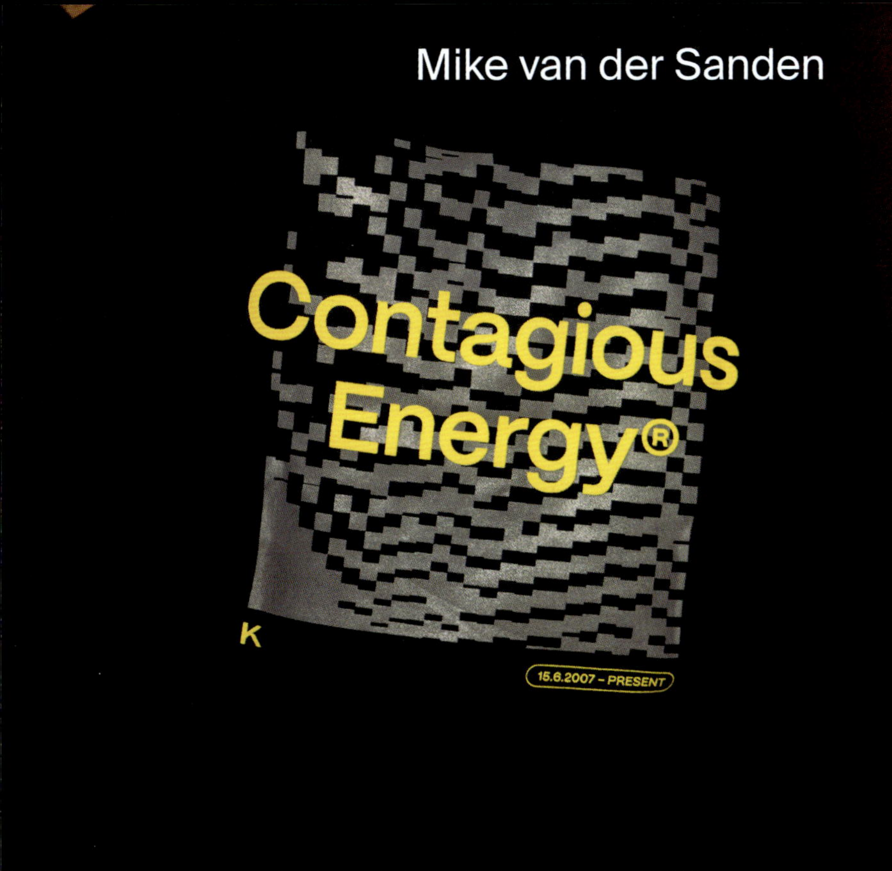

Komma's brand identity centres around dynamic energy and the idea of shared excitement. A generative system was developed to create diverse visuals, where backgrounds and contrasting colours evoke a sense of motion. By leveraging creative coding, the system generates infinite variations while maintaining consistency, ensuring all visuals stay connected under the same brand identity.

Programming Tools/Languages:
Processing, Typescript

Client:
Komma

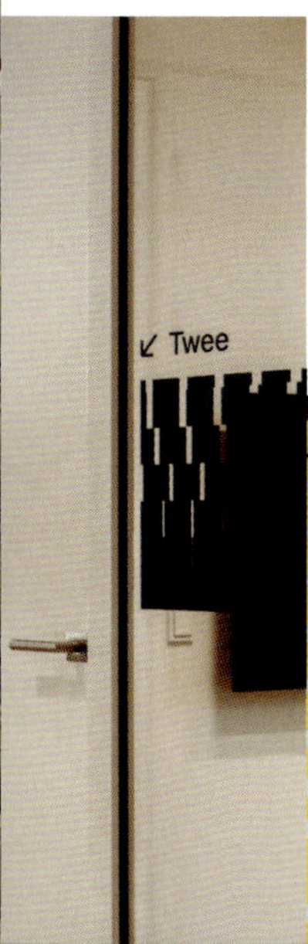

FANÉ.E

Diplomatie Studio designed the identity for FANÉ.E, an ephemeral label by Anetha, inspired by the natural cycle of growth and decay. The visual system evolves in three stages: the blossoming of a plant, partial deterioration, and final erosion. This gradual transformation reflects the label's transient nature, symbolising the fleeting beauty of time and change.

Programming Tool/Language:
Processing

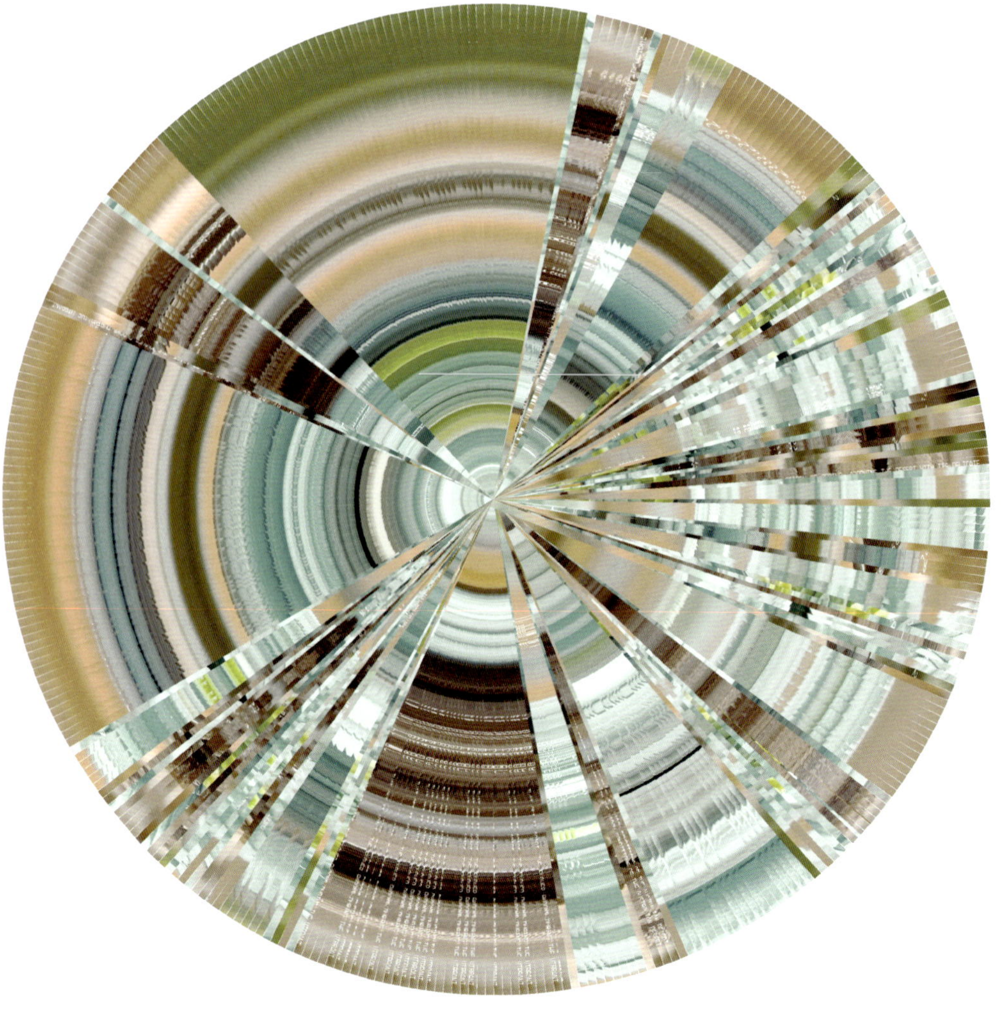

145-147BPM
AVAILABLE 3 MONTHS
PRINTEMPS
FP002
ARTIST
VBK
AUTOMNE
THE PASSIFLORA ZEPHYRE IS A RARE AND STRIKING SPECIES OF
PASSIONFLOWER THAT THRIVES IN THE LUSH, TEMPERATE REG
EUROPE. THIS CLIMBING, PERENNIAL VINE IS PARTICULARLY KNOWN
FOR ITS MESMERIZING TURQUOISE AND FIERY ORANGE BLO
UNIQUE COMBINATION THAT DISTINGUISHES IT FROM OTHER MEMBERS OF THE PASSIFLORA GENUS. WITH ITS EXOTIC BEAUTY AND VIVID HUES, THE PASS
ZEPHYRE IS A CAPTIVATING ADDITION TO GARDENS, BALCONIES, AND CONSERVATORIES, ENCHANTING ANYONE WHO ENCOUNTERS ITS OTHERWORLDLY BLOSSOM

fal
Generative media platform for developers.
Build the next generation of creativity with fal. Lightning fast inference.
Documentation
Get Started
No coldstarts. Pay only for what you use.
fal has the most capable generative media models.
Optimized by fal's inference experts.
AuraFlow
FLUX
Explore more models

MACHIN

fal
Generative media platform for developers.

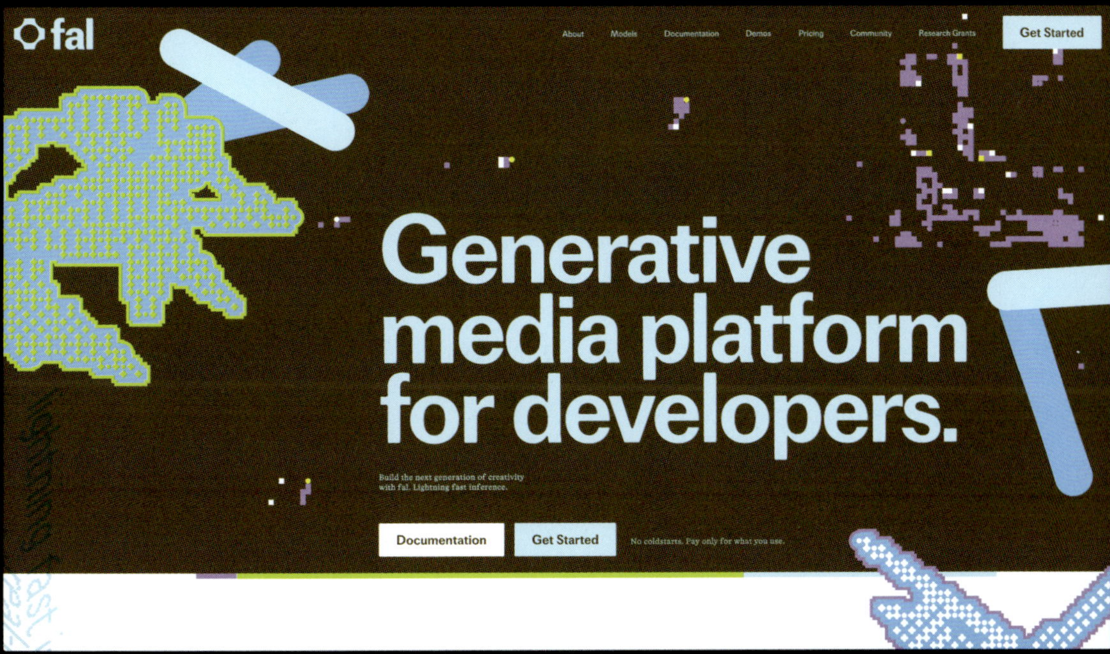

Designed by Adam Ho, I.S.P., fal is an exciting generative media platform for developers. Its identity is built around a distinctive typographic system inspired by the camera, typewriter, and processor. To bring the concept to life, generative techniques are used to add depth and evolution to the visual identity, reflecting the platform's cutting-edge, dynamic nature.

Programming Tool/Language:
p5.js

Client:
fal

fal
AI inference faster than you can type.
lightning fast inference
real-time applications

fal
Generative media platform for developers
Lightning fast Speed
Under ~120ms

Do not hold
fal
AI inference faster than you can type.

Gorkem Yurtseven
fal

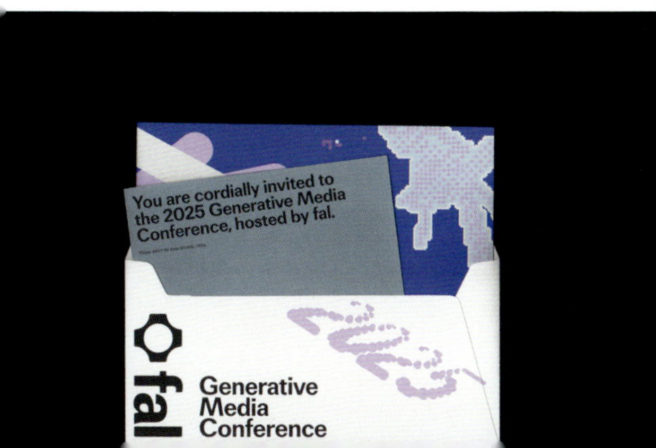
You are cordially invited to the 2025 Generative Media Conference, hosted by fal.
fal
Generative Media Conference

Inform Architecture

The identity for Inform Architecture, created by Dimitris Lelakis and Maria Tsilomitrou, features a dynamic visual system reflecting the relationship between form and architecture. It incorporates elements of positive-negative, light-shadow, and transparency-opacity. Through a custom algorithm, grid and content parameters generate unique forms for each application. The typographic system is also influenced by these generated forms, enhancing the overall design.

Programming Tool/Language:
Processing

Client:
Inform Architecture

Dimitris Lelakis (Lelism), Maria Tsilomitrou (Studio Chill)

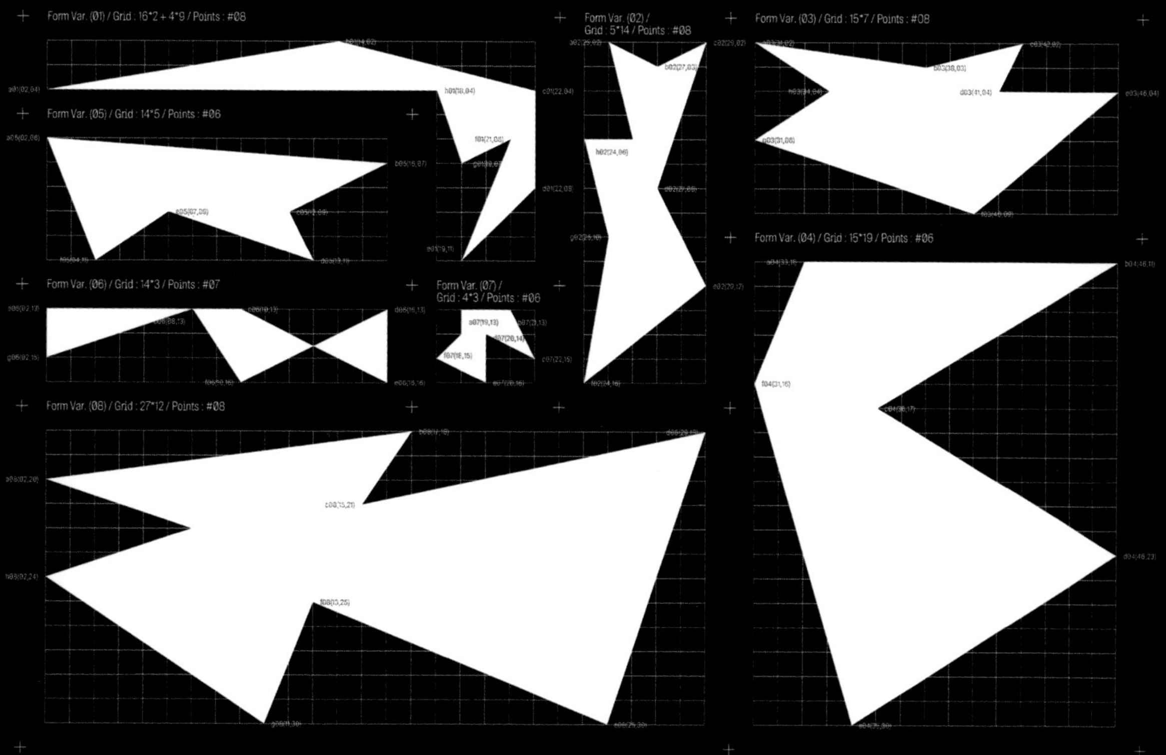

Inform Architecture

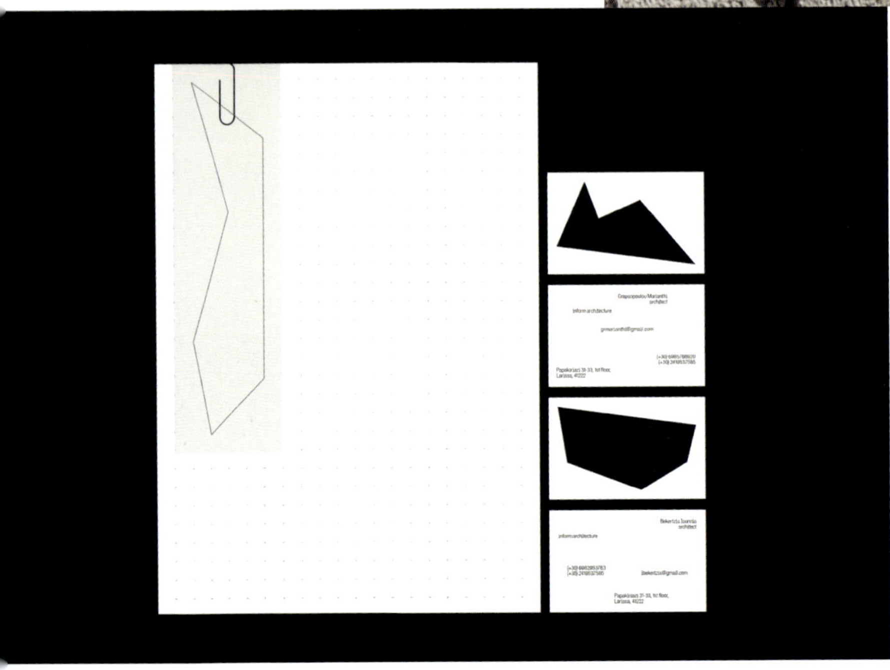

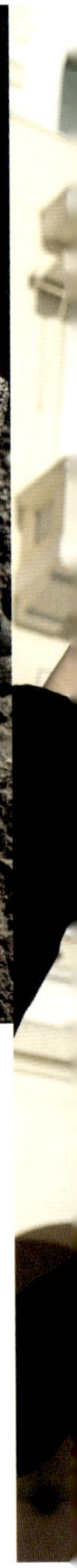

ΟΛΥΜ

ONEFOOTBALL
SAME GAME. NEW VIBE.
Better stats, better graphics, better hype.
OneFootball
THE ULTIMATE
FOOTBALL PLATFORM

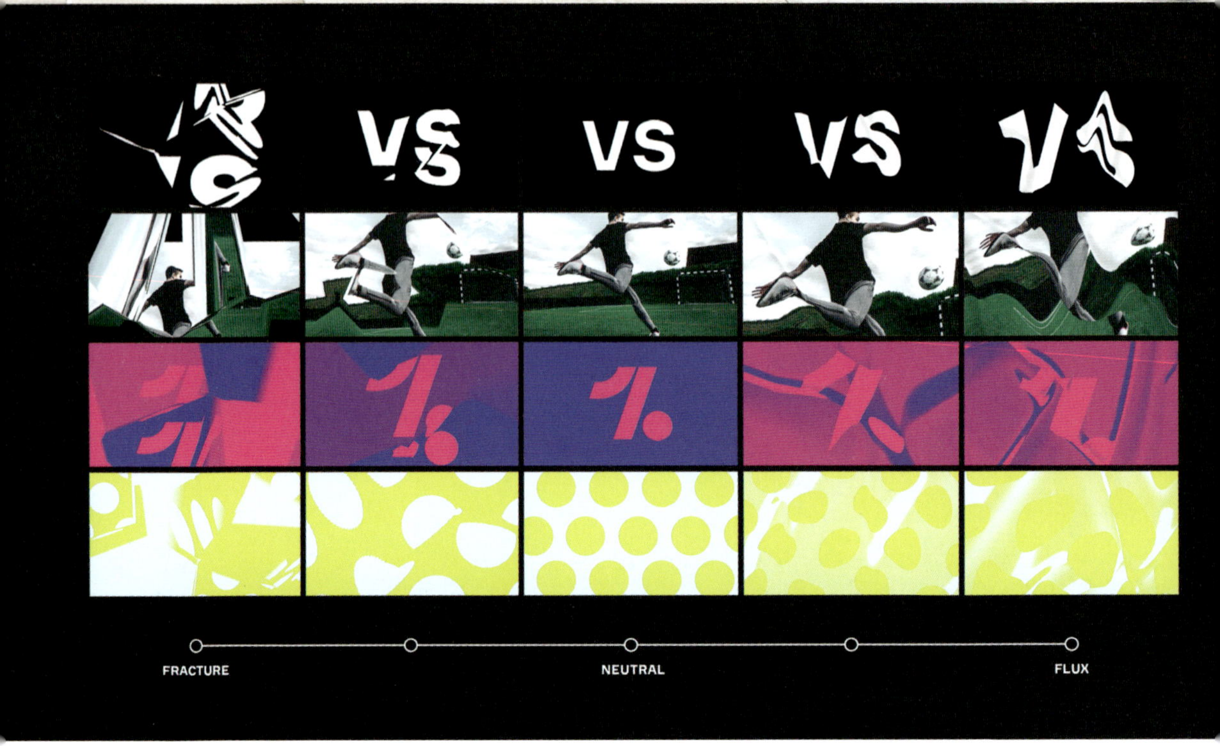
VS
VS
VS
VS
VS
FRACTURE
NEUTRAL
FLUX

DesignStudio rebranded OneFootball, the global football media platform, with a strategy called "Hype the Game". This dynamic approach adapts to fan moods, using a "hype generator" created with Artificial Rome. The tool generates three visual states—Fracture, Neutral, and Flux—affecting everything from the logo to typography and imagery, creating an engaging, responsive experience for fans.

Programming Tools/Languages:
Processing, p5.js

Client:
OneFootball

Scalability
with
difference

CHAIN

B

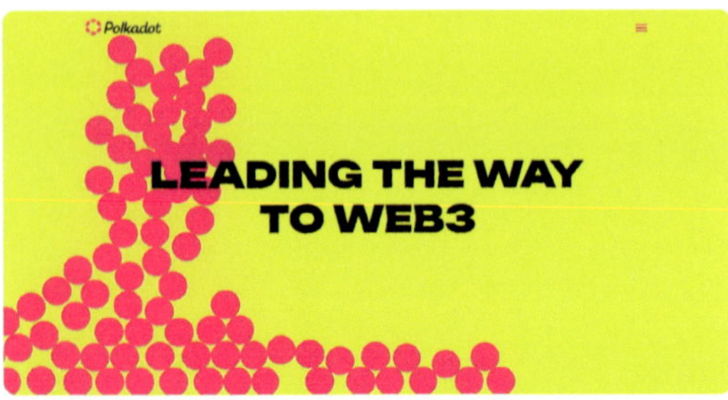
Polkadot
LEADING THE WAY
TO WEB3

Polkadot
MANY CHAINS, ONE
NETWORK. ENDLESS
POSSIBILITIES

Polkadot
THE FUTURE IS
MULTICHAIN

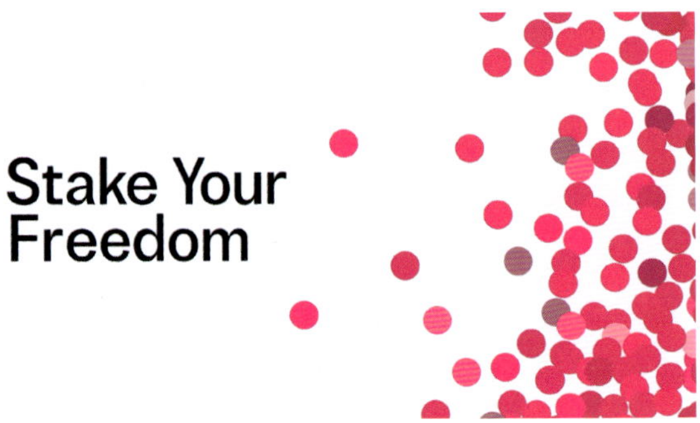
Stake Your
Freedom

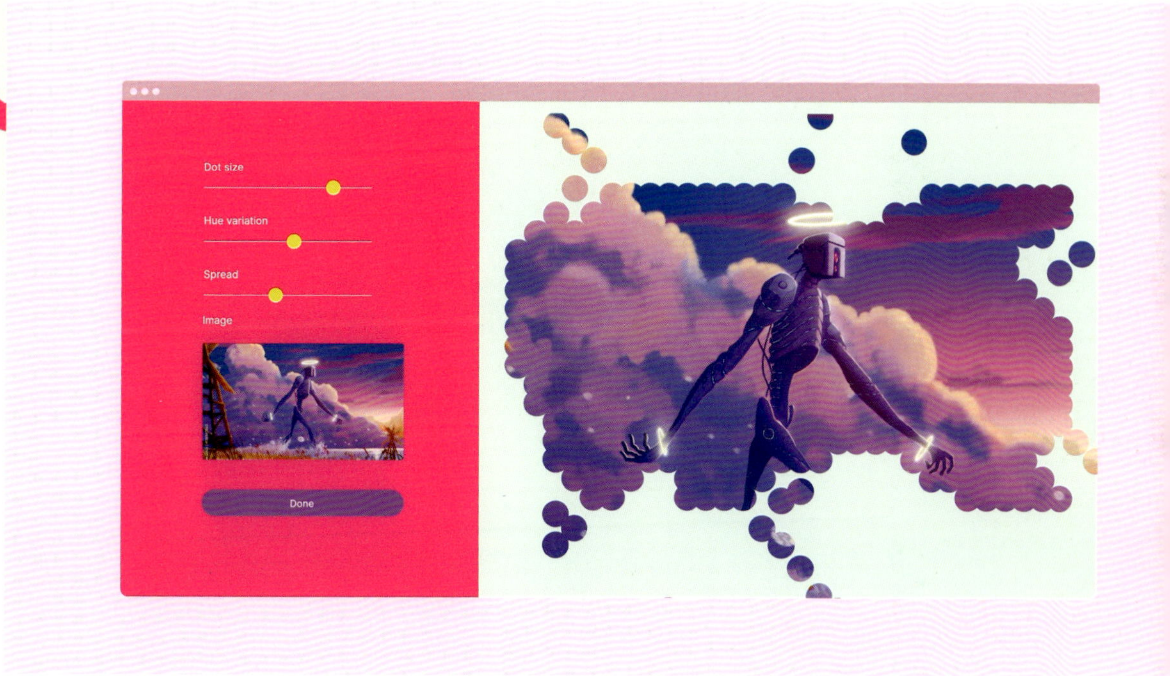

Polkadot, a blockchain network focused on decentralisation and community-driven innovation, was refreshed with a dynamic brand identity system created by Koto Berlin and Patrik Hübner. The generative design system allows users to create unique visuals within a consistent framework, guided by modular, algorithmic rules. This flexible, scalable approach fosters collaboration and grows with the blockchain revolution.

Programming Tools/Languages:
JavaScript, WebGL, GLSL, Vue.js

Client:
Polkadot

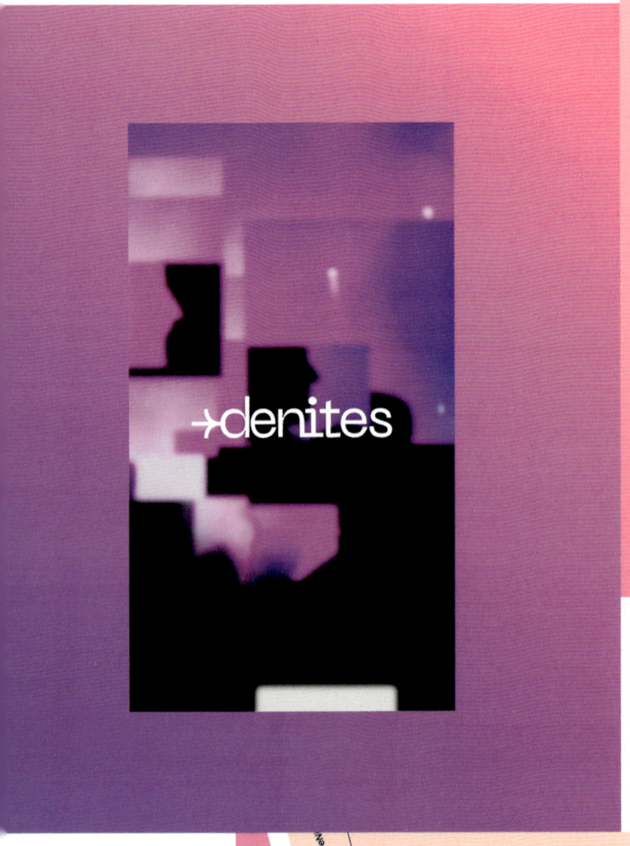
→denites

→denites

Join us
Hosts
Why they exist
What are DeNites
Next events
and party like a local
Join us
Hosts

DeNites needed a bold identity to break through the noise of official crypto afterparties. The branding captures the electric energy of a must-attend event, where vibrant colours reflect the lively atmosphere, while deconstructed imagery nods to the digital world. This dynamic visual language makes DeNites the ultimate destination for those seeking an unforgettable night.

Programming Tool/Language:
Webflow

Client:
Talent Protocol

IBM Quantum
Super Position
Entanglement
Interference
Composition
Palette
Resolution
Qubit Phase
Warm Glow
Balance
Strength
Phase
Reset

Sarah
McDonague
Tyra
Sandford

IBM Quantum
Summit 2023

FIELD.IO developed a cohesive visual brand for IBM Quantum, spanning digital, product, and events. A generative brand tool was designed to create dynamic assets that reflect the adaptable nature of quantum computing. Drawing inspiration from quantum principles, the design explores the interplay of quantum states through interactive visuals. FIELD.IO also crafted visual explainers to simplify complex quantum concepts, bridging science and design for deeper understanding.

Programming Tools/Languages:
GLSL, TouchDesigner

Client:
IBM

Prescience [colour shift : colour shift distance : prescience opacity : line thickness : particle amount]

Planning [visibility : monochrome : swing duration : swing interval : quantise angles]

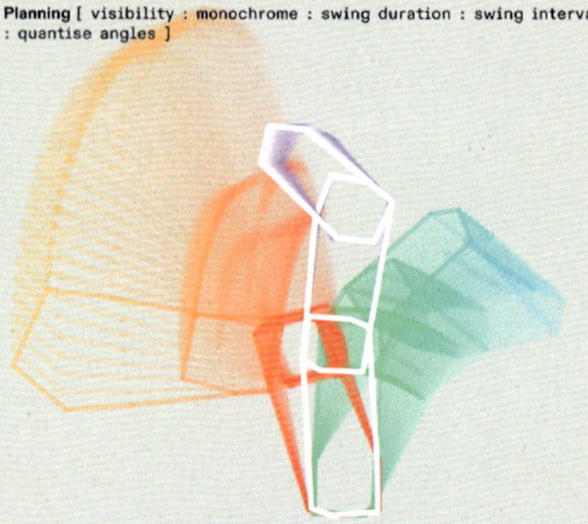

Simulation [simulation colour : swing duration : swing inte : quantise angles]

Sensing [sense colour : sense thickness : sense grid size : sense distance : sensing radius]

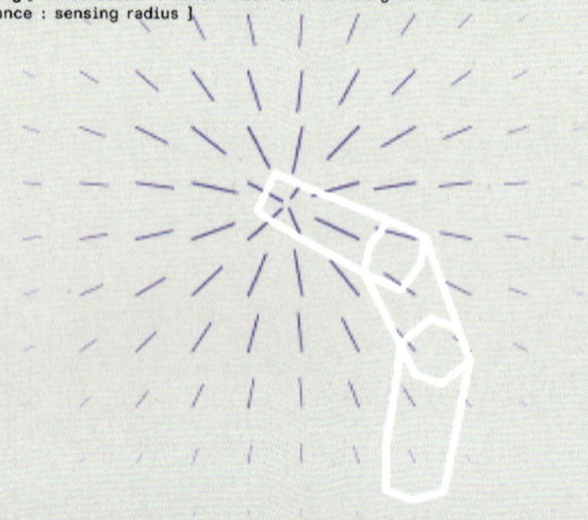

Learning [line visibility : line colour : swing duration : swing interval : quantise angles]

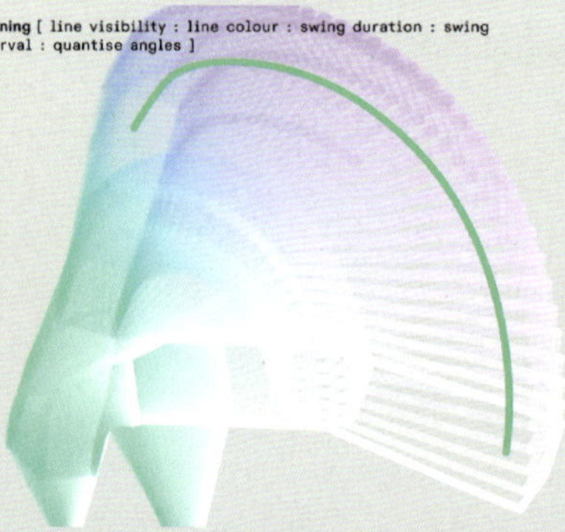

Collaboration [grid width : grid height : grid spacing : grid randomisation : randomisation colour]

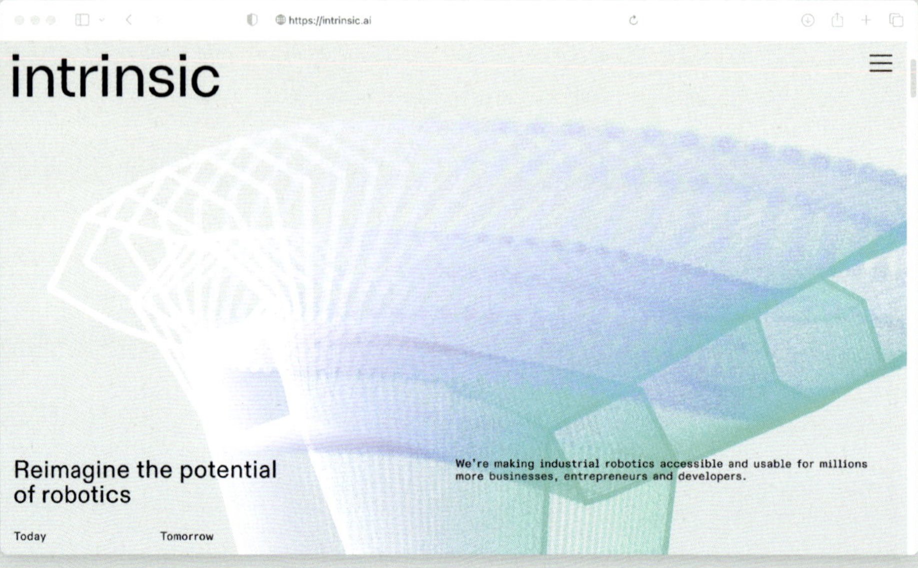

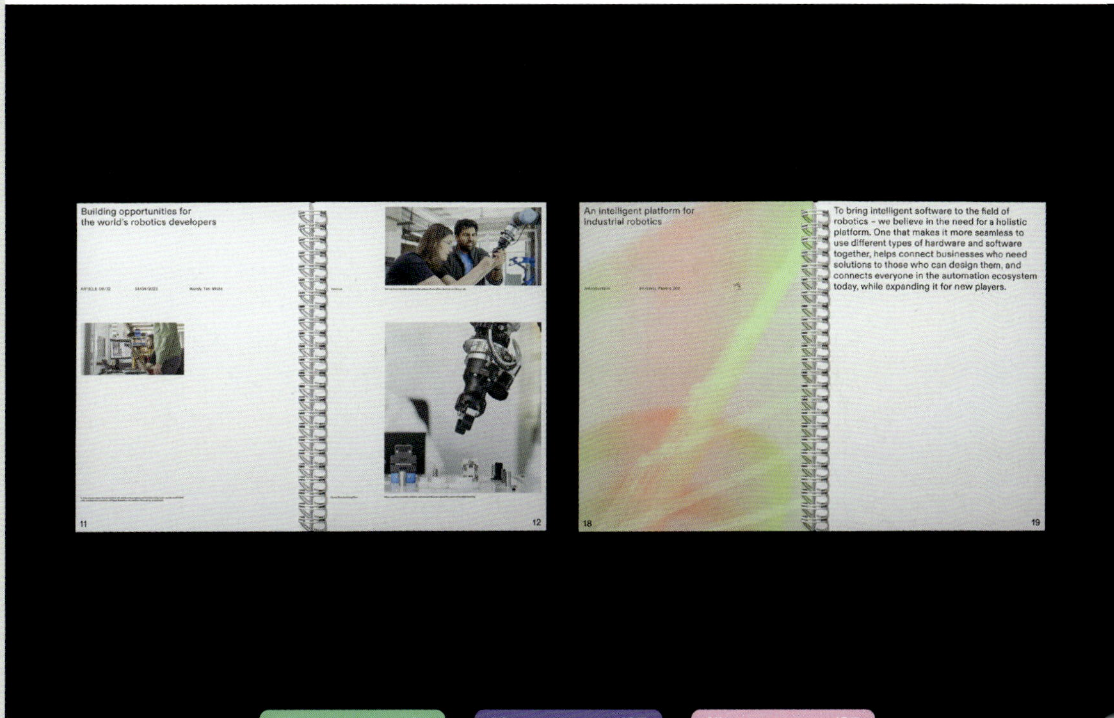

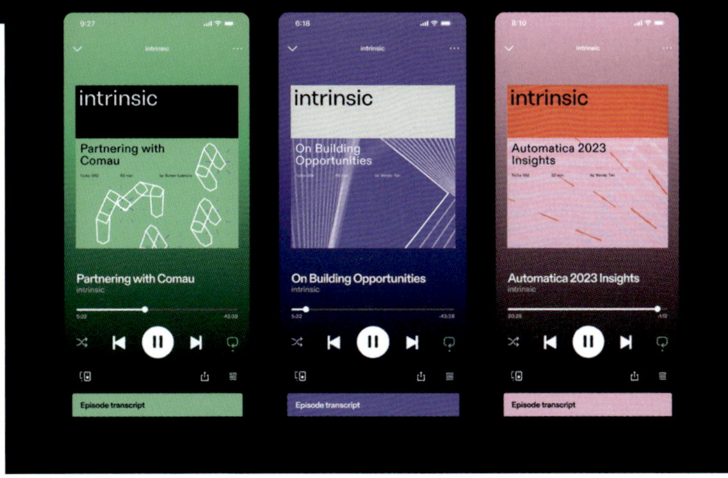

Pentagram developed the brand identity and a generative visual tool for Intrinsic, an AI-driven robotics software company within Google's Alphabet. The identity centres on prescience, reflecting Intrinsic's ability to simulate thousands of outcomes. A custom-built tool generates semi-abstract robotic arm visualisations, animated through inverse kinematics to mimic real-world motion, showcasing the platform's problem-solving capabilities.

Programming Tools/Languages:
JavaScript, Google Chromium (via Electron), WebGL, FFmpeg, custom code

Client:
Intrinsic

intrinsic

ntrinsic

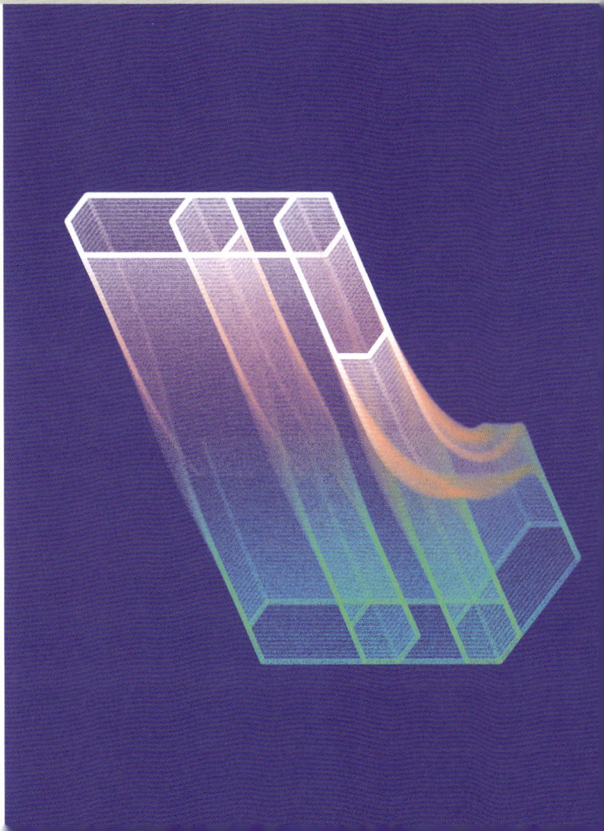

studio_veh
Design
Intern
Winter
2023/2024

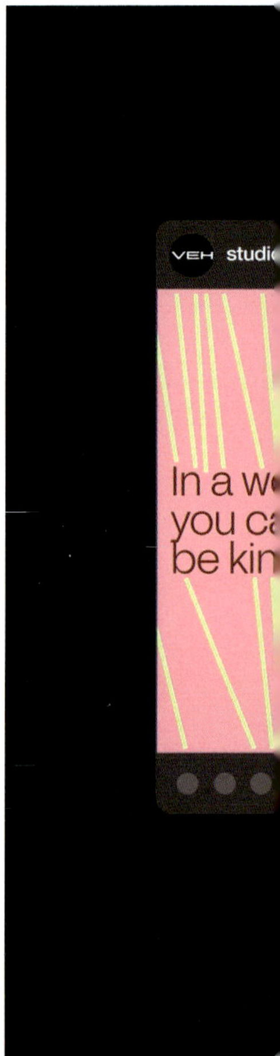

made
with love
and
Creative
Coding

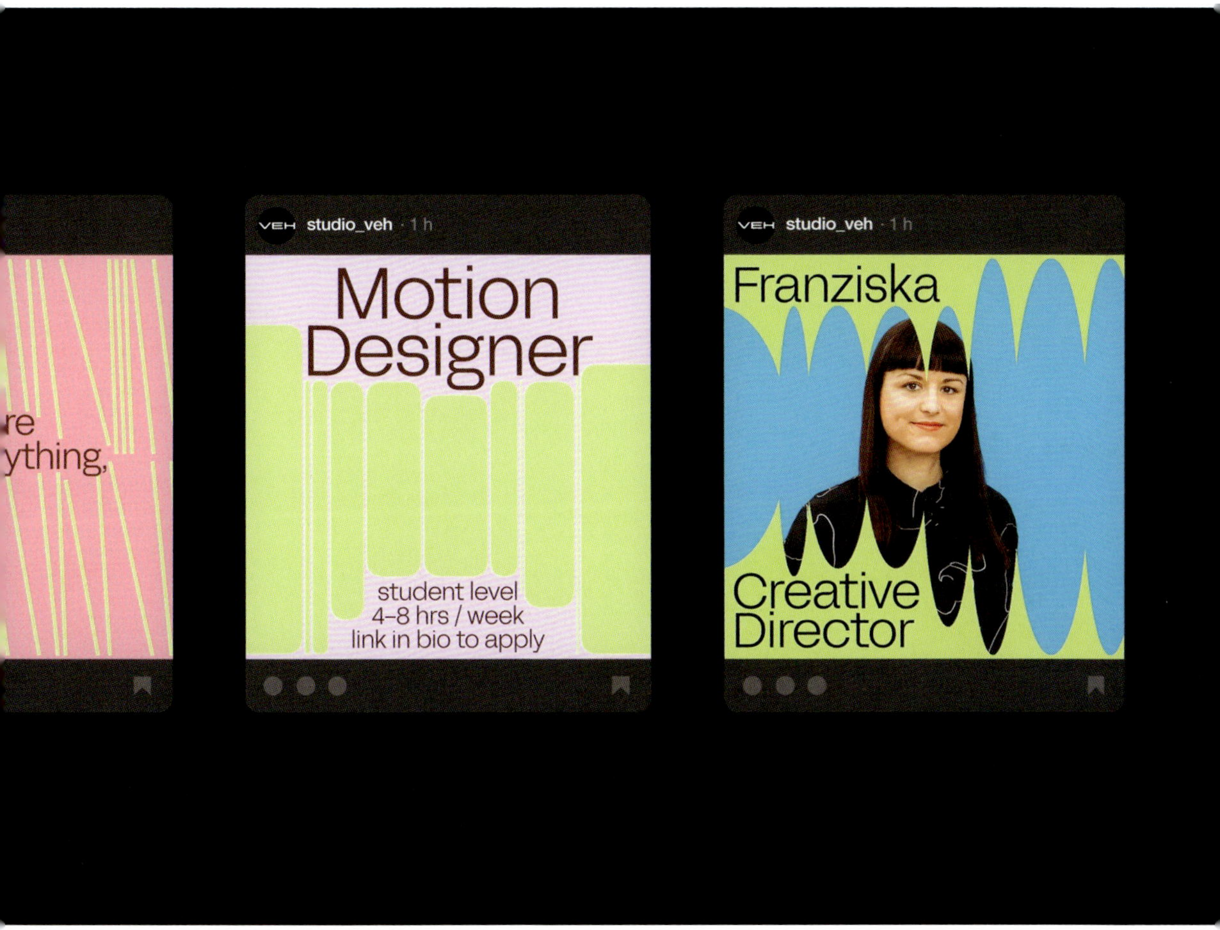

Afterimage collaborated with Studio VEH, experts in brand strategy and communication, to create a generative motion identity for their social media and presentations. The result was a suite of four code-based tools designed to generate videos, enhancing Studio VEH's ability to communicate their brand in a dynamic and engaging way across various platforms.

Programming Tool/Language:
Processing

Client:
Studio VEH

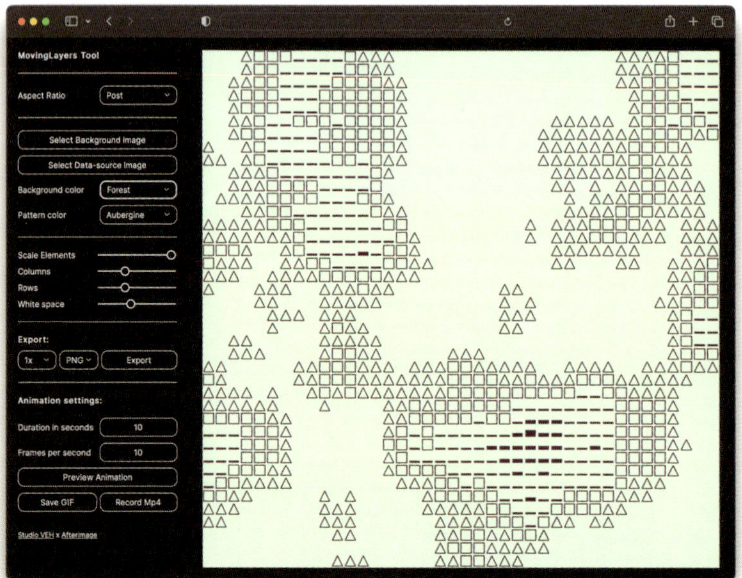
MovingLayers Tool
Aspect Ratio
Post
Select Background Image
Select Data-source Image
Background color
Forest
Pattern color
Aubergine
Scale Elements
Columns
Rows
White space
Export:
1x
PNG
Export
Animation settings:
Duration in seconds
10
Frames per second
10
Preview Animation
Save GIF
Record Mp4
Studio VEH x Afterimage

Afterimage partnered with Studio VEH to develop a web tool for MovingLayers, a Vienna-based company that transforms raw geographical data into dynamic, immersive visualisations. The tool enables users to create static and animated graphics from maps, supporting communication across various channels. This helps businesses make informed decisions, uncover hidden patterns, and gain a deeper understanding of the world around them.

Programming Tools/Languages:
JavaScript, p5js, HTML+CSS

Client:
MovingLayers

Mascot

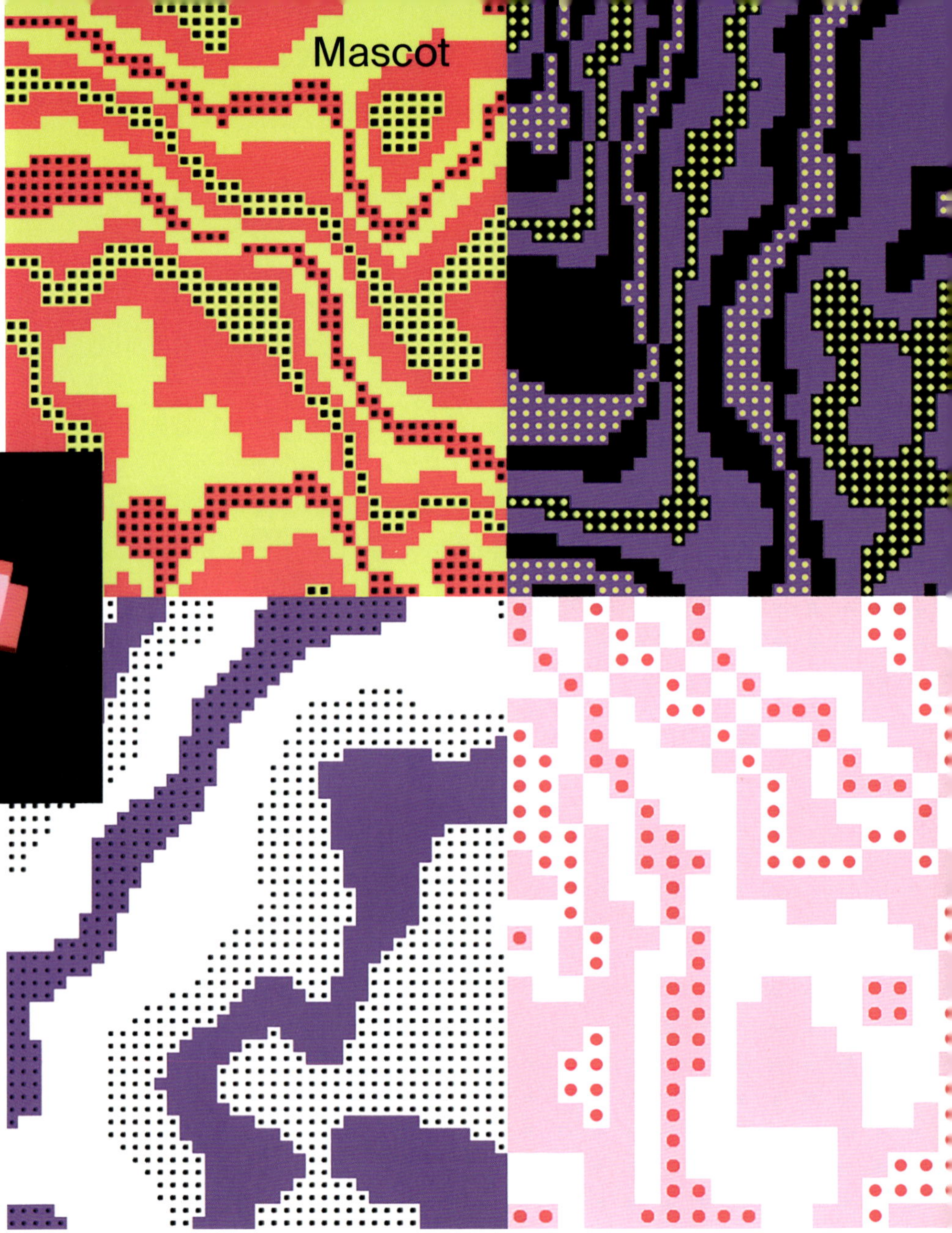

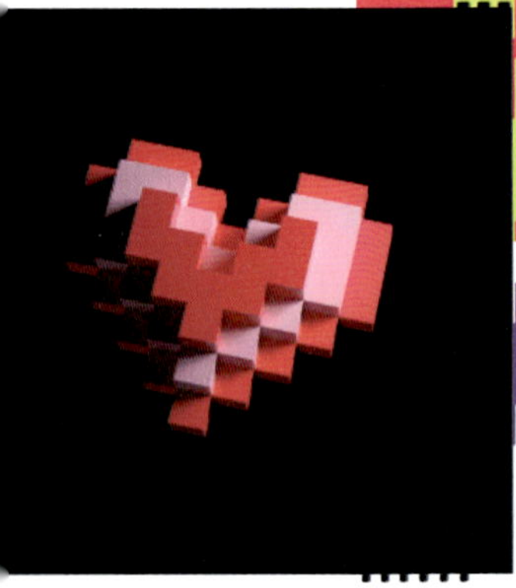

Mascot Agency's branding system merges creativity and technology through a flexible, generative identity. With 729 logo variations and dynamic graphics, the design adapts in colour, size, and animation, ensuring a fresh look for every application. This customisable approach reflects the agency's mission to craft unique, emotionally resonant ideas that connect with audiences in innovative ways.

Programming Tool/Language:
Processing

Client:
Mascot Agency

mascot
mascot
mascot
mascot
mascot

enjoei

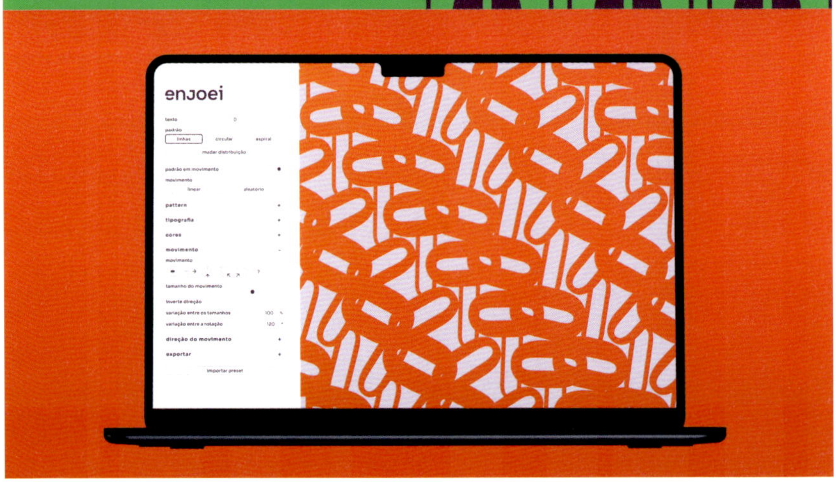
enjoei
texto
padrão
linhas
circular
espiral
mudar distribuição
padrão em movimento
movimento
linear
aleatorio
pattern
tipografia
cores
movimento
movimento
tamanho do movimento
inverte direção
variação entre os tamanhos
100
variação entre a rotação
120
direção do movimento
exportar
importar preset

André Burnier's project for Enjoei, a platform revolutionising Brazil's fashion scene, centres on a custom typeface designed to enhance the digital craft experience. Enjoei Display, a versatile family of five weights, offers a flexible system with adjustable width and weight, creating a range of moods. This dynamic type generates infinite patterns, boosting sales and elevating the brand's cool factor.

Programming Tool/Language:
p5.js

Client:
Enjoei

SPOTLIGHT
02

DIA Studio
Meg Donohoe & Mitch Paone

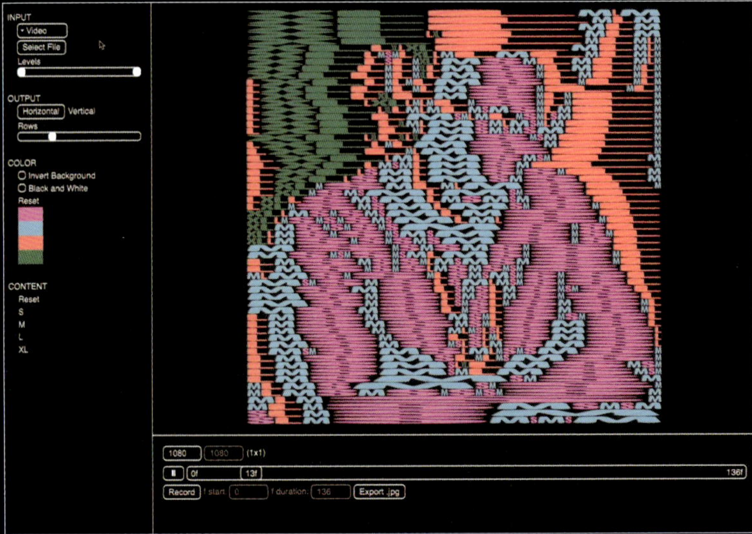

For the technology start-up smlXL, we had fun creating a generative design system that embodied the brand's essence of scale, exponential growth, and momentum – all using just the five characters in 'smlXL'. The playful concept was brought to life through motion behaviours, which we developed into a custom tool for efficiency, consistency, and creative control. This tool allowed for the seamless import of images, videos, and live camera feeds, with the capability to export a variety of formats suitable for both digital and print media. Built using After Effects, Cinema 4D, Cavalry, and finalised with JavaScript, the project allowed us to explore how typography alone could convey the idea of exponential growth and size (S, M, L, XL). We also learned how to overcome technical challenges in rendering video within a web-based tool.”

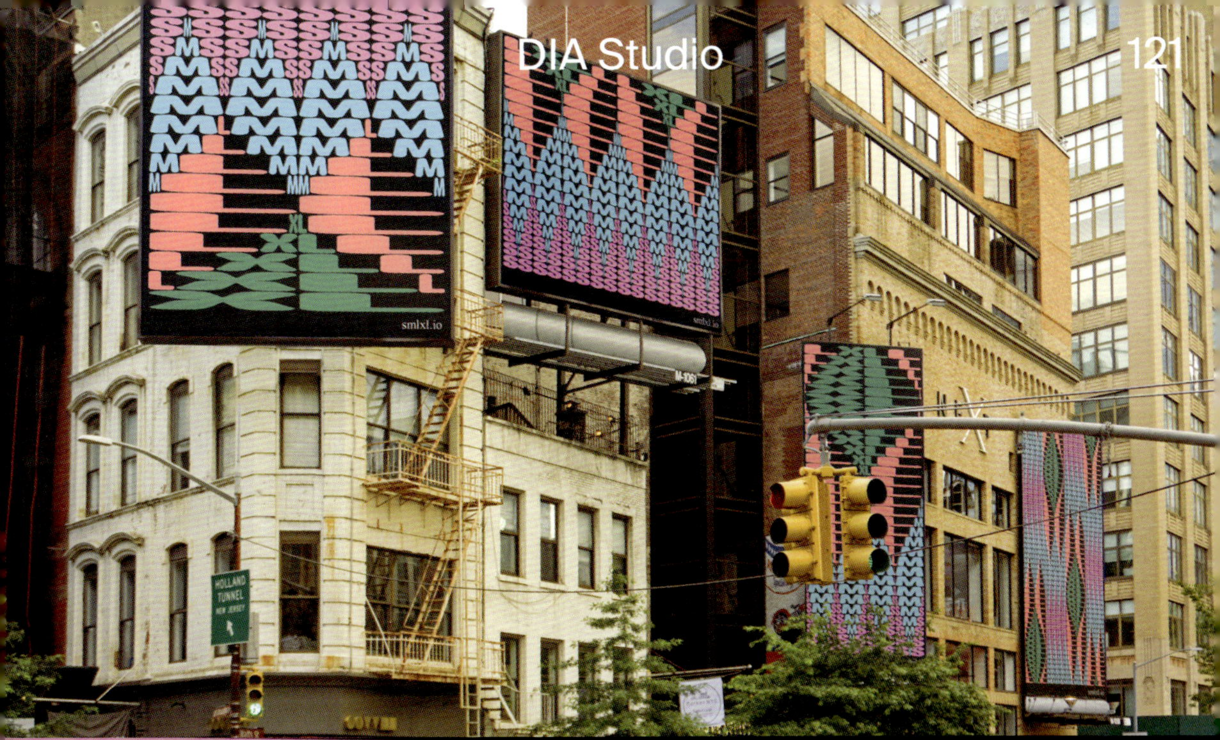
smlxl.io
smlxl.io
HOLLAND TUNNEL
NEW JERSEY

We build products that help groups align and better achieve their collective goals in a rapidly changing world.
smlxl.io
sMLXL

programming language
JavaScript

client
Adidas London

project year
2019

"For the Adidas flagship stores launched in London, we created a generative identity system that could deliver a dynamic and immersive customer experience. The content was programmed to ensure no repetition during a store visit, offering fresh visuals throughout the day. Using Cinema 4D and After Effects, we took on an exploratory role where we pushed the boundaries of the brand's existing assets to create a unique look that worked seamlessly across a variety of screens in unconventional formats.

In terms of the creative concept, we drew inspiration from the rhythmic actions of sports—starting and stopping—ensuring all movement had a non-continuous energy. As we partnered with Field.io for the development of the custom CMS, we had to maintain close oversight to ensure the design direction remained consistent. Ultimately, the system, which spans both motion and static signage, is now being implemented across Adidas flagship stores worldwide."

REPEAT

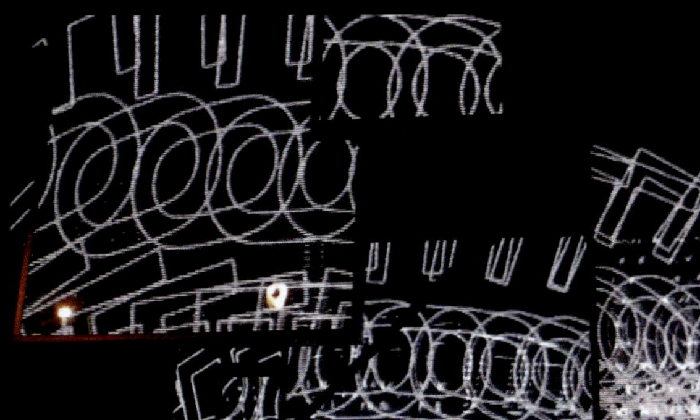

programming language
JavaScript

client
A-DA

project year
2021

"The team at Listen in New York sought to expand their business by founding an experience innovation design agency, which they named A-DA. Drawing inspiration from the one and only Ada Lovelace, we developed a generative design system that could adapt seamlessly across various formats and media. The creative concept centred on an animation that cycled through a curated list of relevant words beginning with 'A' and 'D', reflecting the agency's focus and capabilities. Alongside this, we also designed an image-based motion behaviour to bring their case studies to life in a distinctive and ownable way. Using After Effects and JavaScript, we followed our established process from design strategy to R&D, implementation, refinement, and delivery."

A________________DA
A________________DA
A__________DA
A___DA
A_DA

ALLOY
DEMOCRATIC
ASTROPHYSICS

A D________________A
A_D________________A
A_______D_______A
A_______________D_A

A____RCHITECTURE
D__________ISPENSE
A_______UTOMOTIVE

A-DA.CO
A____DA
A____DA

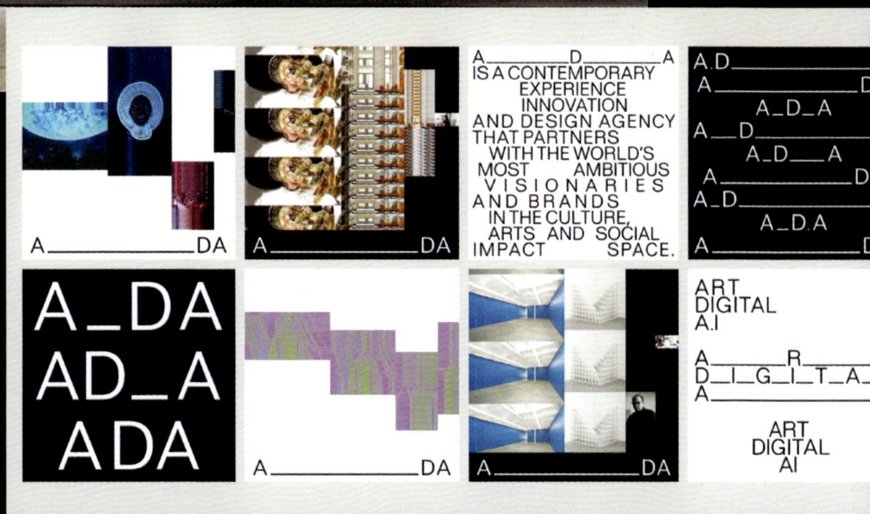
A____DA
A____DA
A____D____A
IS A CONTEMPORARY
EXPERIENCE
INNOVATION
AND DESIGN AGENCY
THAT PARTNERS
WITH THE WORLD'S
MOST AMBITIOUS
VISIONARIES
AND BRANDS
IN THE CULTURE,
ARTS AND SOCIAL
IMPACT SPACE.
A_D_A
A_D___A
A_D.A
A_DA
AD_A
ADA
A____DA
A____DA
ART
DIGITAL
A.I
A____R
D_I_G_I_T_A
ART
DIGITAL
AI

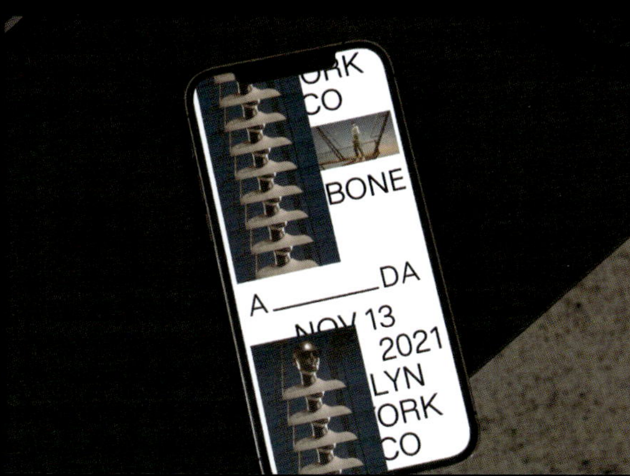
CO
BONE
A____DA
13
2021
LYN
ORK
CO

programming language
JavaScript

client
Space10

project year
2020

"Space10 approached us with the challenge of translating their basic brand identity into a more practical and versatile system for internal creative teams. To address this, we designed and developed a proprietary generative tool capable of handling full layouts, images, and real-time adjustments. The tool also enabled the seamless exporting of 4K videos, looping GIFs, PNGs, and high-resolution stills, reducing creative friction while ensuring consistency across teams.

Since the project was primarily focused on building this tool, we spent the first half dedicated to R&D, where we developed motion behaviours and their parameters. We then moved into prototyping, designing the tool, and finally development and testing. Inspired by the concept of illustrating space using only typography, we utilised Cinema4D and After Effects during the design phase, with the final tool built using THREE.js. A small team at Space10 tested the tool, helping us refine it by addressing bugs and questions. Ultimately, we learned a lot from harnessing our organisational skills to set up a system for housing a content library and streamlining the export process."

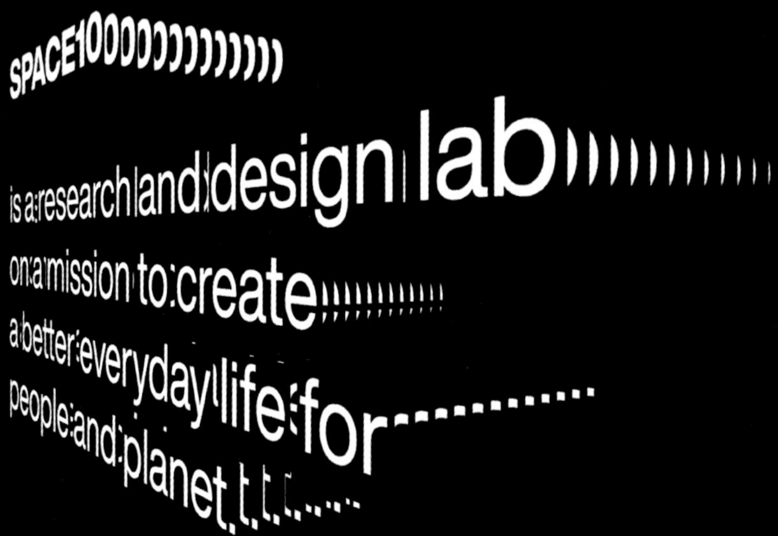

SPACE10
Session:
Designing Politics, with
Nanjala Nyabola
Online
18.08.20

Everyday
Online
18.08.20

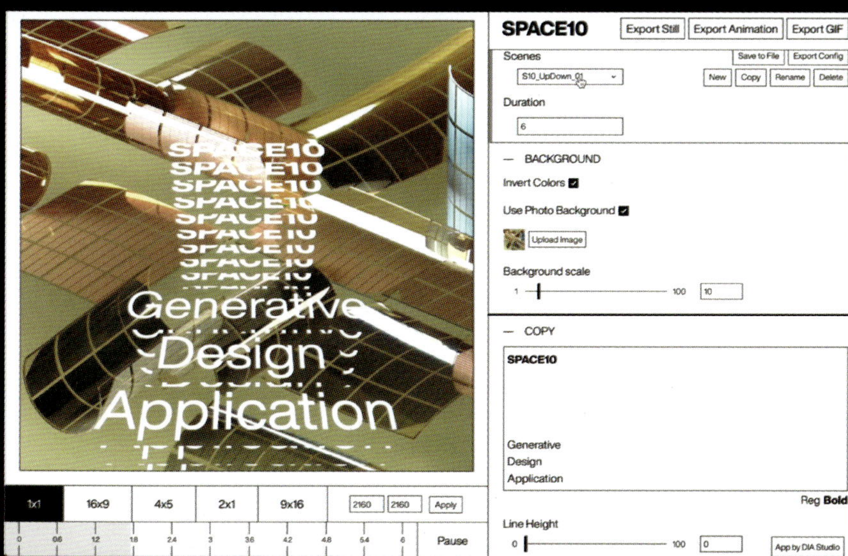
SPACE10
Export Still
Export Animation
Export GIF
Scenes
Save to File
Export Config
S10_UpDown_01
New
Copy
Rename
Delete
Duration
6
— BACKGROUND
Invert Colors
Use Photo Background
Upload Image
Background scale
1
100
10
— COPY
SPACE10
Generative
Design
Application
Reg Bold
Line Height
0
100
0
App by DIA Studio
1x1
16x9
4x5
2x1
9x16
2160
2160
Apply
Pause
0 0.6 1.2 1.8 2.4 3 3.6 4.2 4.8 5.4 6
SPACE10
Generative
Design
Application

programming language
JavaScript

client
Le Signe - Centre National du Graphisme

project year
2021

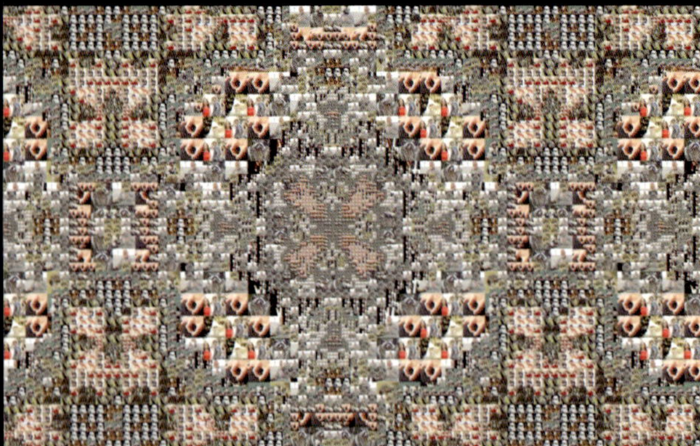

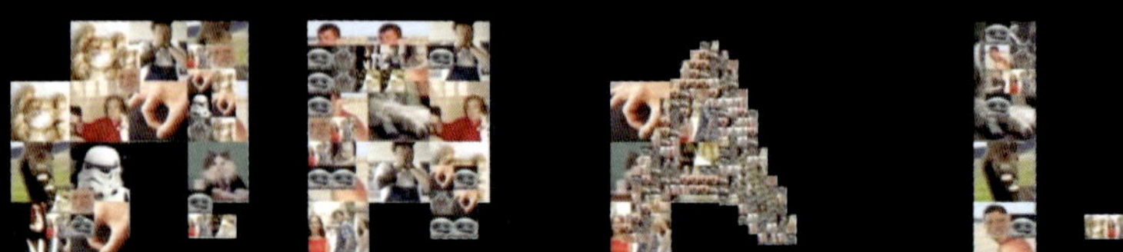

"The team at Le Signe in Chaumont, France, commissioned us to create an identity system for the Chaumont Biennale Internationale de Design Graphique 2021, titled 'Viral'. To authentically embody the concept of 'viral' through design, we relinquished manual control in favour of a system that could produce unexpected and dynamic results. Using After Effects and JavaScript, we developed a custom tool that combined memes and kinetic typography to evoke a sense of virality.

The use of technology allowed us to curate and select iterations that would have been impossible to create by human craftsmanship. Our process followed a structured flow, beginning with a design strategy to establish a clear purpose, followed by research and development, implementation, and finally refinement for delivery. The creative concept was deeply inspired by the theme itself, and the project reinforced the value of technology in accelerating tactical aspects of our work."

VIRAL
Biennale
internationale
DE DESIGN
GRAPHIQUE
de Chaumont
27. 5-
21.11.21

Graphique
NATIONAL

Concours international
Concours étudiant
Studio Kargah
Michiel Schuurman
Fanette Mellier
Michel Lepetitdidier
Raphaël Garnier
Chantal Jacquet
DEMO festival
Formes de collaboration
Club Collecte
Le prix unique du livre
Prospectives graphiques
Le Signe
Centre National du Graphisme
1 Place Émile Goguenheim
52000 Chaumont 03.25.35.79.01 France
@lesigne_cndg
VIRAL
Biennale
Internationale
DE DESIGN
GRAPHIQUE
de Chaumont
27. 5-
21.11.21

Biennale
Internationale
DESIGN GRAPHIQUE

YOUR STUDIO HAS REDEFINED HOW BRANDS USE TYPOGRAPHY AND MOTION. WHAT DO YOU THINK MAKES KINETIC DESIGN AND CREATIVE CODING SO POWERFUL IN TODAY'S DIGITAL-FIRST WORLD?

Graphic design's history is directly tied to its media. Long before founding DIA in 2009, we created motion-based design, typically in longer formats like 30- or 60-second TV spots for advertising. While historically overlooked, network TV branding shaped how brands behave in today's digital-first world. These brands acted as containers for their content—lower thirds, transitions, end tags, logo animations – much like brand systems today.

With social media now the primary channel and attention centred on mobile screens, design has evolved to fully integrate motion. No longer just an attention-grabber, motion is embedded in the design itself, allowing time to create form. This fusion of design and motion was the "redefinition" moment we introduced to the industry around 2016 which opened up the doors for other designers and studios to follow suit.

Creative coding pushes design beyond standard software, seamlessly integrating motion and interaction. It enables toolkits that automate visual identity production across formats – renders, GIFs, stills, and code snippets – while balancing consistency with creative flexibility. Motion and creative coding aren't just enhancements; they're essential tools for modern graphic designers.

WHAT ROLE DOES MOTION PLAY IN ENHANCING STORYTELLING THROUGH TYPOGRAPHY, AND HOW DO YOU MAINTAIN HARMONY BETWEEN FORM AND FUNCTION THROUGH CREATIVE CODING?

Motion enhances storytelling in typography by bringing it to life without adding extra elements – it shifts focus, guides the eye, and reinforces meaning. When thoughtfully executed, motion, typeface selection, and composition work together to be either practical or expressive, depending on the design's intent. Whether reinforcing clarity or pushing creative boundaries, motion should always have a strong conceptual and functional framework.

Creative coding ensures harmony between form and function by integrating motion directly into the design system. This maintains consistency while allowing flexibility across formats. By embedding motion into typography through code, we can create dynamic, responsive assets that remain purposeful – whether structured and utilitarian or fluid and experimental. Ultimately, motion and creative coding fuse typography with movement, making it both functional and alive.

HAVING WORKED WITH MAJOR BRANDS LIKE NIKE, ADIDAS, AND YOUTUBE, HOW DO YOU NAVIGATE THE CREATIVE EXPECTATIONS OF GLOBALLY RECOGNISED CLIENTS, AND WHAT ROLE DOES COLLABORATION PLAY IN SHAPING THE FINAL PRODUCT?

Collaboration is key, but trust is even more important. Clients seek us out for our studio's unique point of view. We've remained small and highly focused on design innovation through motion and code, with a strong emphasis on typography. In some ways, we even find it hard to define exactly what DIA Studio is!

This commitment to innovation translates into a diverse range of projects – branding, TV commercials, speculative research, campaigns, and more, but we don't see ourselves as a studio defined by any one type of work. Instead, our goal is to push the boundaries of what's possible in design.

This approach has consistently attracted large clients. When approached for a project, there's often an element of education in how we work. If a client is simply looking for a predefined list of deliverables from an RFP, it won't be a good fit. True collaboration happens when we develop the project brief together, allowing space for exploration and experimentation. We then present our research and findings, gradually refining the work into a practical execution.

It's fair to say that once you've proven successful projects for large clients and demonstrated that even radical experimental ideas can scale, gaining trust from new partners becomes easier, creating a positive feedback loop.

FOR OUR READERS WHO ARE UNAWARE, WHAT INSPIRED THE FOUNDING OF DIA AND HOW HAS YOUR CREATIVE ETHOS EVOLVED OVER THE YEARS – IF AT ALL? WHAT ARE THE CORE VALUES THAT DEFINE YOUR STUDIO AND YOUR VISION OF "SUCCESS"?

DIA was founded 15 years ago with the goal of creating an environment that fosters creativity. From the start, we drew on our diverse experiences – both positive and challenging – at various agencies and studios to shape how we operate. While our work has evolved, our commitment to a nurturing and inspiring workspace remains unchanged. Alongside client projects, we've always prioritised experimentation and research, ensuring innovation stays at the heart of what we do.

For us, "success" isn't defined by a client list, accolades, or awards. It all comes back to our core value: cultivating a comfortable, supportive environment. Waking up happy, minimising stress, feeling content, exploring and experimenting, collaborating with inspiring people, and working with like-minded clients. You could call that success.

AS DEMONSTRATED BY THE DIA TOOLS PLATFORM, YOUR STUDIO EMPHASISES A PROCESS ROOTED IN R&D. HOW DOES THIS APPROACH INFLUENCE THE WAY YOU TACKLE CREATIVE CHALLENGES AND DERIVE SOLUTIONS? HOW DO YOU BALANCE THE EXPERIMENTAL NATURE OF R&D WITH THE PRACTICAL NEEDS OF CLIENT PROJECTS?

At DIA, R&D isn't a separate initiative; it's the foundation of our creative process. We actively set aside time for research and experimentation, even turning down work to ensure it remains a priority. This commitment allows us to build an internal library of ideas, rather than relying on external design references, except in a historical context.

R&D directly informs how we tackle creative challenges, shaping the conceptual groundwork for every project. The creative development phase is inherently experimental, where we explore abstract ideas and unconventional approaches. Through collaboration with our clients, these experiments are refined into actionable, practical solutions tailored to their needs.

By integrating R&D into our workflow, we maintain a balance between exploration and execution – ensuring our work remains innovative while meeting the demands of real-world applications.

HOW DOES THE PLATFORM ALIGN WITH YOUR BROADER MISSION? WHAT EDUCATIONAL VALUE DOES IT OFFER, AND HOW DO YOU SEE IT BEING USED BY STUDENTS, CREATIVES, OR RESEARCHERS?

DIA Tools aligns with our broader mission by fostering transparency, creativity, and innovation in the design process. It serves as a space where we share the experimental tools we've developed, offering a behind-the-scenes look at how we work and the methodologies that drive our practice. By making these tools accessible, we aim to demystify aspects of our creative process, encouraging others to experiment, iterate, and develop their own unique approaches.

Beyond just sharing insights, DIA Tools also serves as a critique of the dominance of large design software companies like Adobe and Figma. Inspired by the experimental and open-ended nature of synthesisers and independent music software, our platform challenges the idea that creativity must be confined to rigid, corporate-driven tools. By introducing more exploratory and unconventional resources, we hope to empower students, creatives, and researchers to think beyond mainstream software, fostering a spirit of play, discovery, and independent innovation.

YOUR PLATFORM EXPLICITLY PROHIBITS UNAUTHORISED COMMERCIAL USE. HOW DO YOU BALANCE OPENNESS FOR EDUCATIONAL PURPOSES WITH PROTECTING YOUR INTELLECTUAL PROPERTY?

We strive to maintain a balance between openness for educational purposes and protecting our intellectual property by ensuring that each tool explicitly cites its reference source material. These tools are not just standalone utilities; they are iterations or replicas of existing projects we've developed. If someone were to use them, their output would inherently carry the DNA of our original design work.

A common misconception is that tools exist separately from the design itself. However, in our case, these tools are a direct result of extensive creative development, prototyping, and experimentation that led to the final design direction. In that sense, even though they function as tools, they embody the creative and conceptual work that is unique to DIA. By restricting unauthorised commercial use, we aim to protect the integrity of our creative process while still allowing others to learn from, explore, and be inspired by our approach.

HOW DO YOU CULTIVATE AN ENVIRONMENT THAT FOSTERS CREATIVE EXPERIMENTATION WITHIN YOUR TEAM? HOW DO EACH MEMBER'S INDIVIDUAL SKILLS AND EXPERIENCES – FOR EXAMPLE, MITCH'S JAZZ TRAINING AND MEG'S STRATEGIC EXPERTISE – COMPLEMENT EACH OTHER?

Creating the right balance between structured timelines and open exploration is key to fostering creative experimentation. At DIA, we make sure to leave space for deep iteration alongside client work, allowing ideas to be pushed to their limits rather than simply executed for efficiency's sake. This balance ensures that experimentation remains a core part of our process rather than an afterthought.

Our team's strengths complement each other in a way that fuels both strategy and creativity. Meg serves as the guardian of the studio, bridging the gap between clients and the creative process. She ensures expectations are met while also protecting the integrity of the work, maintaining high quality and ensuring that every project reaches its full potential. With her ability to see both the big picture and the creative details, she plays a crucial role in refining and elevating the work.

Mitch, on the other hand, brings an improvisational approach to design, influenced by his background in jazz and music composition. The DIA design philosophy is rooted in this perspective – akin to beat-making and production, but applied visually. His process encourages fluidity, experimentation, and spontaneity, pushing the work beyond conventional design methods.

While Meg's role leans more managerial and Mitch's more creative, there is significant overlap. Meg has a strong creative voice, particularly in refining the work through a strategic lens. This dynamic – balancing structure with improvisation, strategy with creativity – is what allows DIA to operate in a way that is both experimental and intentional, ensuring that every project is developed to its fullest potential.

HOW DO YOU STAY AHEAD OF EMERGING CREATIVE TOOLS/TECHNOLOGIES AND EVALUATE THEIR RELEVANCE TO YOUR WORK? COULD YOU SHARE EXAMPLES OF RECENT WORK OR OTHER STUDIOS THAT HAVE INSPIRED YOU?

This is an ongoing process at DIA, but it's not about chasing trends or adopting new software for the sake of it. Instead, we see innovations in the media our work lives in as a natural force that shapes how design evolves. As these media shift, our tools must also adapt to ensure design remains responsive and relevant. However, at the core, great work still comes down to strong creative concepts and well-crafted design. Technology is simply a tool to aid or amplify intent, not replace the fundamentals of good design.

We evaluate the relevance of new tools by testing, learning, and integrating them into our workflow, but always through the lens of solid design principles and good taste. The goal is never just to use new tech, but to find ways it can enhance or expand what we're already doing. If a tool offers a new way of thinking about motion, form, or interaction, then it's worth exploring. But ultimately, the idea and execution matter more than the tool itself.

When it comes to inspiration, we tend to look back rather than forward. Our work is built on a long lineage of designers and thinkers who have shaped the field. Many of the most impactful figures for us were deeply involved in design academia, meaning their work is well-documented and provides a rich source of knowledge. Key influences include Karl Gerstner, Wolfgang Weingart, 8vo-Octavo, and Tomato. More recently, we've been inspired by studios and artists like Universal Everything and Jürg Lehni, who approach design through a technological and conceptual lens. Mitch also had the opportunity to teach alongside Jürg at HEAD Geneva, which reinforced the importance of blending education, research, and practice in pushing design forward.

Ultimately, while tools and technology evolve, our focus remains on the ideas, execution, and the historical context that informs our work. Understanding where design has been is just as important as where it's going.

WHAT EXCITES YOU MOST ABOUT THE FUTURE OF CREATIVE CODING AND ITS INTEGRATION INTO GRAPHIC DESIGN? DO YOU HAVE ANY ADVICE FOR ASPIRING CREATIVES/CODERS LOOKING TO TAP INTO ITS POSSIBILITIES AND CARVE OUT A UNIQUE NICHE FOR THEMSELVES?

With AI lowering the barrier to entry for coding and software development, we expect to see a surge of innovative work in creative coding and graphic design. As these tools become more accessible, creatives without traditional coding backgrounds will be able to experiment, iterate, and push boundaries in new ways. This shift will democratise creative coding, making it less about technical gatekeeping and more about ideas and execution.

That said, while new tools can unlock potential, understanding the history and fundamentals of design remains essential. The most groundbreaking work comes from those who know where design has been and use that knowledge to shape where it's going. Mastering principles like composition, typography, and motion – along with an awareness of past innovations – ensure that technology is used with intention rather than novelty.

For aspiring creatives and coders, our biggest piece of advice is to look beyond design itself. The most interesting work happens at the intersection of disciplines, where personal interests, hobbies, or other fields of study merge with design. Whether it's music, architecture, science, or gaming, fusing design with something unique to you creates work that is both personal and original.

OSESP –
Orquestra Sinfônica de São Paulo

In 2023, the São Paulo State Symphony Orchestra (OSESP) underwent a rebranding to showcase its historical significance, appeal to younger audiences, and highlight its Latin American identity. The new identity merges rational design, inspired by musical scores, with emotional layers reflecting the music's sensations. It offers flexibility and dynamism across platforms, ensuring OSESP's legacy and excellence shine through every brand interaction.

Programming Tool/Language:
JavaScript

Client:
São Paulo State Symphony Orchestra (OSESP)

osesp
Orquestra Sinfônica do Estado de São Paulo
Temporada 2024
Osesp 70 anos
7 de abril
Temporada 2024
Osesp 70 anos
21, 22 e 23 de março
Temporada 2024
Osesp 70 anos
23, 24 e 25 de maio

OSESP – Orquestra Sinfônica de

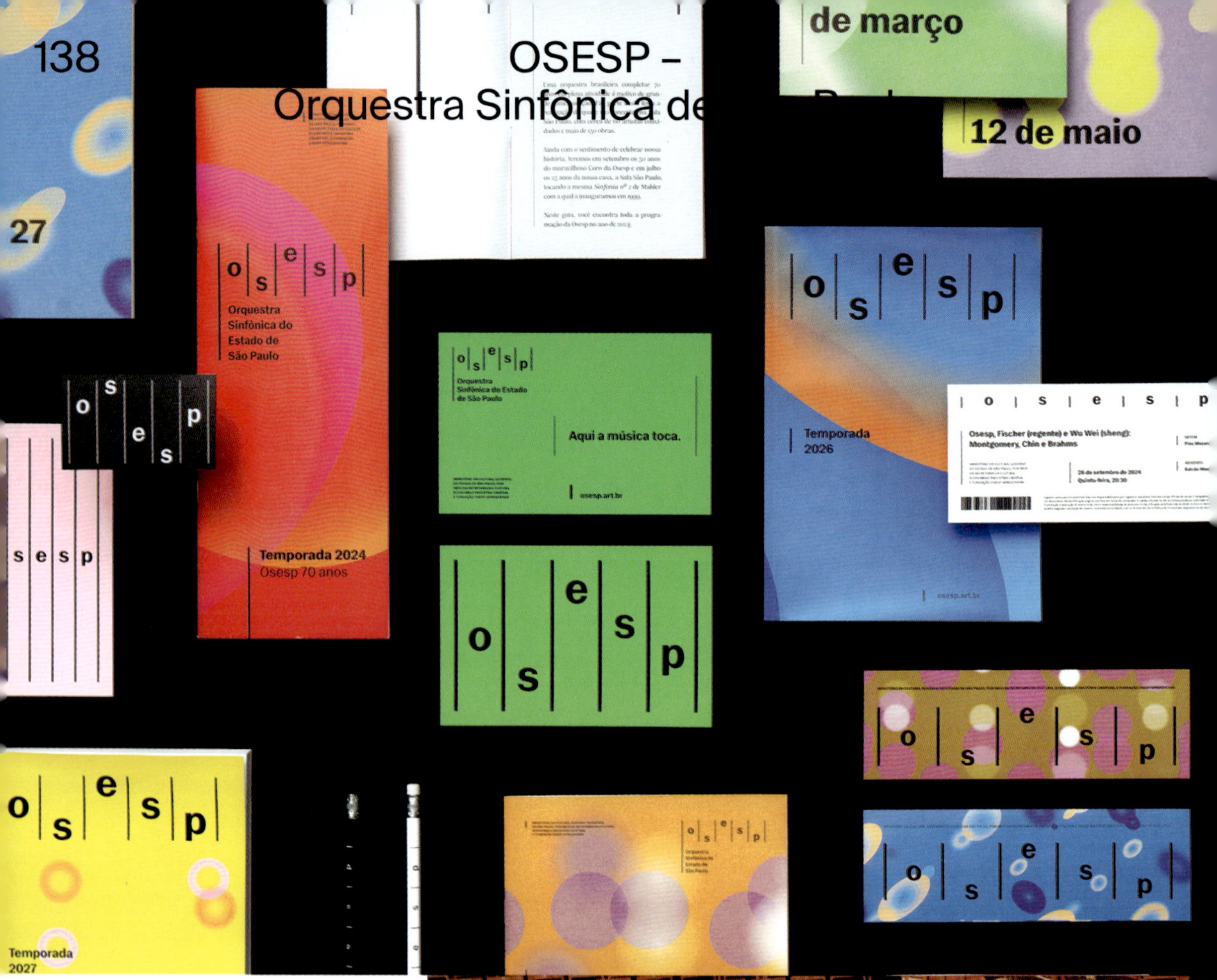

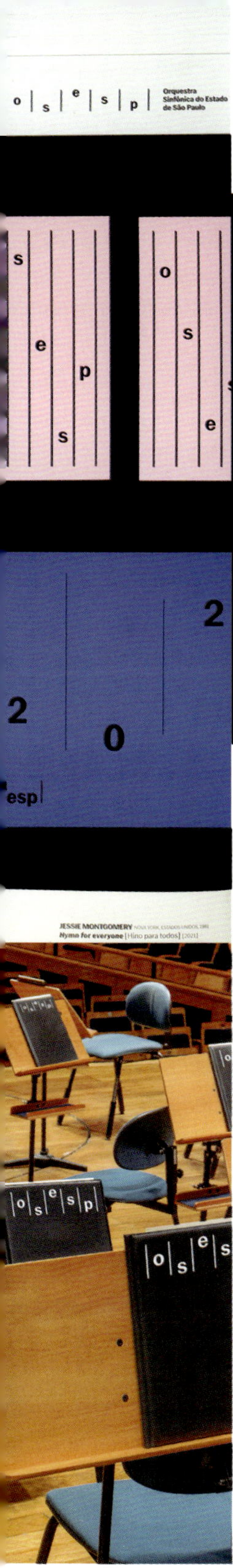

Thierry Fischer
Conductor

Emmanuele Baldini
Concertmaster

Elena Klementieva
Violin

Regina Vasconcellos
Cello

Ana Valéria Poles
Double Bass

Liuba Klevtsova
Harp

Claudia Nascimento
Flutes

Arcadio Minczuk
Oboe

Giuliano Rosas
Clarinets

José Arion Linarez
Bassoon

Nikolay Genov
Horn

Antonio Carlos Lopes Júnior
Trumpets

Darrin C. Milling
Bass Trombone

Filipe Queirós
Tuba

Elizabeth Del Grande
Timpani

Rubén Zúñiga
Percussion

The Philharmonie Luxembourg's brand refresh, developed by NB Studio London and Patrik Hübner, aimed to connect with a younger audience while preserving its prestigious reputation. The new identity system incorporates dynamic, generative design inspired by the venue's iconic columns, translating music and performance energy into a visual format. This adaptable design enables quick, tailored visuals for events, enhancing engagement across media platforms.

Programming Tools/Languages:
JavaScript, WebGL, GLSL, Vue.js

Client:
Philharmonie Luxembourg

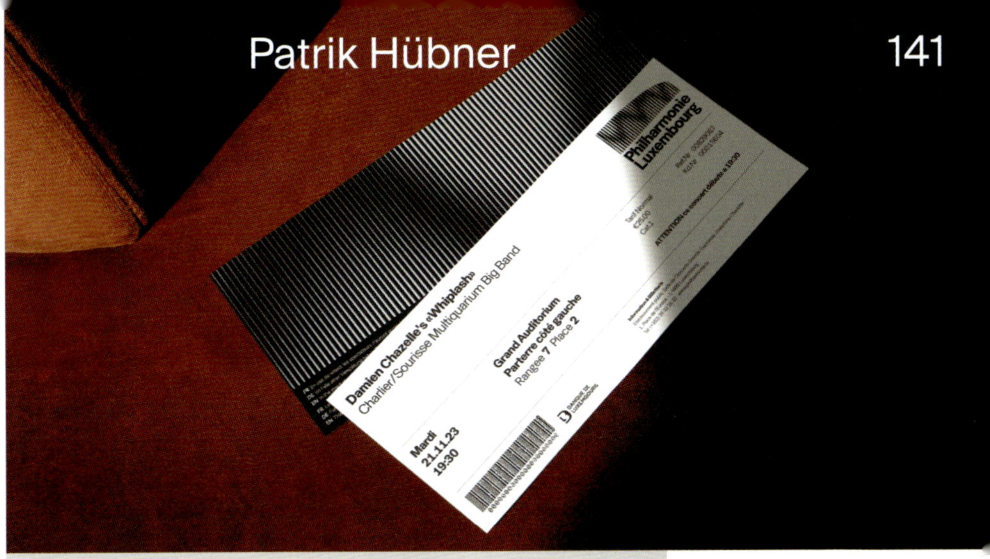
Philharmonie
Luxembourg
Damien Chazelle's «Whiplash»
Charlier/Sourisse Multiquarium Big Band
Mardi
21.11.23
19:30
Grand Auditorium
Parterre côté gauche
Rangee 7 Place 2

Saison 23/24

Philharmonie
Luxembourg

Philharmonie Luxembourg
Un mois de
Symhonies
Solidarité
& Soul
Février 2023
Un mois de
Le Jazz
Baroque
& Électro-pop
Mai 2023
Mai 2023

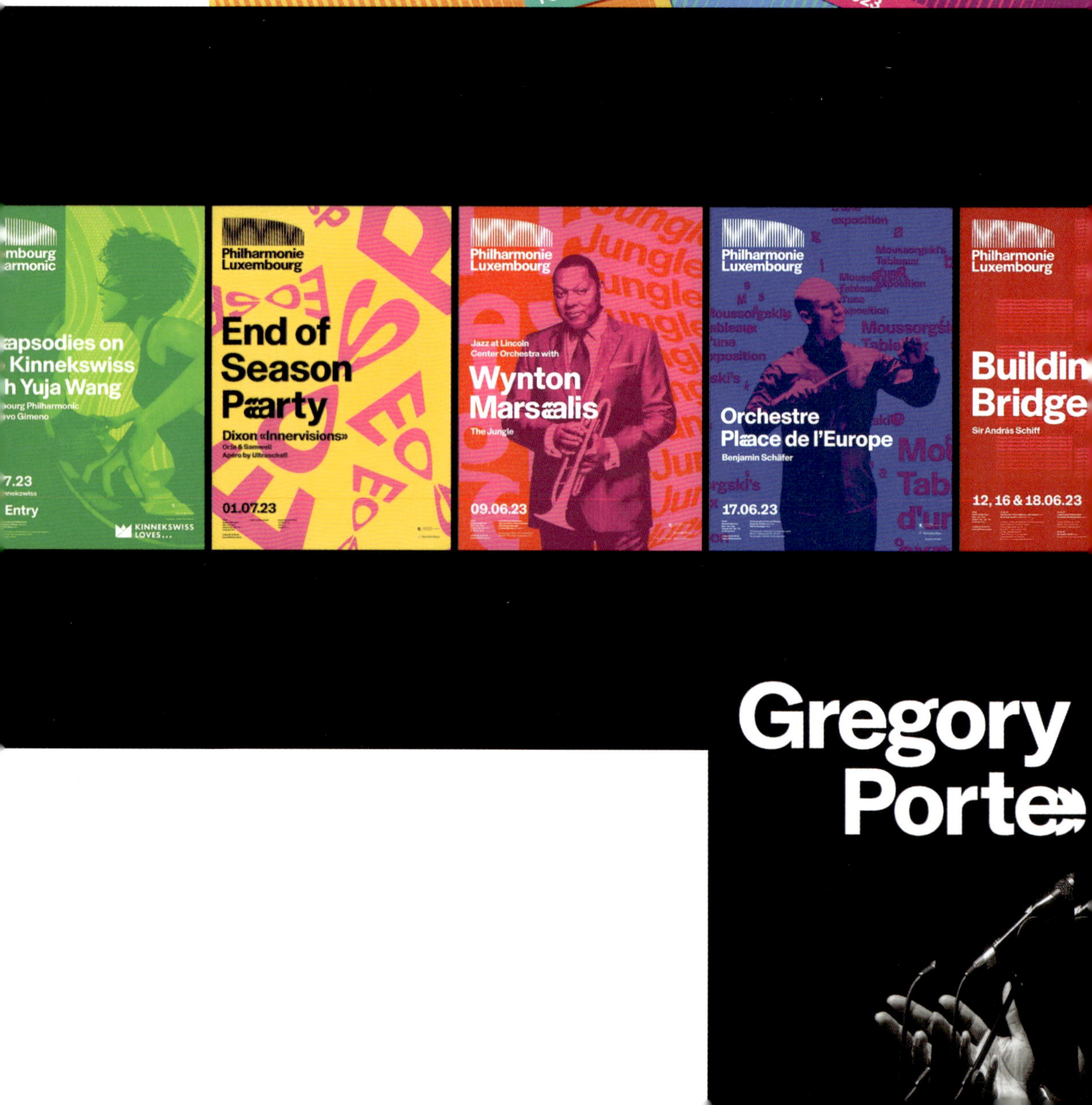
Philharmonie Luxembourg
End of Season Party
Dixon «Innervisions»
01.07.23
Jazz at Lincoln Center Orchestra with
Wynton Marsalis
The Jungle
09.06.23
Orchestre Place de l'Europe
Benjamin Schäfer
17.06.23
Sir András Schiff
12, 16 & 18.06.23
Gregory
Porter

Philharmonie
Luxembourg

OVO Energy Forecast

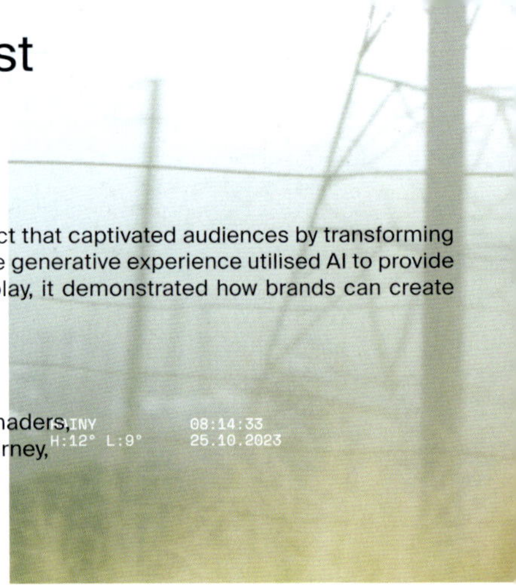

FIELD.IO created the OVO Energy Forecast, a groundbreaking data visualisation project that captivated audiences by transforming abstract data into a human story. Using live power grid data and commuter surveys, the generative experience utilised AI to provide an emotional perspective. As the world's first monumental use of AI in a public display, it demonstrated how brands can create lasting impact by putting audiences at the heart of their experiences.

Programming Tools/Languages:
React, Vanillatool, Three.js, Remotion, custom shaders, Vercel, Carbon Intensity, AWS Lambda, Midjourney, ChatGPT, custom trained models

Client:
OVO Energy

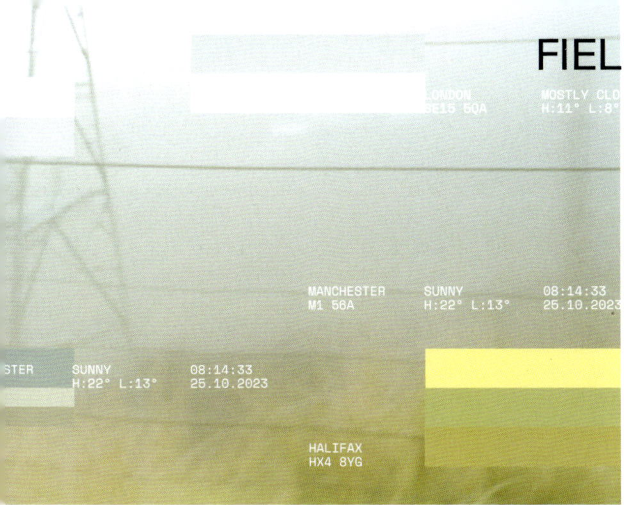

LONDON
SE15 5QA

06:12:32am

LONDON
SE15 5QA

Waking up to the crack of dawn

LONDON
SE15 5QA

LONDON
MOSTLY CLOUDY

11:48
kro ncrv
Overzicht Media Liefdesprikkelsvideo's
Festival van de liefde
In Festival van de liefde zetten Anita en Edson iedere keer een andere plaats in Nederland centraal. Zij zijn daar op zoek naar de mooiste liefdesverhalen en helpen de liefde ter plekke een handje.
Toon meer
Recente media van

11:48
kro ncrv
Overzicht Media Gemist
Keuringsdienst van waarde
Doet aan huishoudjournalistiek. Simpele vragen, verbazingwekkende antwoorden. Fascinerende televisie over de verhalen uit ons boodschappenmandje.
Recente media van

11:48
kro ncrv
Overzicht Media
Volgen
BinnensteBuiten
In het lifestyleprogramma BinnensteBuiten wordt de kijker dagelijks, op TV én online, getrakteerd op een gepassioneerde en duurzame dosis huis en interieur, tuin en natuur, eten en drinken.
Toon meer
Recente media van

KRO-NCRV's rebranding introduced a vibrant new identity, uniting 270 programmes with a dynamic, colourful system. Its focal point is a multi-coloured circle, with each programme adopting its own unique colour combination. Featuring a magenta centre and green-cyan halo, it uses a spectrum of over 14 million colours and was made to be easily customisable with an innovative online tool.

Programming Tool/Language:
Processing

Client:
KRO-NCRV

Freeform

COLLINS partnered with Freeform, a Disney division, to redefine its brand and narrative in a saturated streaming market. Embracing young adult stories that challenge conventions, Freeform redefined its audience as individuals in a constant state of becoming. Their new promise, symbolised by a reimagined typeface, encourages fresh perspectives and deeper storytelling from emerging voices.

Programming Tools/Languages:
JavaScript (Three.js, Node.js), Kinect,
Adobe Illustrator, Adobe After Effects

Client:
Freeform / Disney

9:41
HAPPY BIRTHDAY
Yara
Shahidi
Super
Custom Variable Typeface
New voices.
Now.
Hero
New voices.
Now.
Bold
New voices.
Now.

Mystery

Will Smith
Genie

GOOD TROUBLE
New Episode

Brie Larson
Captain Marvel

Tweet us
@grownish

Kunststipendien der Stadt Zürich 2022

The curators of the Zurich Art Grants annual exhibition (Kunststipendien der Stadt Zürich) sought an inclusive and diverse visual identity to showcase emerging artists' work to a broader audience. To fulfill this request, Skala Design created a multilayered and dynamic design, inspired by the concept of contrasting positions that complement one another. The work reflected the richness of countless voices and perspectives that shape both the creation and appreciation of art.

Programming Tool/Language:
p5.js

Client:
Helmhaus Zürich

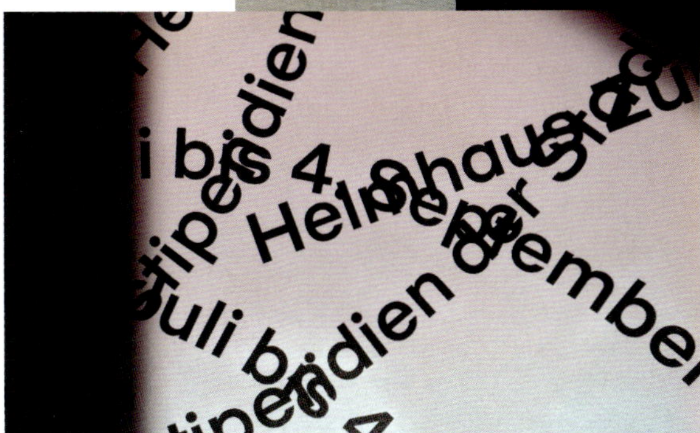

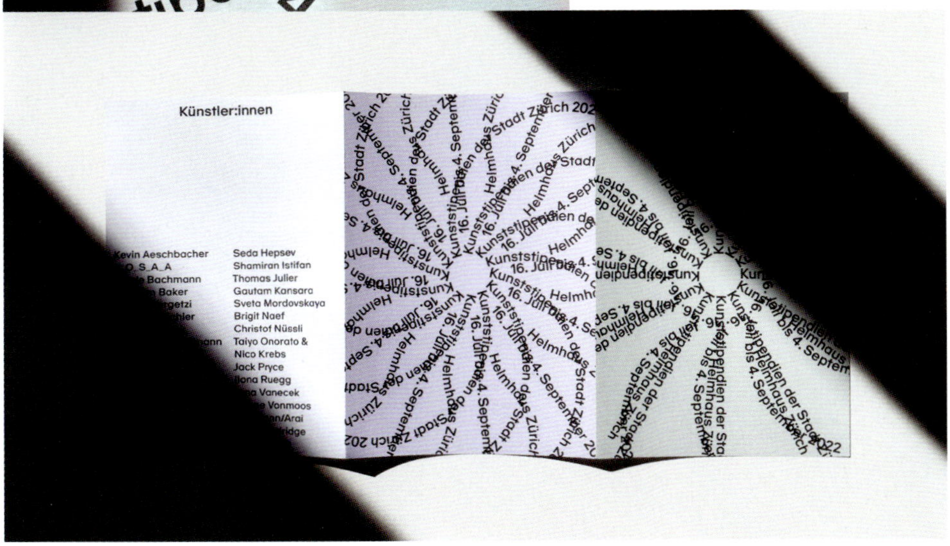
Künstler:innen
Kevin Aeschbacher
Seda Hepsev
Shamiran Istifan
Thomas Julier
Gautam Kansara
Sveta Mordovskaya
Brigit Naef
Christof Nüssli
Taiyo Onorato &
Nico Krebs
Jack Pryce
Ilona Ruegg

Creative Week, hosted by The One Club for Creativity, is a week-long festival in New York City uniting global creatives to celebrate top advertising and design. Its 2024 visual identity, a kinetic and generative system, reflected the concept of diverse voices. The One Club's team used a custom generator to craft varied graphics—static or animated—for coffee cups, signage, Instagram stickers, merchandise, and interactive sticker sheets.

Programming Tool/Language:
p5.js

Client:
Creative Week

CREATIVE WEEK

THE
ONE CLUB
FOR
CREATIVITY

CREATIVE
WEEK
MAY 13–17
2024
NEW YORK
CITY
COME
ONE
COME
ALL
THE
ONE CLUB
FOR
CREATIVITY

theoneclubforcreativity
SPEAKER
CREATIVE WEEK
MAY 13–17, 2024
DAMIEN ESCOBAR
GLOBAL CHIEF MUSIC OFFICER, HAVAS

theoneclubforcreativity
CREATIVE
WEEK
MAY 13–17
2024
NEW YORK
CITY

Creative Week
May 13–17, 2024
New York City
CREATIVEWEEK
Brooklyn Br
ONE WAY
Chambers Street

CREATIVE WEEK BRINGS TOGETHER THE GLOBAL CREATIVE COMMUNITY TO CELEBRATE THE BEST IN ADVERTISING AND DESIGN WITH AWARDS CEREMONIES, WORKSHOPS, AND MORE, FOR ONE WEEK ONLY IN THE HEART OF NEW YORK CITY.
CREATIVE WEEK 2024
For free events, tickets, and more information, visit creativeweek.com
THE ONE CLUB FOR CREATIVITY

Vietnam Festival of Creativity & Design 2023

Behalf Studio's collaboration with the Vietnam Festival of Creativity & Design (VFCD) explored the theme "Mind & Machine", addressing AI's role in creativity. Responding to the question *"will AI replace creative workers?"*, Behalf Studio highlighted human creativity's irreplaceable essence. In a playful approach, they used AI to create a digital avatar, the "AI-generated creative" or "Persona", emphasising technology as an enhancer, not a replacement.

Programming Tools/Languages:
JavaScript (Three.js, Node.js), Kinect,
Adobe Illustrator, Adobe After Effects

Client:
Vietnam Festival of Creativity & Design (VFCD)

I AM A...
Lateral Thinker
I AM A...
Systemic Thinker
I AM AN...
Aesthetic Thinker
I AM A...
Nonconformist Thinker

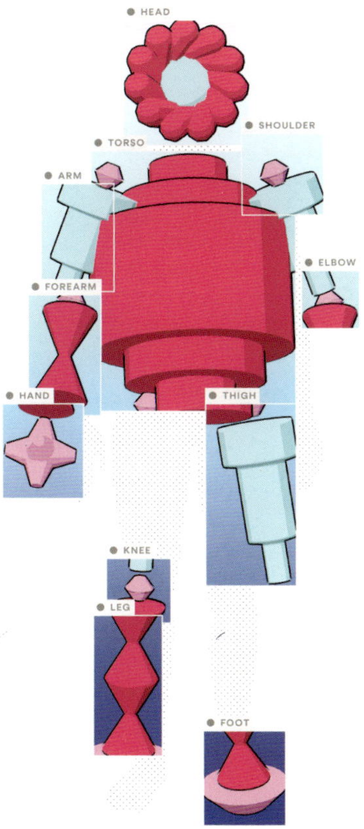
HEAD
SHOULDER
TORSO
ARM
ELBOW
FOREARM
HAND
THIGH
KNEE
LEG
FOOT

ORGANISER
Ms
Hằng
Nguyễn

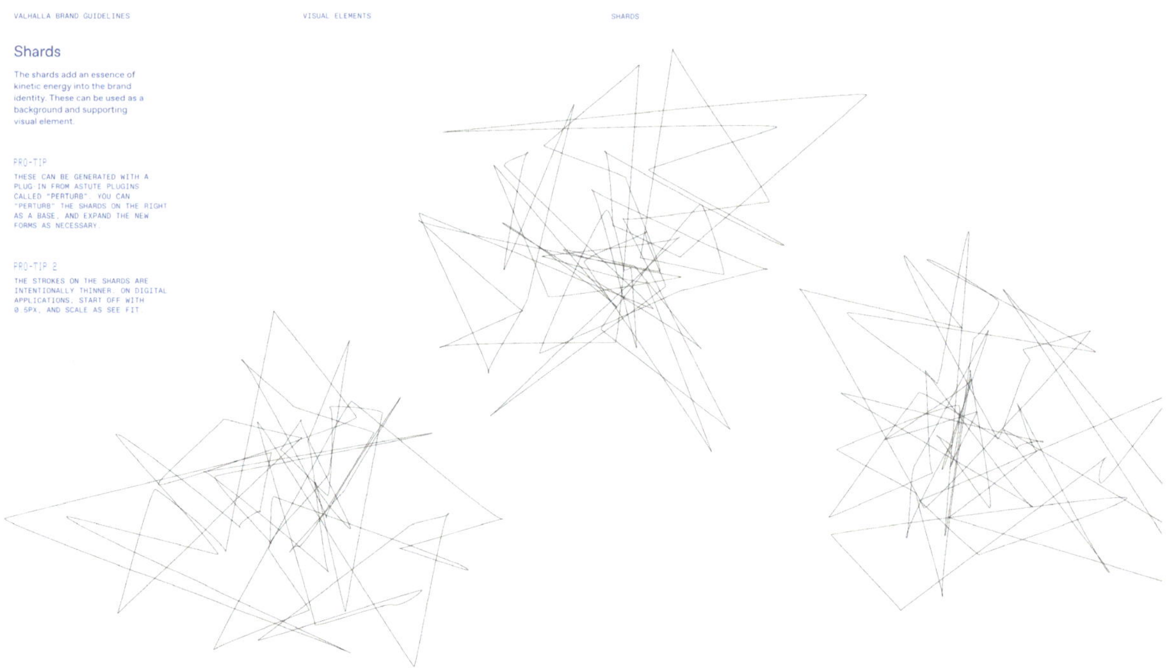

VALHALLA BRAND GUIDELINES   VISUAL ELEMENTS   SHARDS

Shards

The shards add an essence of kinetic energy into the brand identity. These can be used as a background and supporting visual element.

PRO-TIP

THESE CAN BE GENERATED WITH A PLUG-IN FROM ASTUTE PLUGINS CALLED "PERTURB". YOU CAN "PERTURB" THE SHARDS ON THE RIGHT AS A BASE, AND EXPAND THE NEW FORMS AS NECESSARY.

PRO-TIP 2

THE STROKES ON THE SHARDS ARE INTENTIONALLY THINNER. ON DIGITAL APPLICATIONS, START OFF WITH 0.5PX, AND SCALE AS SEE FIT.

Adam Ho's Valhalla project uses a core blue and generative visual techniques to express character. Featuring dynamic "shards" with infinite possibilities, the design conveys a sense of urgency and excitement, creating a visually engaging experience.

Programming Tool/Language:
p5.js

Client:
Valhalla

International Festival of Architecture

FIELD.IO envisioned a brand that evolves while maintaining consistency, inspired by architecture biennales and events. To showcase the potential of generative AI in brand design, the team created a fictitious architecture festival. By developing a generative tool, they translated architectural visual libraries into custom identity systems, offering limitless creative opportunities to shape brands with cohesive, dynamic visual outputs.

Programming Tools/Languages:
FIELDKIT.AI, various AI models for image analysis, Houdini,
Midjourney, custom Python scripts

FESTIVAL
OF ARCHITECTURE
2025
WARREN AND
MAHONEY
FESTIVAL
OF ARCHITECTURE
2025
I
F
A
5-22
NOV 2025
DANIEL STATHAM
STUDIO
FESTIVAL
OF ARCHITECTURE
2025
I
F
A

IFA
FESTIVAL
OF ARCHITECTURE
2025
NATIONAL STAR
OBSERVATORY
KYRIAKOS
TSOLAKIS
ZHUHAI JINWAN
CIVIC ART CENTRE
ZAHA HADID
ARCHITECTS

UBISOFT+

ubisoft
BUNNY
PACK
UNLOCK
ubisoft
PLAY
PLAY
PLAY
PLAY
ubisoft
JINN
PACK
UNLOCK

DesignStudio rebranded Ubisoft+ to create a distinctive identity while staying connected to the Ubisoft master brand. The new design features an immersive spiral graphic, inspired by the master brand's logo, evoking the sense of navigating through diverse gaming worlds. In collaboration with Mata, they also developed a tool to help the in-house team efficiently create dynamic 3D visuals.

Programming Tools/Languages:
Processing, p5.js

Client:
Ubisoft

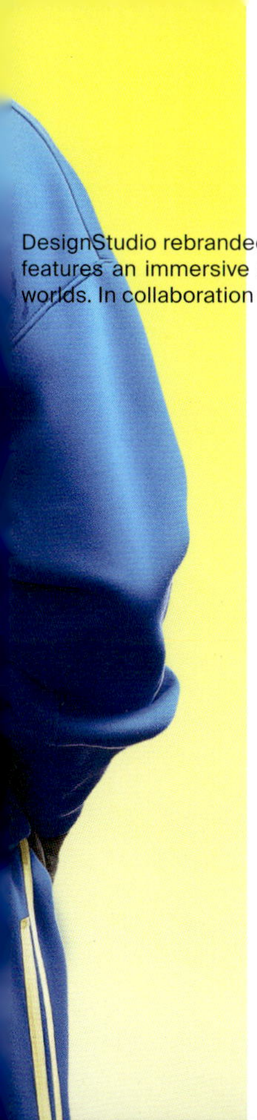

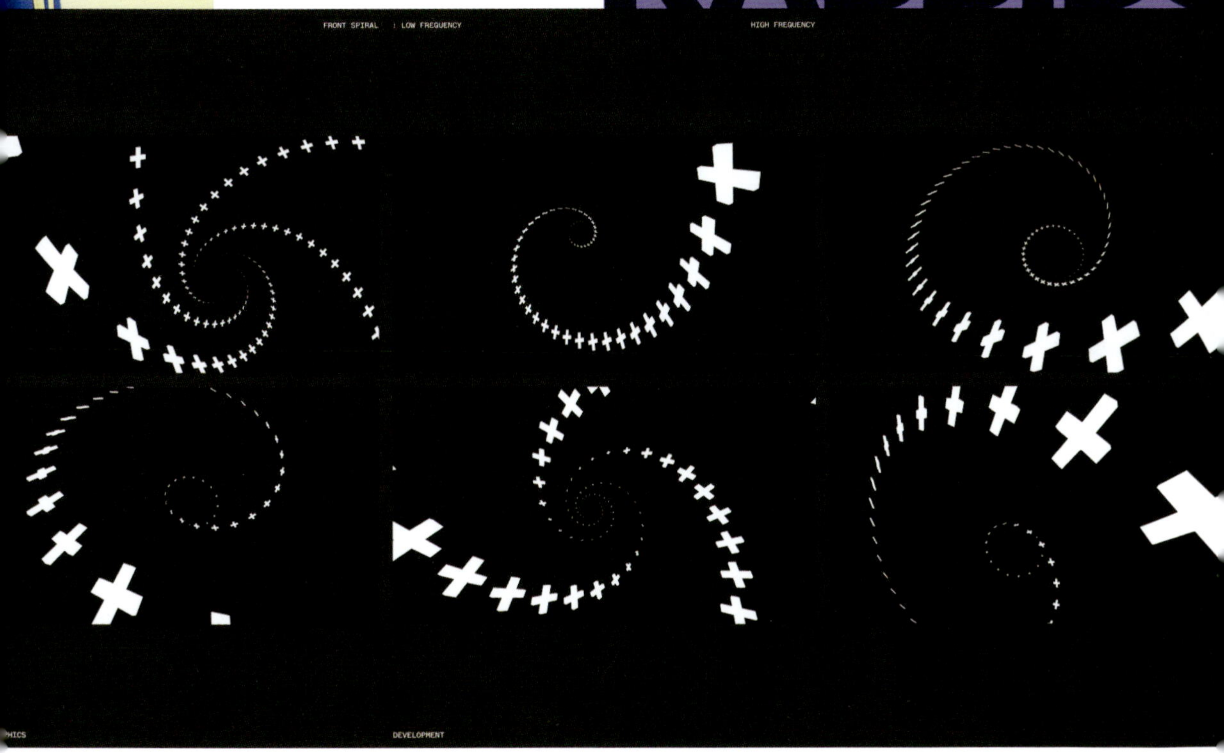

Accept & Proceed joined forces with Dark Matter Labs and Hard Art to reshape venture capital with Hard Imagination. In response to Marc Andreessen's Techno-Optimist Manifesto, this initiative encourages venture capitalists to focus on long-term, transformative possibilities instead of short-term returns. The project, spanning 27 pages, features dynamic graphic elements within a structured grid system.

Programming Tool/Language:
Processing

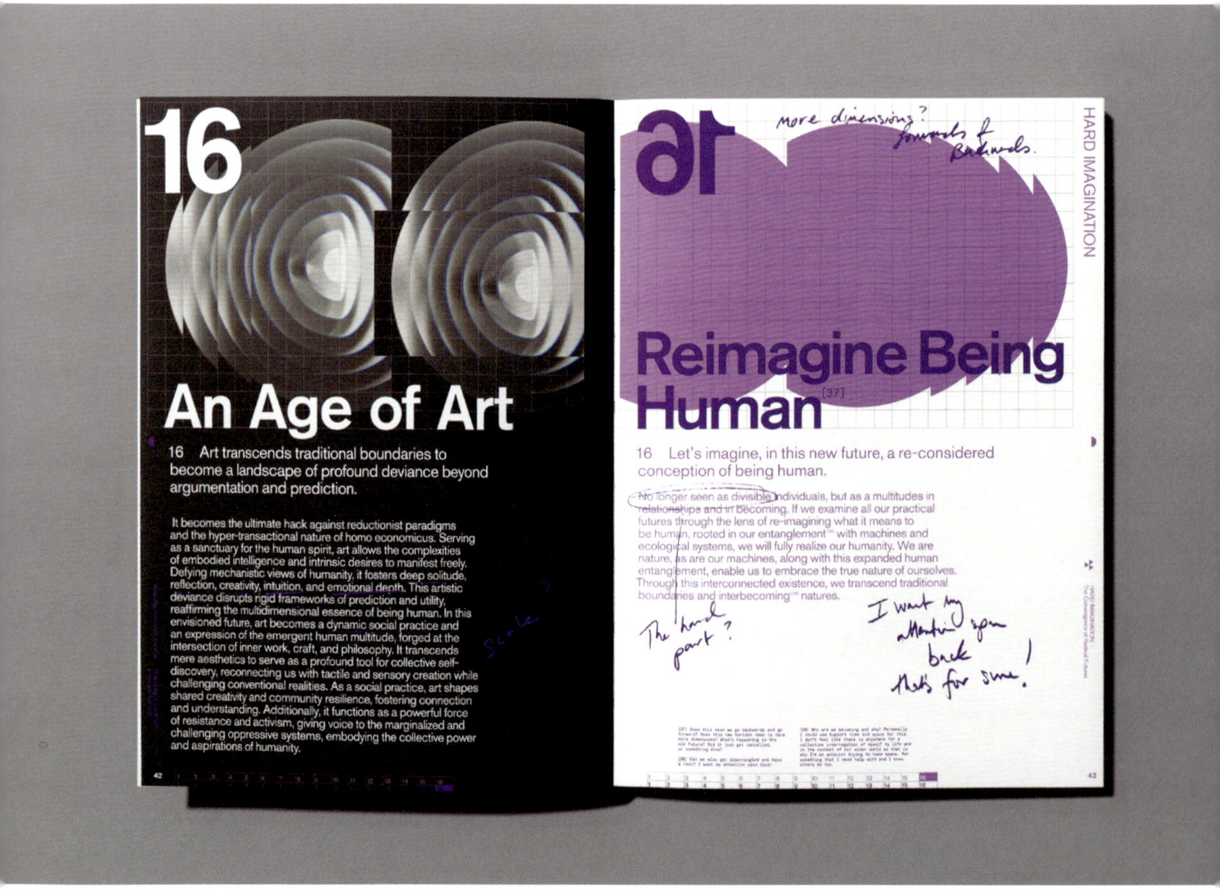

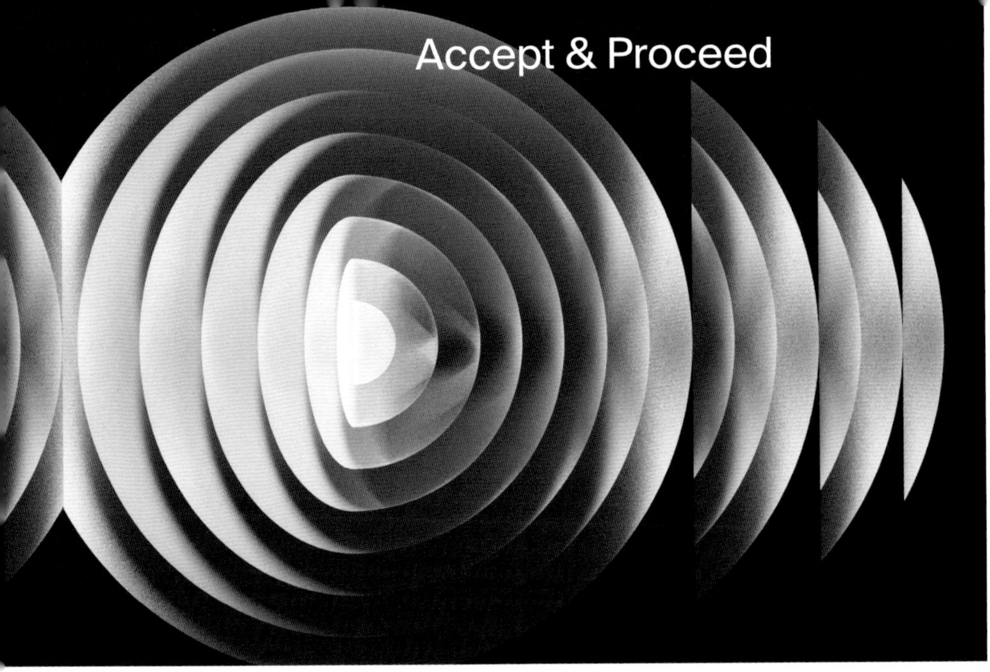

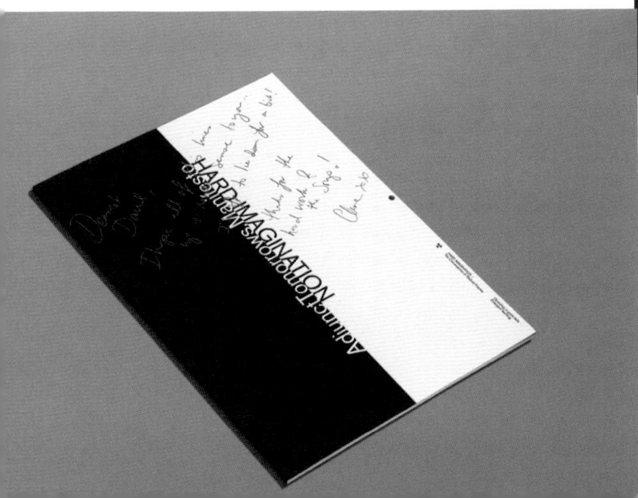
HARD IMAGINATION
Adjunct Tomorrows Manifesto

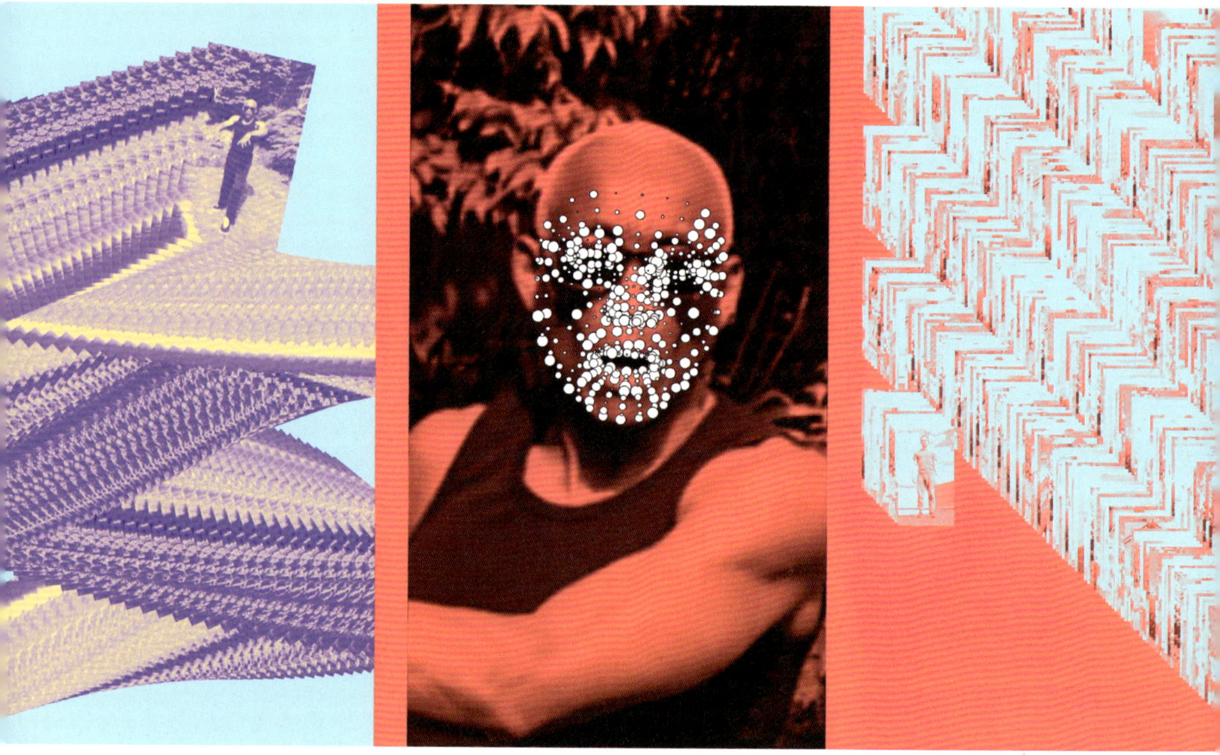

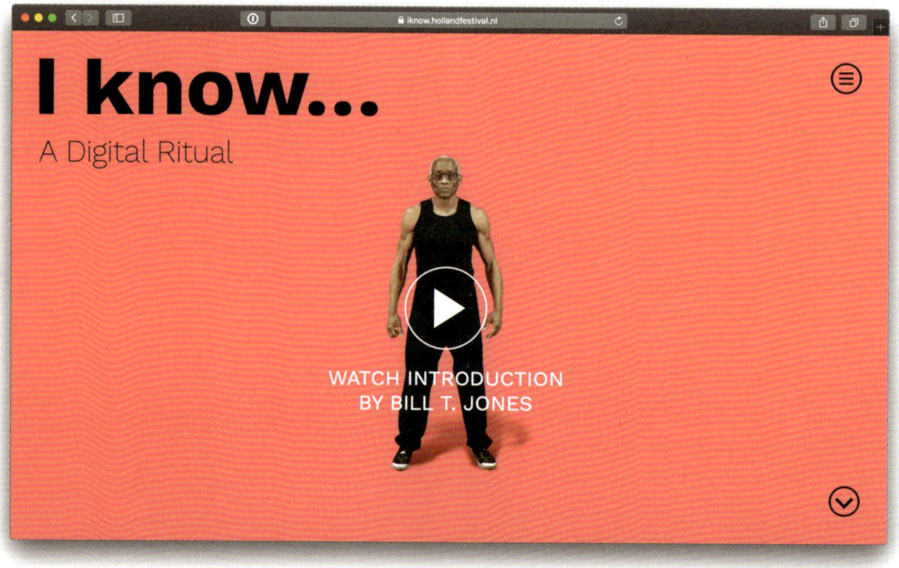
iknow.hollandfestival.nl
I know...
A Digital Ritual
WATCH INTRODUCTION
BY BILL T. JONES

During the pandemic, Holland Festival shifted to an online format focused on “In Pursuit of the We” by Bill T. Jones. The project invited global participation by uploading videos starting with “I know...”. These contributions formed a growing mosaic, showcasing personal expressions. The project also featured dynamic design, complex data visualisation, and sound design to compile a catalogue of knowledge, translating strong words and gestures.

Programming Tool/Language:
OPENRNDR

Client:
Holland Festival

MANQUE DE RECUL

The exhibition MANQUE DE RECUL held in the Pearl Art Museum in Shanghai showcased artists whose work is shaped by the internet, technology, and commerce. The key visual featured a bold neon purple and green palette with dynamic, fast-moving text bars that expanded and contorted, reflecting the exhibition's theme of immediate, unfiltered artistic expression.

Programming Tool/Language:
Processing

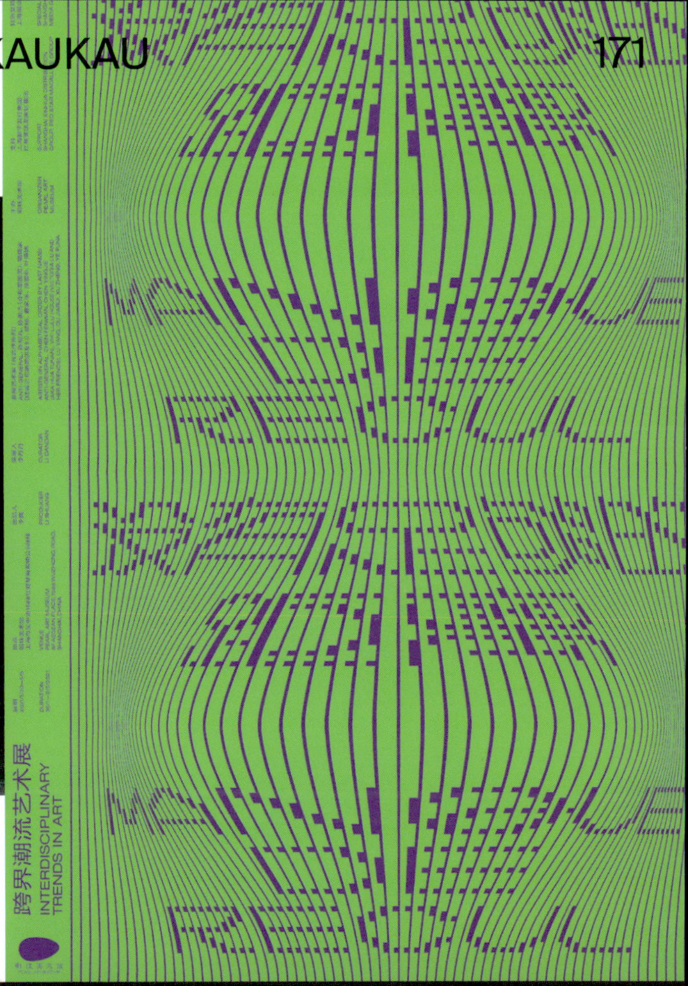
跨界潮流艺术展
INTERDISCIPLINARY
TRENDS IN ART

Paris Electronic Week 2024

Diplomatie Studio's design for Paris Electronic Week 2024 celebrated electronic music's evolution at the Cité Fertile in Pantin. The event brought together artists, industry professionals, and music fans, offering immersive performances and insightful panels. Highlighting data's role in music's growth, the festival showcased the vibrant, ever-changing electronic music scene, leaving a lasting mark on France's music culture.

Programming Tools/Languages:
Processing, p5.js

Client:
Technopol (l'association des musiques électroniques)

Electronic Week
septembre 2024
Fertile
Edouard Vaillant,
Pantin
Vaillant,
Paris Electronic Week

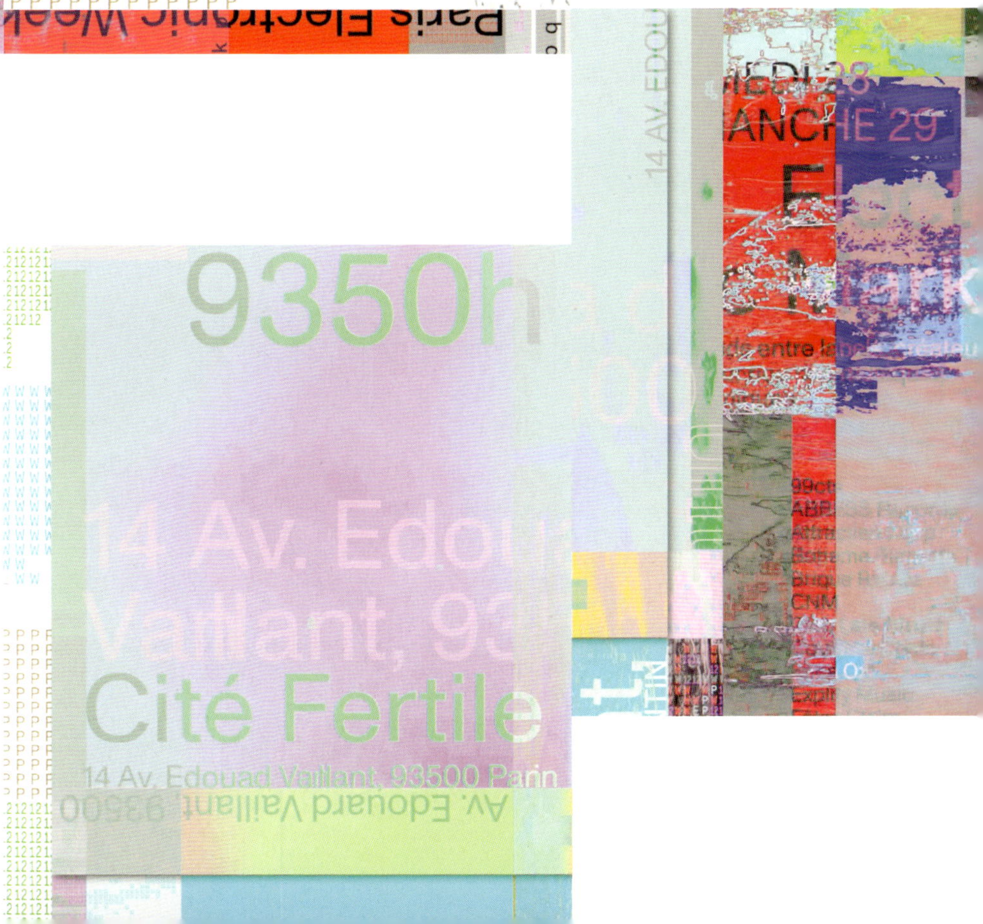
9350h
14 Av. Edou
Vaillant, 93
Cité Fertile
14 Av. Edouard Vaillant, 93500 Parin
Av. Edouard Vaillant 93500

Paris Electronic Week 2023

Diplomatie Studio directed the artistic vision for the 11th edition of Paris Electronic Week, an electronic music festival at Parc de la Villette. Utilising TouchDesigner's dynamic capabilities, they created a memorable visual identity through generative tools, exploring themes of organic shapes, geometric patterns, and fluidity to capture the essence of musical diversity.

Programming Tools/Languages:
TouchDesigner, Processing

Client:
Technopol (l'association des musiques électroniques)

Convention et festival des cultures électroniques
20 — 22 septembre 2023
Parc de la Villette 75019 Paris
Masterclass, Workshops, Talks, Apéros pros,
Soirées, Electronic Market

Convention et festival des cultures électroniques
Talks - Workshops - Soirées
Apéros pros - Electronic Market
Parc de La Villette
75019 Paris
Convention et festival des cultures électroniques
Jeudi 21.09
Vendredi 22.09

Paris Electronic Week
11e éditic
Convention et festival des cultures électroniqu
20 — 22 septembre 2023
Parc de la Villette 75019 Paris
Masterclass, Workshops, Talks, Apéros pros,
Soirées, Electronic Market
Infos & préventes sur pariselectronicweek.com
Un événement produit par Technopol
#PEW23
technopc

Beazley Designs of the Year Poster Campaign

In collaboration with the Design Museum, Accept & Proceed developed the print and digital campaign for the annual Beazley Designs of the Year exhibition. The concept, *Designing a Better Tomorrow*, highlighted the role of designers as problem solvers, tackling global challenges. Using Processing, a kaleidoscopic filter was created as a visual metaphor for fragmentation and exploration, symbolising the journey from problem to solution.

Programming Tool/Language:
Processing

Client:
Design Museum

ARCHITECTURE
DIGITAL
FASHION
GRAPHIC
PRODUCT
TRANSPORT
TICKETS ON SALE NOW
#BEASLEYDESIGNSOFTHEYEAR
BEAZLEY
DESIGNS OF
THE YEAR
18 OCTOBER 2017
28 JANUARY 2018
the
DESIGN
MUSEUM
beazley
dezeen
ARCHITECTURE
DIGITAL
FASHION
GRAPHIC
PRODUCT
TRANSPORT
TICKETS ON SALE NOW
#BEASLEYDESIGNSOFTHEYEAR
BEAZLEY
DESIGNS OF
THE YEAR
18 OCTOBER 2017
28 JANUARY 2018
the
DESIGN
MUSEUM
beazley
dezeen
ARCHITECTURE
DIGITAL
FASHION
GRAPHIC
PRODUCT
TRANSPORT
TICKETS ON SALE NOW
#BEASLEYDESIGNSOFTHEYEAR
the
DESIGN
MUSEUM

become a member today
enjoy it first
members
Ferrari
UNDER THE SKIN
BEAZLEY
DESIGNS OF
THE YEAR

Barcelona Design Week 2023
Design for Human Future
16-28.10.23
18th Edition
B
DW
(23)
barcelonadesignweek.com
Instal·lacions, Exposicions, Showrooms,
Xerrades, Tallers, Rutes...
#BDW23
Design
for
Human
Future

16-28.10.23

LEÓN ROMERO developed the identity and campaign for the 18th Barcelona Design Week, introducing SDG 18 to promote a more humanistic future. The design balances humanism and technology through generative artworks that make the number 18 iconic and dynamic. The result is a bold, recognisable identity that visually communicates the event's forward-thinking vision.

Programming Tools/Languages:
TouchDesigner, Adobe After Effects

Client:
Barcelona Centre de Disseny
(Barcelona Design Center)

Expos
MULTIPLE EXPOSITIONS AND INTERACTIVE INSTALLATIONS.
Café
COLD DRINKS VEGAN FOOD COFFEE & TEA
Lobby
ENTRANCE EXIT TOILETS
LIVING ART LAB

LIVING ART LAB
01.09
21.09
2024
Johannes Vermeer
Tickets online

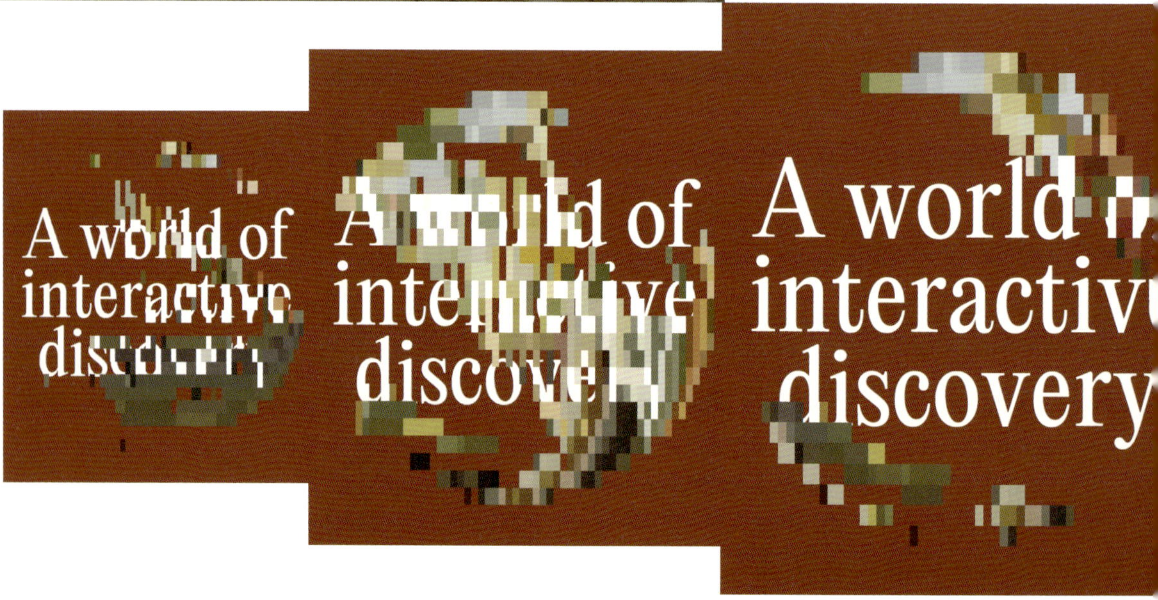
A world of interactive discovery

The Living Art Lab's visual identity, created by Mike van der Sanden, explores interactive play to teach art history. Using Processing, the identity is built around colours drawn from famous paintings, creating a dynamic visual language. The concept envisions a fictional museum where all ages can engage with the stories behind iconic artists and their works.

Programming Tool/Language:
Processing

smanship. We are "Computational Pottery Brand" that combines computational process and cr
about
EC_shop
01 02 03
instagram

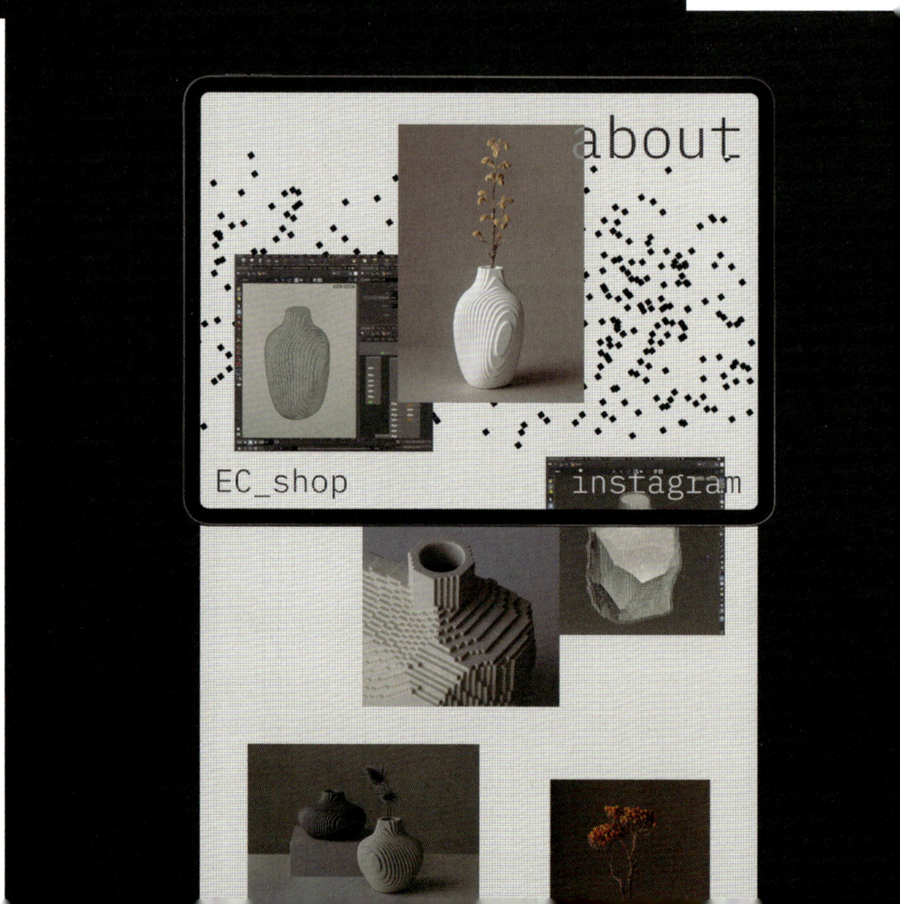
about
EC_shop
instagram

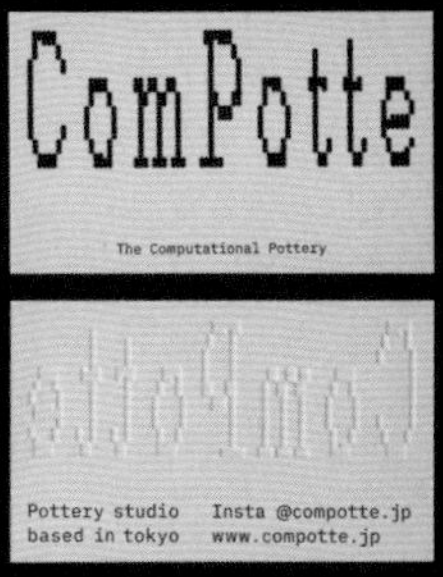

For the ceramics brand ComPotte, DIGRAPH crafted a logo using 3DCG software to design a pixel font of cubes, reflecting the organic essence of pottery. The web design employs programming to create dynamic animations that articulate a unique digital worldview, emphasising the brand's innovative approach to blending craftsmanship with technology.

Programming Tool/Language:
Houdini

Cafeteria ↑
Restrooms ←
Elevator ←
Auditorium →
TBWA\ The Disruption® Company

is
up
on®
N DISRUPT
2022
DE&I
Creative
bravery
inspired
by data
Pirates

TBWA\
We are the
Disruption
Company.

WE ARE
A GLOBAL
TBWA\ Group Canada
The Disruption Company®
Unseen, Unexpected,
We don't follow cultural and market conventions.
AGENCY
LOCATED IN
33 Bloor Street East
Toronto ON
M4W 3H1
Canada
TORONTO

André Burnier collaborated with TBWA and Plau to design the TBWA Grotesk typeface for their brand refresh. Inspired by the backslash in TBWA's logo, the typeface features a distinctive 20-degree slant. A standout innovation, the Font Disruptor— a custom tool by Burnier—adds dynamic effects, enhancing the type's evolving, disruptive personality to reflect TBWA's bold vision.

Programming Tool/Language:
p5.js

Client:
TBWA

Formless Twins designed an evolving identity system for the Busan Museum of Contemporary Art, blending technology, typography, and ecology. Inspired by rhizomatic structures and Eulsuk Island's biodiversity, the system invites visitor participation through generative design. Users could create personalised letterforms, forming a dynamic, ever-growing archive. Interactive digital elements transform the identity into an organic, living entity that redefines museum branding.

Programming Tool/Language:
JavaScript

Client:
Busan Museum of Contemporary Art

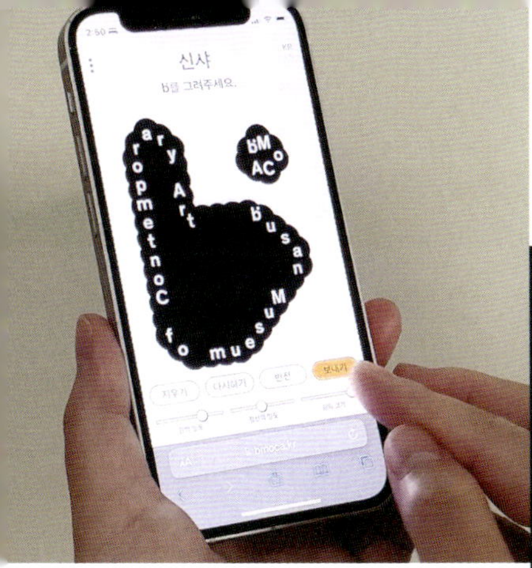

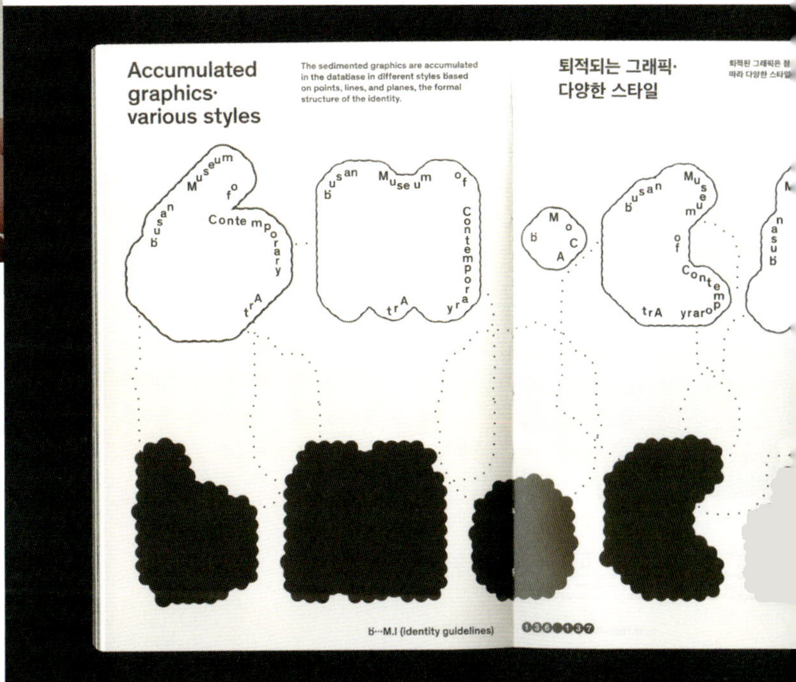
Accumulated graphics· various styles
The sedimented graphics are accumulated in the database in different styles based on points, lines, and planes, the formal structure of the identity.
퇴적되는 그래픽· 다양한 스타일
b···M.I (identity guidelines)

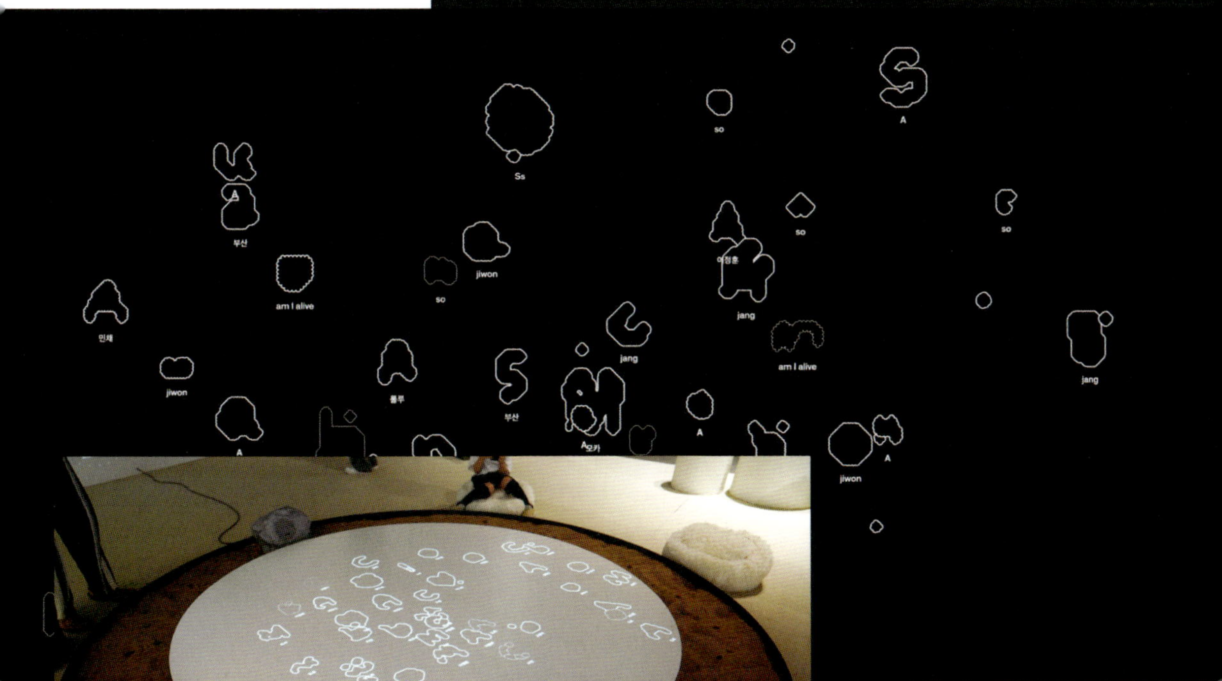
so
A
Ss
부산
jiwon
am I alive
민재
jang

Digital Culture Index

Andstudio's design for the Digital Culture Index (DCI) uses open-source data from Spotify, YouTube, and Google to capture Europe's cultural landscape. By identifying six archetypes, the DCI informs targeted marketing strategies. The design process pixelates national flags, symbolising each country's unique identity. Portrait photography ties the visual identity together, blending data with human culture to create a compelling narrative.

Programming Tool/Language:
Python

DE

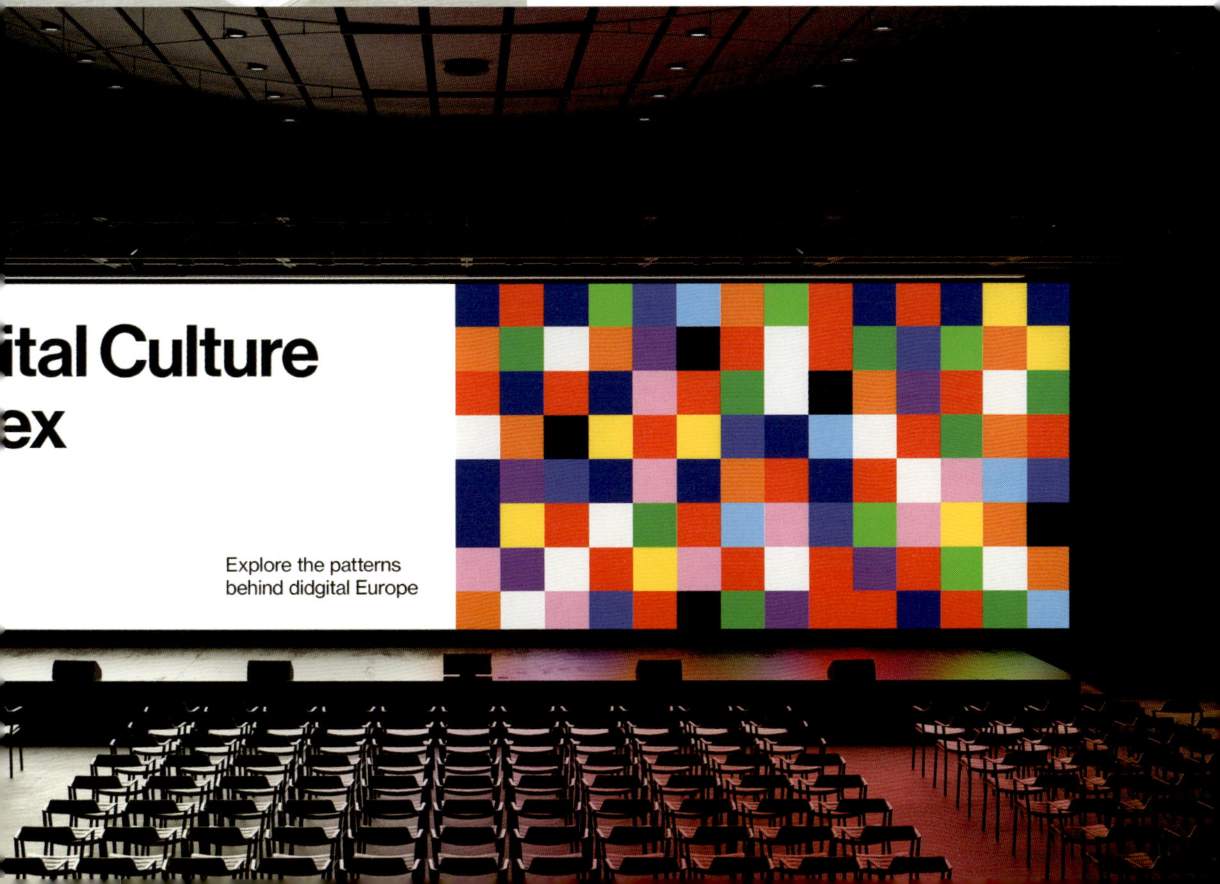
ital Culture
ex
Explore the patterns
behind didgital Europe

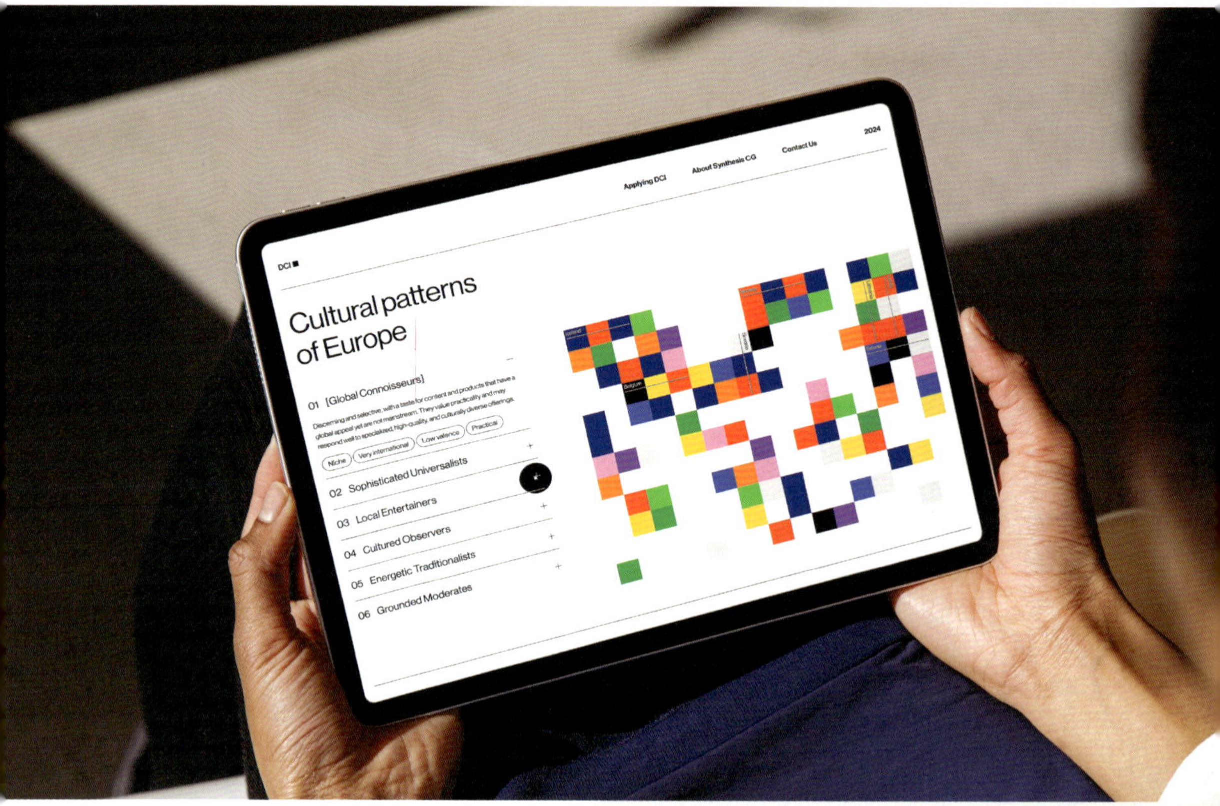
Applying DCI
About Synthesis CG
Contact Us
2024
DCI
Cultural patterns of Europe
01 [Global Connoisseurs]
Discerning and selective, with a taste for content and products that have a global appeal yet are not mainstream. They value practicality and may respond well to specialized, high-quality, and culturally diverse offerings.
Niche
Very international
Low valence
Practical
02 Sophisticated Universalists
03 Local Entertainers
04 Cultured Observers
05 Energetic Traditionalists
06 Grounded Moderates

DCI
BE

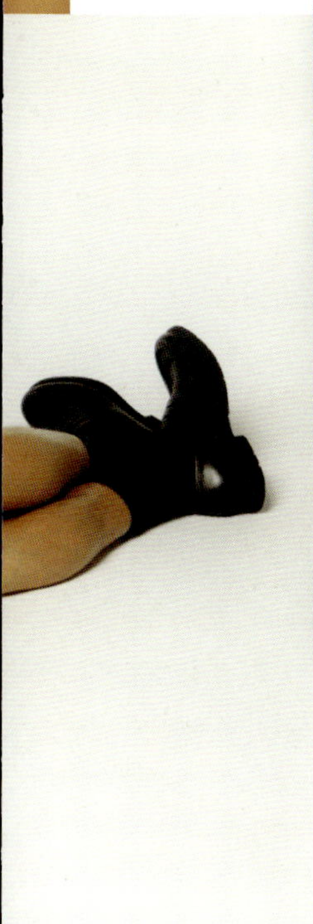

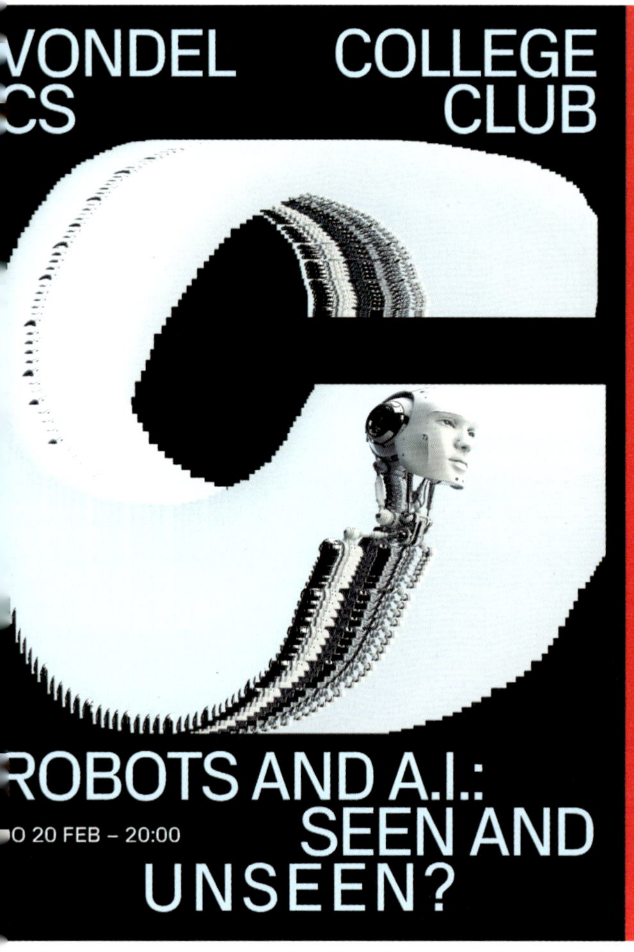
VONDEL
CS
COLLEGE
CLUB
ROBOTS AND A.I.:
20 FEB – 20:00
SEEN AND
UNSEEN?

VONDEL
CS
COLLEG
CLU
ECSCAPING
DI 26 NOV – 20:0
BLACKMIRRO

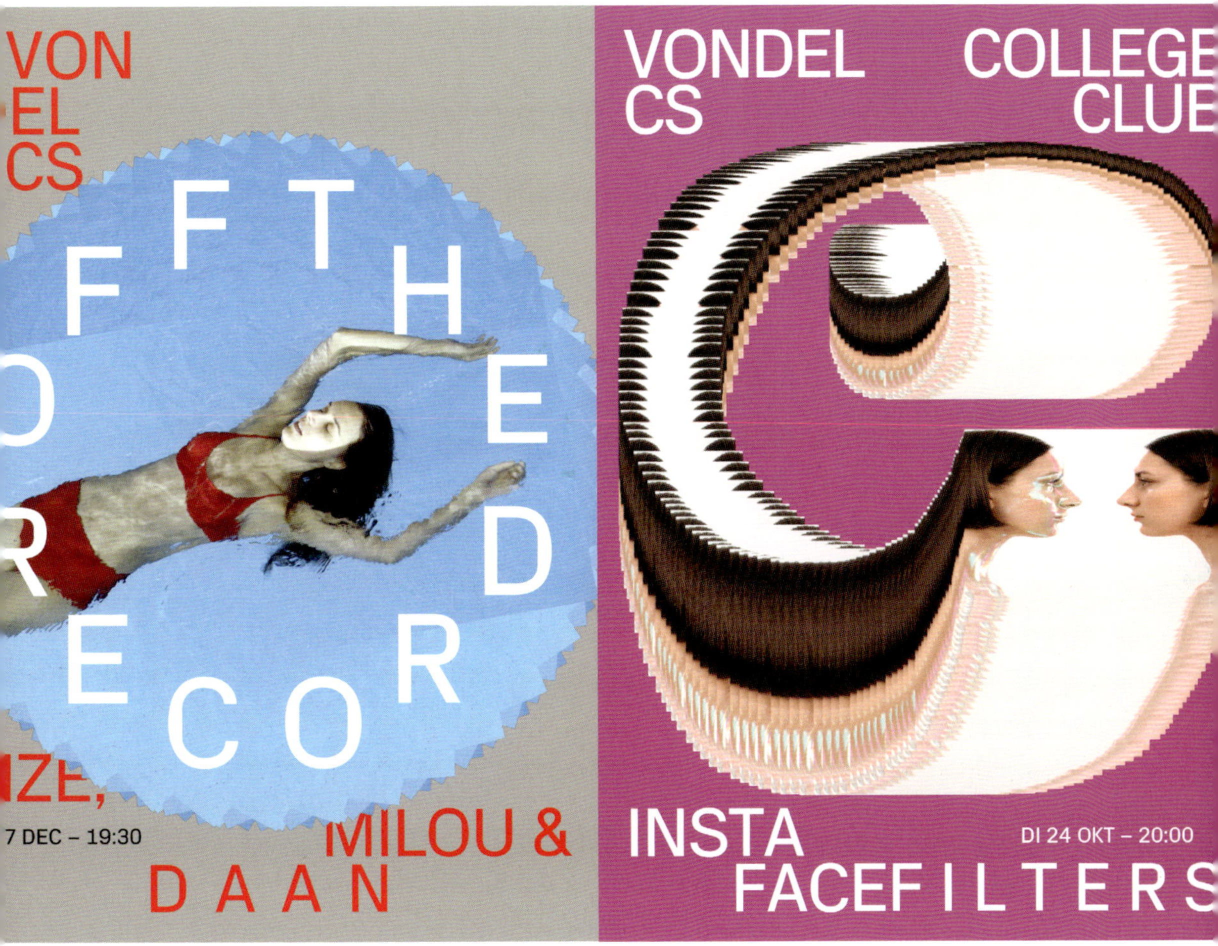

Cccclone sssssystem is a generative tool created for the new visual identity of VondelCS, a media and culture lab by AVROTROS in Amsterdam's Vondelpark. Designed to accommodate diverse events, the system transforms unedited photos and simple illustrations into dynamic poster visuals, reinforcing VondelCS's role as an innovative platform for media and cultural experimentation.

Programming Tool/Language:
p5.js

Client:
VondelCS

SPOTLIGHT 03

Lava

de Kromhouthal
Amsterdam Noord
Lava
07 – 10 july

programming language
JavaScript

client
House of Rubber

project year
2023

"What happens when a studio grows beyond its founder? This was the question Marlou Breuls and her team faced. Initially rooted in fashion, creating designs for artists like Björk and Sia as well as brands like Disney and Vogue, the studio had built a strong reputation with their work being featured at London's Victoria & Albert Museum. As part of its evolution, it sought to focus on expanding beyond fashion to include textures and sculptures, broadening its artistic scope while staying true to its DNA.

For its new identity, we used the behaviour of rubber as the foundation. This created a flexible system that balanced brand visibility with product visibility. Since the studio's work is often intricate, we designed an identity that contrasted with this: brutalist and simple. A rough sketch made in Illustrator was turned into a working tool in just one afternoon. The prototype also quickly became the final version, built in JavaScript with Paper.js to retain vector graphics. It combined a path cleanup algorithm with object distribution and used the k-means algorithm to detect prominent colours, integrated with our colour system. It was exciting to see the team conceptualise and experiment with the tool, finding unexpected uses for it – turning the identity into something dynamic and self-sustaining."

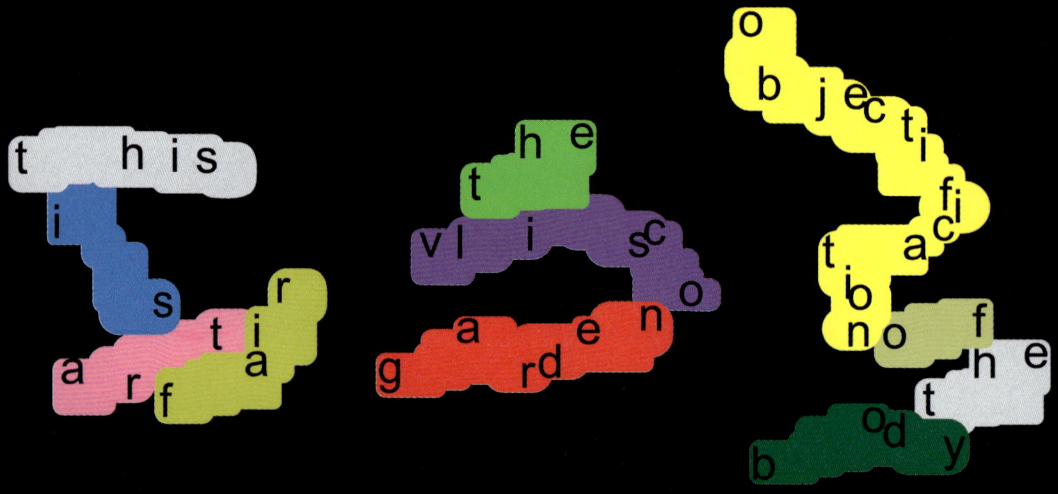

houseofrubber.com
h o us e
o
f
r u bb e r
pretty busy sculptural business

h o u s e
o f
rubber

pretty busy sculptural business
h o u se
o f
house of rubber x metal magazine

Smeerboel Festival

programming languag
JavaScript

client
Elevation Events

project year
2023

“The Dutch techno and house festival Smeerboel brings Utrecht to life every September, featuring a diverse range of artists, a quirky fringe programme, and an electrifying party atmosphere. Attracting around 20,000 visitors aged 20 to 40, the name Smeerboel translates to 'smearing mess' in English.

The organisers tasked us with creating a rebrand that could vary with each edition, capturing the playfulness of both the event and its audience. Our research led to a vibrant design system centred on the behaviour of 'smeren' or smearing. Built entirely in JavaScript with Three.js, the tool uses shaders, generative meshes, and custom UV coordinates to smear photographs. Initially developed in a different form for an art installation compressing images as earth layers, the concept aligned perfectly with the festival's name and energy.

Our main challenge was designing a style and layout that allowed bold smears while remaining readable and recognisable. As Smeerboel encourages audience participation, we incorporated this into the system. Elevation Events, the festival organiser, embraced the idea early on, and the online tooling environment was straightforward to implement. By creating fields of repeating text and layered visuals, we ensured smearing became an integral, recognisable part of the identity, allowing it to connect seamlessly with all festival assets.”

SMEERBOEL
FESTIVAL

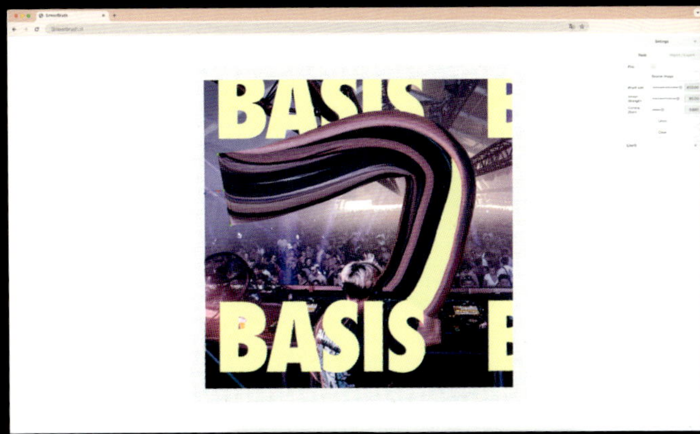
BASIS
BASIS

SMEER
BOEL
FESTIVAL
9 SEPT
GRASWEIDE PAPENDORP
UTRECHT

THE RESONANCE OF A POP STAGE

programming language
JavaScript

client
EKKO

project year
2023

“EKKO is a pop venue and club in Utrecht, showcasing emerging national and international artists such as Franz Ferdinand, Four Tet, and Death Cab for Cutie. Behind the scenes, it nurtures new talent, with learning and development at its core. In 2022, it entered a period of transition, welcoming a new team, fresh perspectives, and audiences from Generations Y and Z.

To reflect these changes, we helped rebrand its identity system using 'resonance' as the central concept. In physics, resonance occurs when an object vibrates at its natural frequency due to an external force, amplifying the effect. It also signifies an emotional connection with music or ideas – both meanings resonating strongly with EKKO’s philosophy. Initial prototypes were developed in C++ with LibCinder, but we shifted to a web-based stack using JavaScript with THREE.js and Paper.js. As existing physics libraries like Bullet proved unsuitable for controlled, stable growth of shapes under tension, we built a computer-heavy but stable faux physics system instead.

We also solved challenges like pre-generating animations and near-live asset generation using AWS batch processing. A workshop with EKKO’s marketing team ensured the tool met their needs, allowing for creative experimentation. Ultimately, the project prioritised behaviour over fixed visuals, offering new creative possibilities for EKKO.”

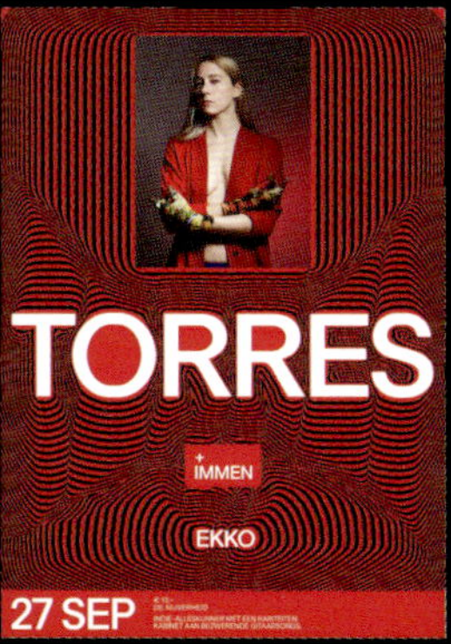
TORRES
+ IMMEN
EKKO
27 SEP

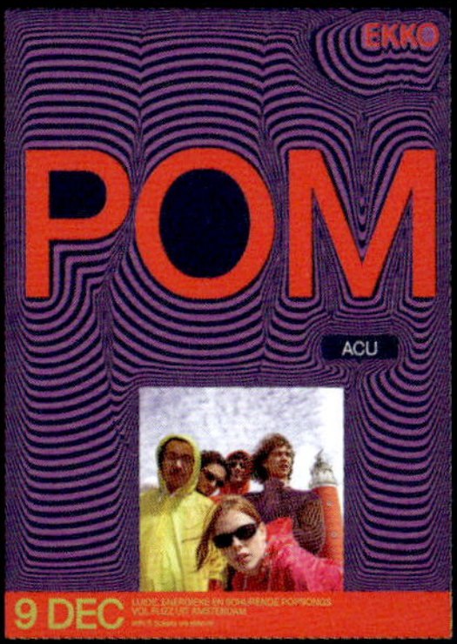
EKKO
POM
ACU
9 DEC

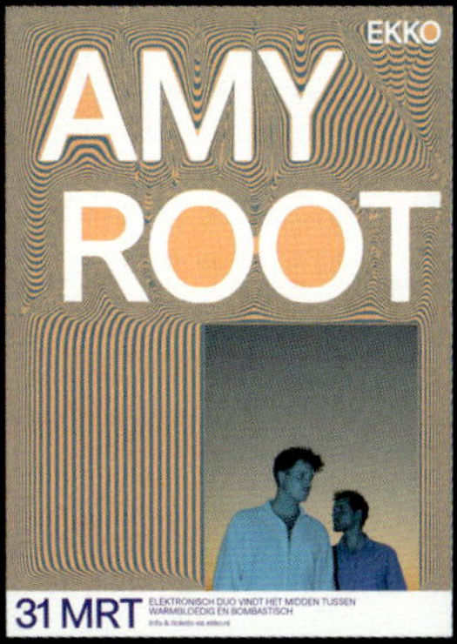
EKKO
AMY
ROOT
31 MRT

+ FFOOSS
IDLES
EKKO
07 JUL

EKKO
MY BODY
MY QUEER
PARTY
21:30 – 04:00
19 NOV

BOB
EKKO
UIT
ZUID
26 NOV

DIT
EKKO
PROTOMARTYR
RAY FUEGO
+ KLEINE CRACK
900 MINUTEN:
CARISTA,
TINLICKER E.A.
MAGNAPOP
FENG
SUAVE
LE GUESS WHO?
2022
BOB UIT ZUID
NAJAAR

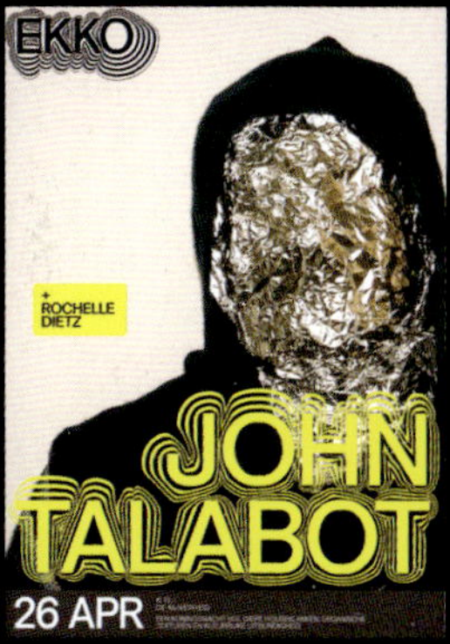
EKKO
+ ROCHELLE
DIETZ
JOHN
TALABOT
26 APR

EKKO
IDLES

SPRING
Performing Arts Festival

programming language
JavaScript

client
SPRING Performing Arts Festival

project year
2023

“The SPRING Performing Arts Festival in Utrecht stands out as a multidisciplinary, international event, attracting thousands of art professionals, students, and adventurous art lovers every year. With a focus on technology and performing arts, it uses its programme to ask urgent societal questions, inviting audiences to challenge their perspectives. Although technology and experimentation have always been part of SPRING’s DNA, after two pandemic years, the team felt it was outdated to simply showcase these elements.

The new artistic director’s interest in technology’s greater impact on human life inspired the creative process. What began as brainstorming for the 11th edition evolved into a new brand identity that reflects the festival’s dynamic and fluid nature. The goal was to ensure strong recognition while allowing flexibility for future programmes.

We first designed a flexible, human-centred typeface which then led to a bespoke tool combining Kinect recordings and AI motion tracking, allowing the SPRING team to merge performances with the brand. Early prototypes used point tracking in After Effects, but as modern dance movements proved too unpredictable for AI models, we switched to Microsoft Kinect sensors. This provided higher resolution and smoother motion tracking. The system consisted of two parts: recording skeleton data and video, then mapping movements onto generative letters. Typography was also adjusted to reflect expressiveness, with added rhythm and spacing to enhance motion. By turning choreography into a design tool, SPRING’s identity captures the festival’s innovative and experimental spirit.”

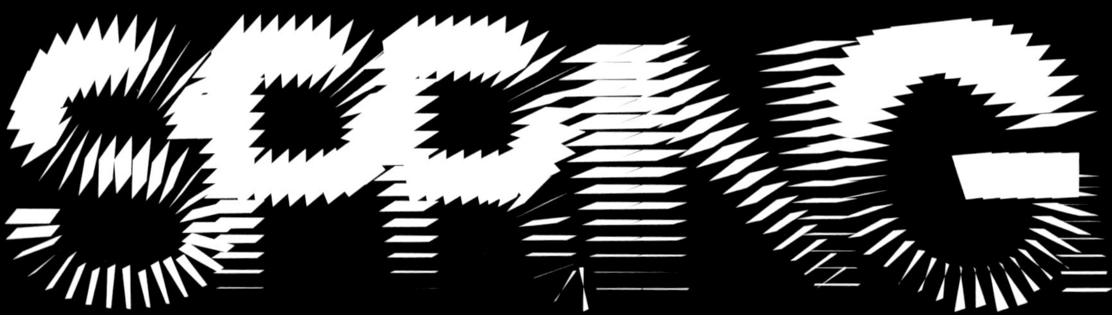

Performing Arts
Festival
Ten Days of
ance, Music
d More
18 - 27
Mei

Ten Days of
Dance, Music
and More
18 - 27
Mei

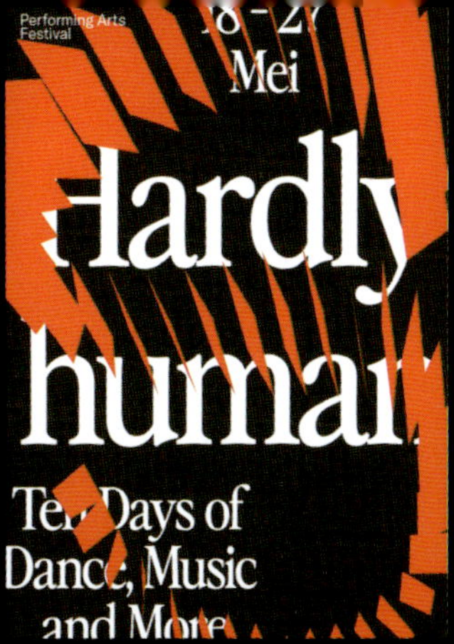
Performing Arts
Festival
Mei
ardly
huma
Days of
Music

programming language	client	project year
JavaScript	VICTORIE	2023

"As the leading venue in the region, Victorie offers an alternative in terms of space, possibilities, and experience, standing apart from larger music venues in and around Amsterdam. Our goal was to craft a new identity that reinforced their strong local reputation while resonating with audiences familiar with the music scenes of bigger cities.

We drew inspiration from the concept of abstracting a flag, aligning with the venue's name and referencing their previous identity. Rather than a literal flag, we reinterpreted its material, construction, and movement in unique ways through sketches and prototypes. In doing so, we built a tool in JavaScript, leveraging shaders for precise letter bending calculations and faster transformations. Besides applying vectors via Paper.js, we generated animation assets in-browser using FFmpeg in WebAssembly. Through several iterations, we were able to explore the idea of adaptability and visual behaviour, aiming to balance artistic expression with recognisability.

Adaptability was key to the identity, reflecting Victorie's pride in tailoring experiences for different artists and audiences, such as custom drinks menus for events. To ensure the artists take centrestage, our system also incorporates colours from their photos as well as custom typography. For its implementation, we held a workshop to explain the tool's features to the Victorie's in-house team, who have limited time and design expertise. Their feedback helped refine the system, such as via the addition of an 'I'm feeling lucky' button, which generates layout options based on content to simplify the process. Users can cycle through designs or adjust them as needed, maintaining high visual standards with minimal effort."

VICTORIE

IPA

VICTORIE
10 SEP

FOR OUR READERS WHO ARE NEW TO LAVA, COULD YOU PLEASE SHARE WHAT SETS YOUR CREATIVE PHILOSOPHY APART FROM YOUR PEERS? WHAT IMPACT DOES YOUR STUDIO HOPE TO MAKE ON THE LARGER BRANDING AND DESIGN LANDSCAPE?

We don't believe in branding that just sits on a shelf. A brand should be something people can use, play with, and make their own. In today's fast-paced world, brands need to adapt and evolve to stay relevant. Too often, design systems are either too rigid to grow or too complicated to use, making it difficult for brands to stay dynamic. When that happens, creativity goes numb, execution suffers, and the brand loses its spark. We're here to change that by pushing branding beyond outdated rules and making it something people can actually use.

We set clear boundaries, but there is plenty of space to explore and evolve within them. A strong brand should not just be a set of rules but a living system that invites interaction and has room to grow. With custom tools, smart templates, and adaptive systems, we make it easy to bring brands to life, so they do not just stand out; they stay relevant and full of energy. In the end, work should also be fun, right?

COULD YOU GIVE OUR READERS MORE INSIGHT INTO WHAT YOU MEAN BY "LIVING BRANDS"? WHAT VALUES OR CHARACTERISTICS DO YOU BELIEVE CLIENTS NEED TO HAVE IN ORDER TO BE "BRAVE" ENOUGH TO PUSH THE BOUNDARIES AND HOW DO YOU HANDLE SITUATIONS WHERE THEY RESIST CHANGE OR EVOLUTION?

We all know what dynamic brands look like, but a living brand is something deeper. It's not just about motion or variation; it's about behaviour. Instead of being locked into a set of predefined graphics, messaging or photography, a living brand reacts, evolves, and responds to the world around it. That could mean a typeface shaped by real-time choreography, a logotype that shifts with the weather, or a layout system that adapts automatically to content. The tools and mechanics change depending on the project, but the goal is the same, to create a system that isn't just designed, but alive.

For this to work, clients need to let go of ego, and so do we. The best outcomes come when both sides can step back and look at the brand objectively, not just as an extension of personal taste or legacy. That's why we start every project with strategy and deep conversations not just about design, but about purpose. When there's trust, we can push boundaries together.

At the end of the day, a brand that isn't willing to stand out is a brand that doesn't need to exist. Because people won't notice it. If you're doing branding, you're doing it for a reason. The best clients understand that. The ones who thrive in this process are open and curious

IN TERMS OF YOUR CREATIVE APPROACH, HOW DO YOU BALANCE AUTHENTIC CREATIVITY WITH THE NEED FOR BRANDS TO BE ADAPTABLE AND RESPONSIVE IN REAL TIME? WHAT'S THE MOST SURPRISING OR UNCONVENTIONAL INSPIRATION YOU HAVE DRAWN UPON WHEN CREATING A BRANDING CONCEPT?

For us, balancing creativity and adaptability isn't much of a struggle, to be honest. It's just how we work. We experiment, push boundaries, and challenge ideas, but it always comes back to solving the client's real communication problem. If the solution works, clients don't need convincing, they're on board. Beyond that, it's about building trust, truly understanding the client and their challenges, and working as equal partners.

As for unconventional inspiration, the key is looking beyond graphic design and branding. New technologies, art, societal movements, or even a piece of nature can completely shift how we approach branding.

HOW DOES YOUR STUDIO FOSTER COLLABORATION BETWEEN STRATEGISTS, DESIGNERS, AND TECHNOLOGISTS TO SEAMLESSLY ALIGN AND CRAFT COHESIVE BRANDING SOLUTIONS THAT DEEPLY RESONATE WITH TODAY'S EVER-EVOLVING AUDIENCES?

We collaborate by keeping things open and fast. No silos, no handovers — just strategists, designers, and technologists working together from the start. We question everything with a "what if" mentality, sketching, coding, and testing ideas in real-time.

Some of our best ideas come from bouncing possibilities between disciplines. R&D is a big part of our projects, but we're also building an experimentation space to push branding behaviours even further, beyond client work, into new territory.

WHEN DEVELOPING A STRATEGY, HOW DO YOU TAILOR-MAKE WORKSHOPS TO HELP CLIENTS UNCOVER THEIR BRAND'S UNIQUE PERSONALITY AND CORE BEHAVIOUR? FOLLOWING WHICH, HOW DO YOU BUILD LONG-TERM RELATIONSHIPS WITH THEM WHILE ENSURING THEIR BRANDS REMAIN DYNAMIC AND INNOVATIVE OVER TIME?

It always starts with understanding the question behind the question. There's often an immediate challenge, but beneath it lies a deeper need. It's crucial to uncover that first, to ensure alignment on the end goal and identify the real pain points.

We balance between methods we often use because they always work and new ideas and approaches that help us uncover deeper insights. Involving people across the organisation is just as important. This ensures a true understanding of what's happening and what's needed while also creating ambassadors and ownership. After all, it's the people within an organisation who ultimately need to implement the change. A top-down approach never works. But when involving people, it's essential to communicate expectations and how their input will be used.

One of the most important part of our experimental approach is guiding our clients in understanding the value of differentiation in a world overflowing with brands competing for attention. Innovation and experimentation come with a phase of uncertainty, where things might feel abstract, and that’s okay. We, and the client, must remain open and vulnerable throughout the process.

What we guarantee is a brand that truly represents your DNA. One that is transferable and usable, even for those without a design background. A key part of this process is giving the client insight into the development along the way, even when things are still unfinished. This helps them understand that branding is a journey we embark on together.

Regarding long-term relationships, we find them very important. We regularly review the work clients create, whether in the early stages or on an ongoing basis. If they have any doubts, they can easily reach out to us. We use collaborative tools to facilitate quick and seamless communication. If we’ve done our job well, this shouldn’t be needed too often, but we often find that after a brand is launched, additional insights emerge during the first phase. Another approach is conducting reviews with all the partners and agencies our clients work with. These sessions act as audits, allowing us to assess the work done over the past few months and ensure everything stays aligned with the brand identity.

And one more thing about long-term relationships: don’t talk about branding and work all the time. Sometimes, it’s nice to go out for a drink or two.

WHAT DOES YOUR TOOLBOX FOR BRANDING ELEMENTS TYPICALLY INCLUDE, AND HOW DO THESE ELEMENTS BRING A BRAND TO LIFE ACROSS DIFFERENT TOUCHPOINTS?

Our toolbox isn’t fixed; it adapts to each project. Of course, we cover the essentials: logos, colours, typography, motion behaviour, tone of voice, illustrations, and image treatment. But the real magic comes from custom tools and templates that make the brand come to life in the real world.

We often create brand-specific tools that empower teams to build and evolve their brand without being constrained by rigid guidelines. In some cases, we even build tools that allow clients to create nearly all their marketing materials. For one client, we even developed an “I’m feeling lucky” button that creates items quickly when there’s little time. Technology is key, but we don’t use it just for the sake of it. Every tool we develop has a clear purpose: to make the brand more fluid, accessible, and alive across different touchpoints.

YOU MENTION THAT TECHNOLOGY SHOULD NOT BE USED "JUST FOR THE SAKE OF TECHNOLOGY". HOW DO YOU DETERMINE WHEN AND HOW TO INCORPORATE TECHNOLOGY INTO A PROJECT – AND HOW DO YOU MEASURE ITS SUCCESSFUL IMPLEMENTATION?

For us, technology isn’t an afterthought; it’s often built into the design process. We don’t ask if we should use it, but how. Sometimes it’s an invisible backbone shaping behaviour, and other times it’s a tool that allows

The key is giving brands what they need. If a brand needs to produce content at scale, we build custom tools that keep it fluid and alive. If a project calls for a more simple identity, we keep it that way. Still, we always try to push it a bit further, surprising the client by showing how it could grow. It's a success when clients no longer need us but continue to create great on-brand work.

WHAT'S THE BOLDEST RISK LAVA HAS EVER TAKEN IN BRANDING, AND HOW DID IT PAY OFF – OR NOT? WHAT LESSONS DID YOU TAKE AWAY FROM THIS EXPERIENCE?

One of our boldest risks was using crowdsourcing as a design tool, letting external input shape a brand's identity. For St. Joost School of Art & Design, we created a custom display typeface built from student contributions. Each year, students design a letter, which we process through an AI system to generate a new typeface for the school's communications.

Great idea, tough execution. Collecting input, ensuring participation, and making the font usable for the school's team were all challenges.

Lesson learned? Bold ideas need strong mechanics. A system isn't just about creativity; it has to function in practice.

WHAT FUTURE TRENDS DO YOU SEE SHAPING THE INTERSECTION OF DESIGN AND TECHNOLOGY? IF YOU COULD INVENT A NEW TECHNOLOGY OR TOOL SPECIFICALLY FOR BRANDING, WHAT WOULD IT DO AND WHY?

Branding is moving beyond static guidelines into living environments and identities that evolve in real time, adapting to context, audience, and external conditions. Another key development is the abundance of tools that allow almost anyone to design. This raises an important question for us: what is our value if everyone becomes a designer? At the same time, how can we facilitate this process for our clients? These questions keep us sharp.

If we could invent a tool, it would be a self-evolving brand system, one that reacts, reshapes, and grows based on real-world inputs. Not just via automation, but with adaptability as a core behaviour.

WHAT ADVICE WOULD YOU GIVE TO UPCOMING DESIGNERS AS THEY EXPLORE THE CONCEPT OF CREATING "LIVING BRANDS"? HOW CAN THEY HARNESS TECHNOLOGY IN STORYTELLING TO BUILD EMOTIONAL CONNECTIONS IN AN INCREASINGLY DIGITISED WORLD?

Forget about making brands look dynamic; make them act dynamic. A "living brand" isn't just motion graphics or clever type; it's about behaviour. Think about how a brand can react, adapt, and evolve in real-time.

When it comes to technology, don't use it just because it's there. Find new ways to use tools instead of following trends. Trends move fast, but a well-chosen toolset grows with you.

Most importantly, break/hack things. Don't focus solely on the end result. It doesn't have to work right away. Experiment. Make ugly things, make stupid things, and have fun.

AMBIENT KYOTO
AMBIENT KYOTO
AMBIENT KYOTO
AMBIENT KYOTO
AMBIENT KYOTO
AMBIENT KYOTO

AMBIENT KYOTO
AMBIENT KYOTO
AMBIENT KYOTO

The AMBIENT KYOTO logo transforms a parallelogram into a spatial metaphor, merging typography with its background. Designed through a C++ algorithm, it evolves autonomously, minimising designer intervention. A motion-based "logo manual" captures this process, showcasing its adaptability. The logo's fluid nature extends across posters and merchandise, mirroring ambient music's ever-changing, immersive qualities.

Programming Tools/Languages:
openFrameworks, C++

Client:
AMBIENT KYOTO 2023 Committee

AMBIENT KYOTO
AMBIENT
2023
AMBIENT KYOTO 2023
MARIKO ASABUKI
SEIICHI YAMAMOTO
RYUICHI SAKAMOTO + SHIRO TAKATANI
BUFFALO DAUGHTER
TERRY RILEY

AMBIENT KYOTO

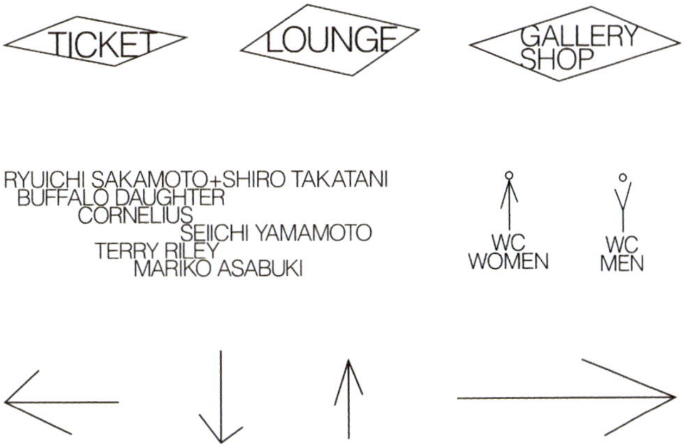
TICKET
LOUNGE
GALLERY SHOP
RYUICHI SAKAMOTO+SHIRO TAKATANI
BUFFALO DAUGHTER
CORNELIUS
SEIICHI YAMAMOTO
TERRY RILEY
MARIKO ASABUKI
WC WOMEN
WC MEN

AMBIENT KYOTO

Design: Vertical & Horizontal Growth. Cumulus Conference

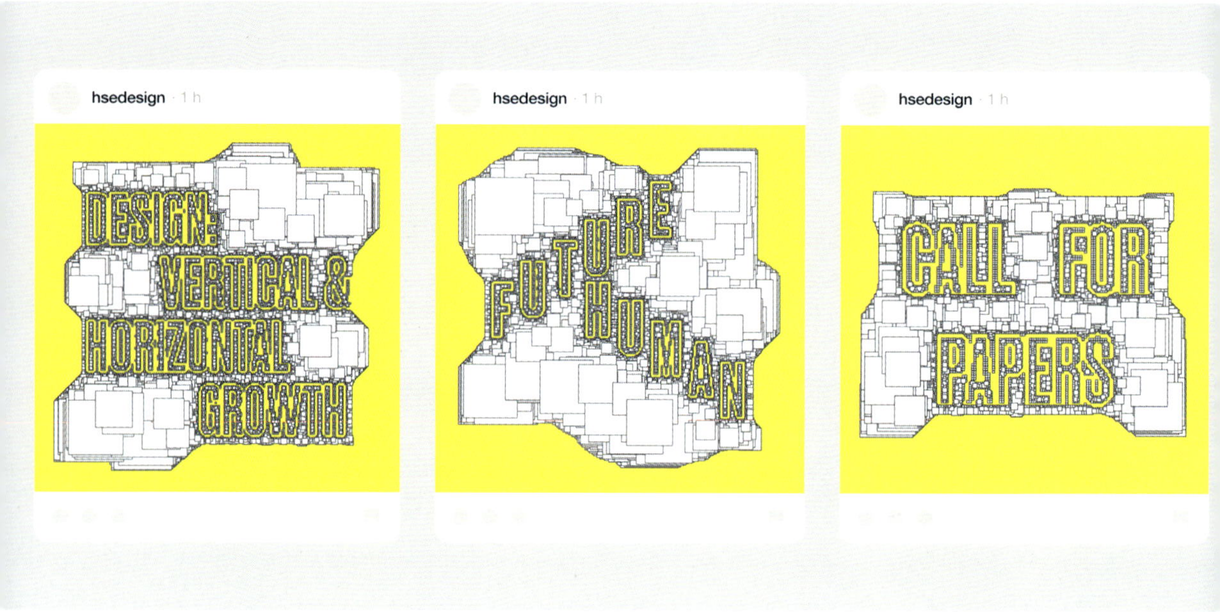

Afterimage created the visual identity for the 2020 Cumulus conference, held online by three Russian universities. The conference, themed "Design: Vertical & Horizontal Growth", explored design's role in addressing development challenges. The identity was generated using a computer algorithm, producing evolving shapes and intricate forms to visually represent the growth central to the theme.

Programming Tools/Languages:
Processing (Prototyping), JavaScript,
p5.js, HTML+CSS

Client:
HSE Art and Design School

DESIGN:
VERTICAL
&
HORIZONTAL
GROWTH
OCT. 28-30
REGISTER NOW

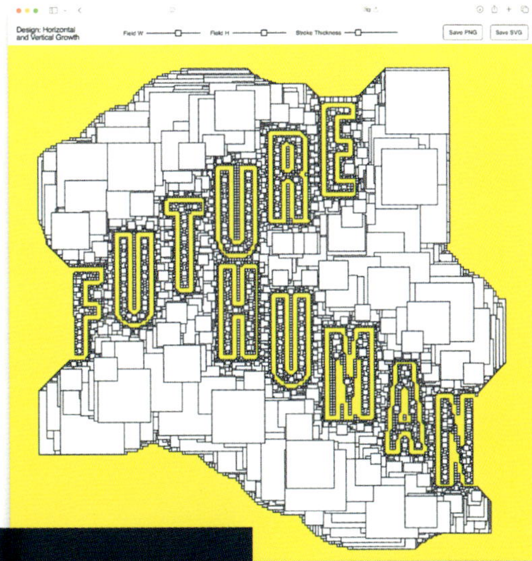
Design: Horizontal
and Vertical Growth
Stroke Thickness
Save PNG
Save SVG
FUTURE
HUMAN

Design: Vertical &
Horizontal Growth
28-30 Oct.
Moscow
St.Petersburg
DESIGN: VERTICAL
& HORIZONTAL
GROWTH

Automatic Music Video Generation System

Hajime Tsunoda developed an automatic music video generation system for his 2023 performance at "Hyper Geek", a Japanese audiovisual event. The system autonomously synchronised visuals with sound, eliminating manual intervention. Designed to anticipate rhythmic pulses, it created a seamless live A/V experience, showcasing the potential for real-time integration of minimal music and motion graphics.

Programming Tool/Language:
Processing

Client:
Hyper Geek

BASS
on Track5,
Vector : 10
Refrence : Model:Cycles

BASS
on Track5,
Vector : 526

BASS
on Track5,
Vector : 563

BASS
on Track5,
Vector : 146

LanPage - ack!

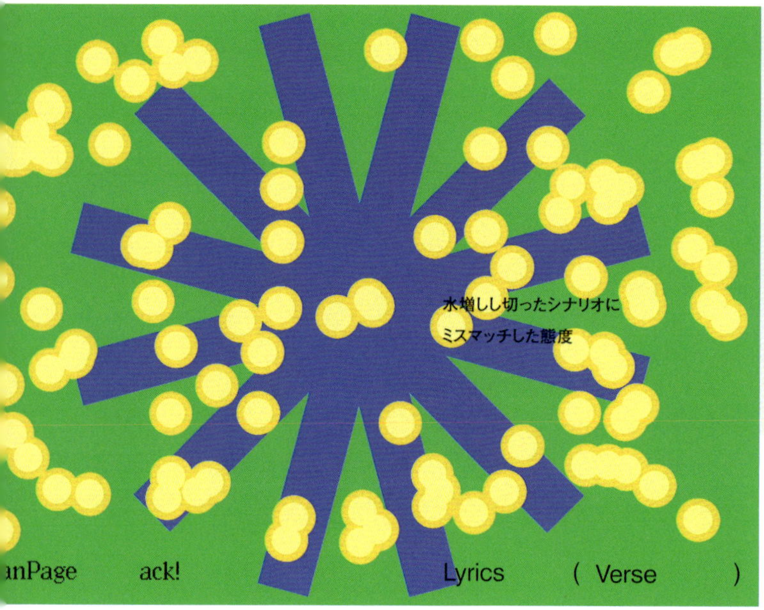

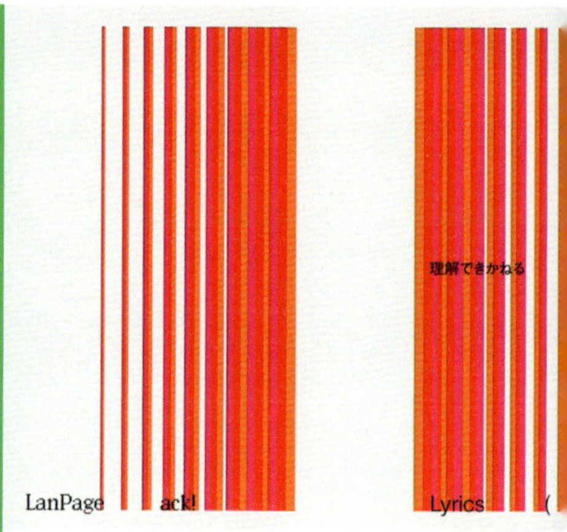

The music video for "ack!", the debut track by Japanese hyperpop unit LanPage, was created using a custom system in openFrameworks. This system generates shapes in real time based on MIDI data, producing a movement style distinct from traditional keyframe animation. The approach also enabled seamless integration into a live audiovisual performance format.

Programming Tool/Language:
openFrameworks

Client:
LanPage

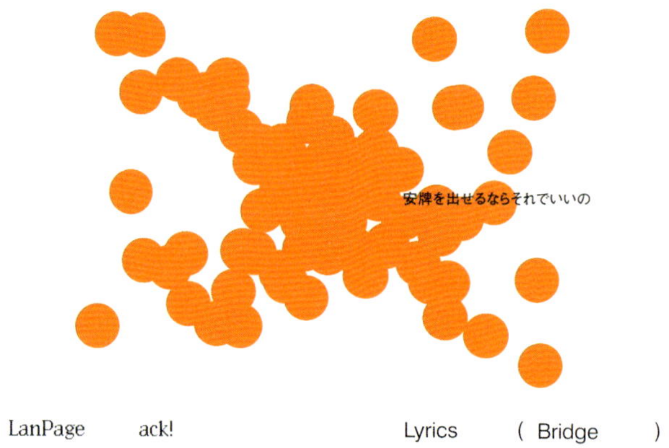

具体性の欠片もない
LanPage
ack!
Lyrics
(Hook 2)

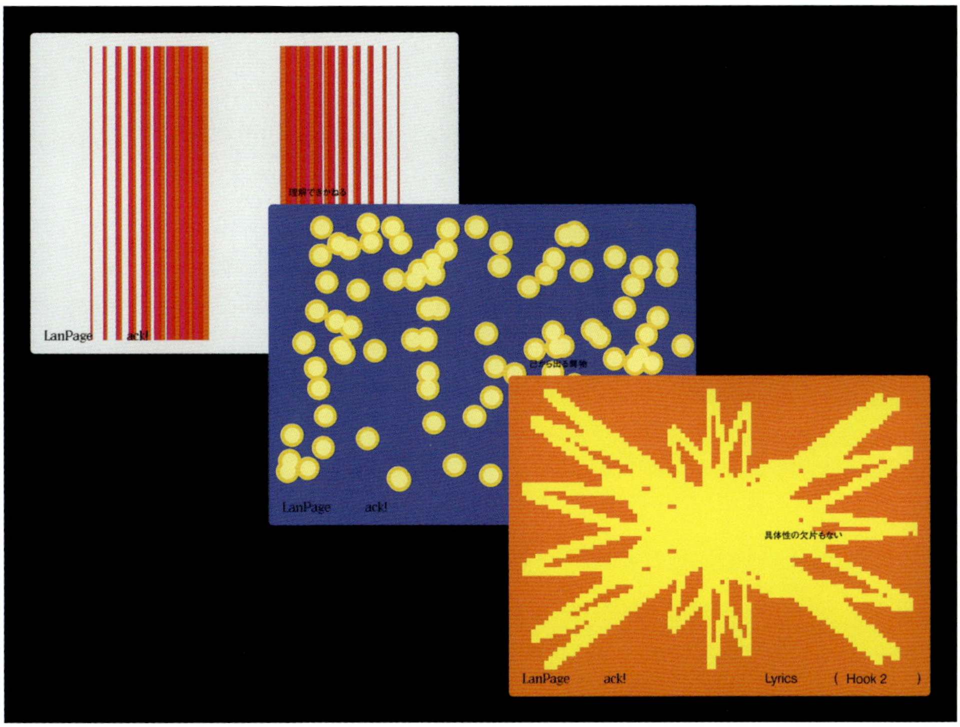
LanPage
ack!
LanPage
ack!
具体性の欠片もない
LanPage
ack!
Lyrics
(Hook 2)

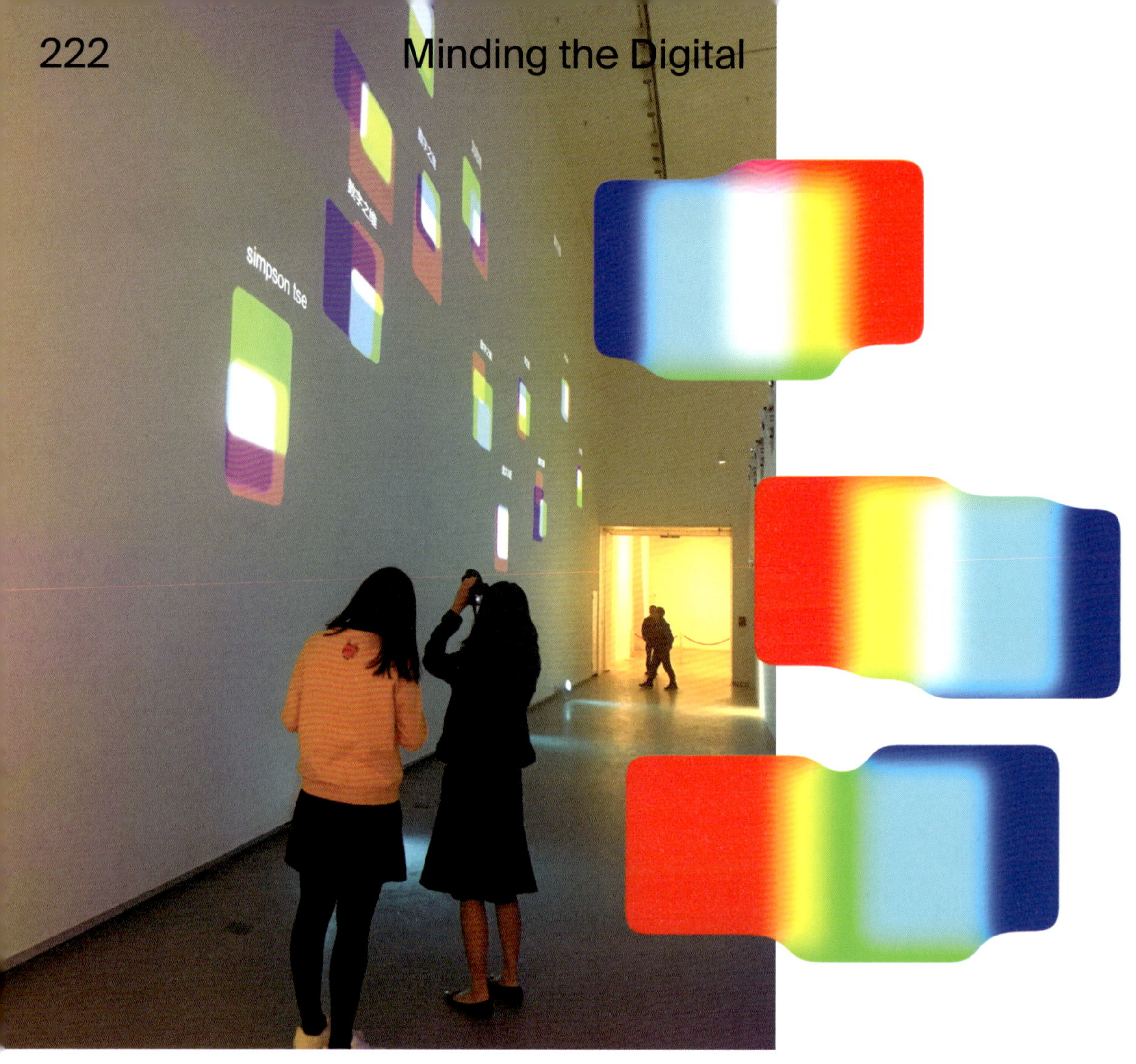

"Minding the Digital", the debut exhibition of Design Society in Shenzhen, featured a striking visual identity with vibrant RGB colour patches floating across the screen, dynamically constrained by computer-generated typography. Inspired by the game of Pong, an interactive JavaScript tool controlled the movement of these elements, echoing early digital aesthetics. The design seamlessly complemented MVRDV's LED-lit exhibition space, blending nostalgia with innovation.

Programming Tool/Language:
JavaScript

Client:
Design Society, Shenzhen

DESIGN
设计
数字之维 MINDING THE DIGITAL
互联
SOCIETY
2017.12.02—
2018.06.31
会场地址 Venue Address
海上世界文化艺术中心主展厅
中国深圳南山区蛇口王海路1187号
Main Gallery
Sea World Culture and Art Center
1187, Wanghai Road, Shekou
Nanshan District, Shenzhen, China
招商蛇口
LASVIT
SWAROVSKI
DESIGNTRUST
www.designsociety.cn

FEEEEL MACAU 2023
Generative Art

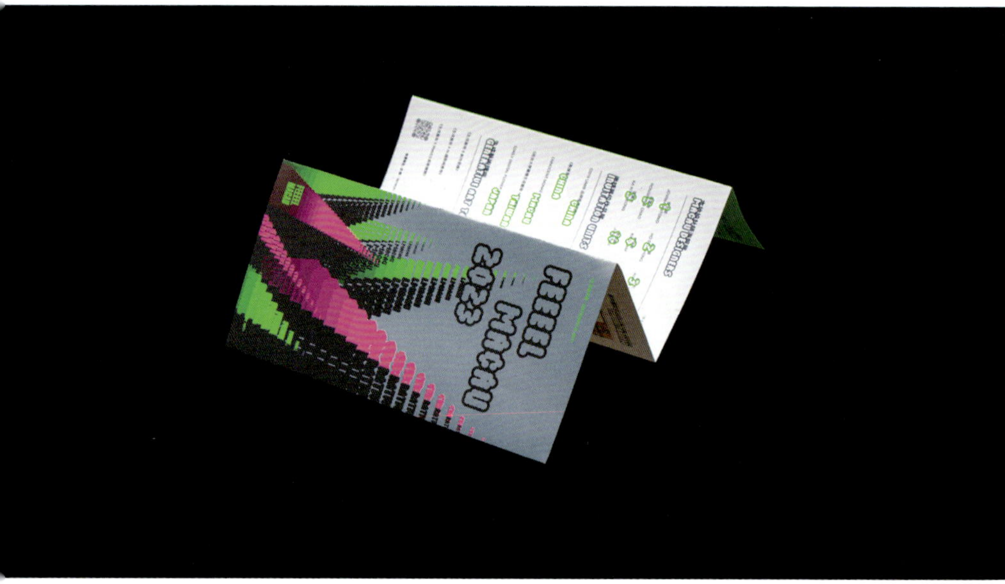

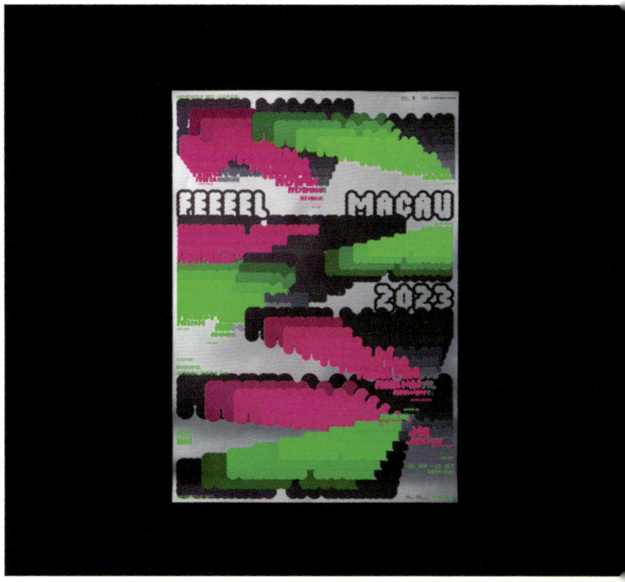

The visual design for the FEEEEL MACAU 2023 exhibition was inspired by the unpredictable and recursive nature of generative art. Using data-driven algorithms, it featured dynamic, evolving visuals based on exhibition details like participant names. These ever-changing compositions were transformed into printed posters and interactive digital products, reflecting the interconnectedness between the exhibition, participants, and audience.

Programming Tools/Languages:
React JS, p5.js, Polygon blockchain

Client:
Macau Poster Design Association

FEEEEL MACAU 2023
Generative Art

FEEEEL
MACAU
2023

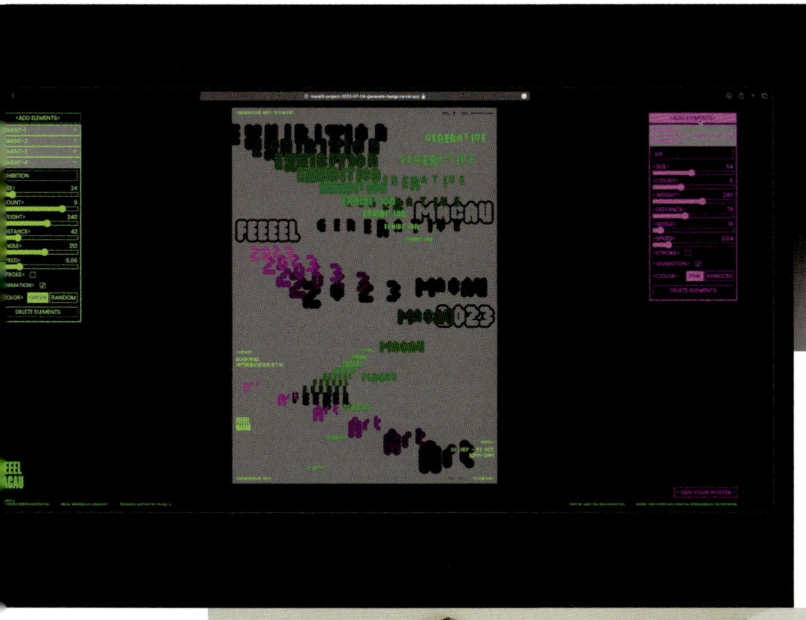

MACAU
2023
GET YOUR UNIQUE POSTER
PLAY
FEEEEL
MACAU

Ode to Benoît Mandelbrot

"Ode to Mandelbrot" is a poster series by Mike van der Sanden inspired by the mathematical beauty of the Mandelbrot set. The posters distort typography through iterations within the set, reflecting the visual complexity and intricacy of fractals. His experimentation with the set's patterns showcases a blend of mathematical and typographic art.

Programming Tool/Language:
Processing

A FRACTAL IS
A WAY
OF SEEING
INFINITY
ODE TO BENOIT MANDELBROT
FATHER OF FRACTALS
LETTERS IMMERSED
IN A SYMPHONY OF
MANDELBROT ITERATIONS

LAB#01: Medios Sintientes

LAB#01: Medios Sintientes at Medialab Matadero explores sensory technologies' impact on health, energy, and the environment. Led by Koln Studio, a custom Processing tool was developed to generate collages from images and videos, visually representing key sensory technologies. The project highlights how digital manipulation and sensory media reshape perception through technology, research, and art.

Programming Tool/Language:
Processing

Client:
Medialab, Matadero Madrid

Medios
Sintientes
LAB#01
Medialab
Matadero
27.01/07.05
Nerea Calvillo
Abelardo
Gil-Fournier
Quadrature
Current
Adam Harvey
Bellingca
Marta Peirano
Luiza Crosman
Gary Zhexy Zhang
and many more...
CENTRO DE CREACIÓN
CONTEMPORÁNEA
MATADERO
MANIFIESTO
GROUCHO
TALLERES
INFANTILES
¡SUENA!
CONCIERTOS EN FAMILIA
QUERIDO
MONSTRUO
21DIC–05ENE
CINETECA

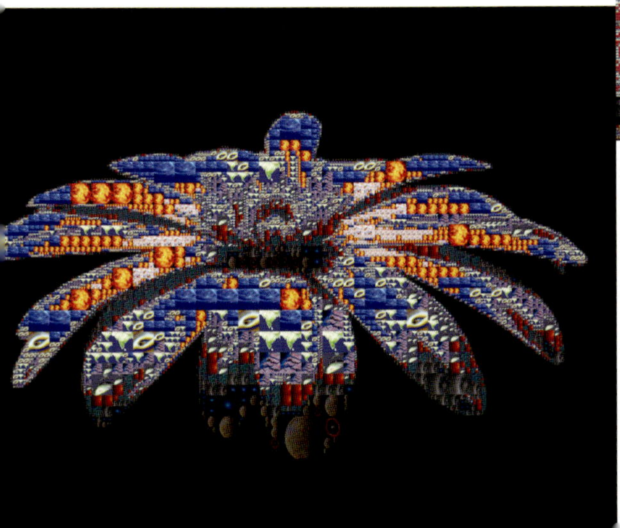

LAUNCH AND GROW
YOUR ONLINE CHANNEL
We are a global tech company that assists our partners in building profitable & scalable online retail businesses
Get in touch

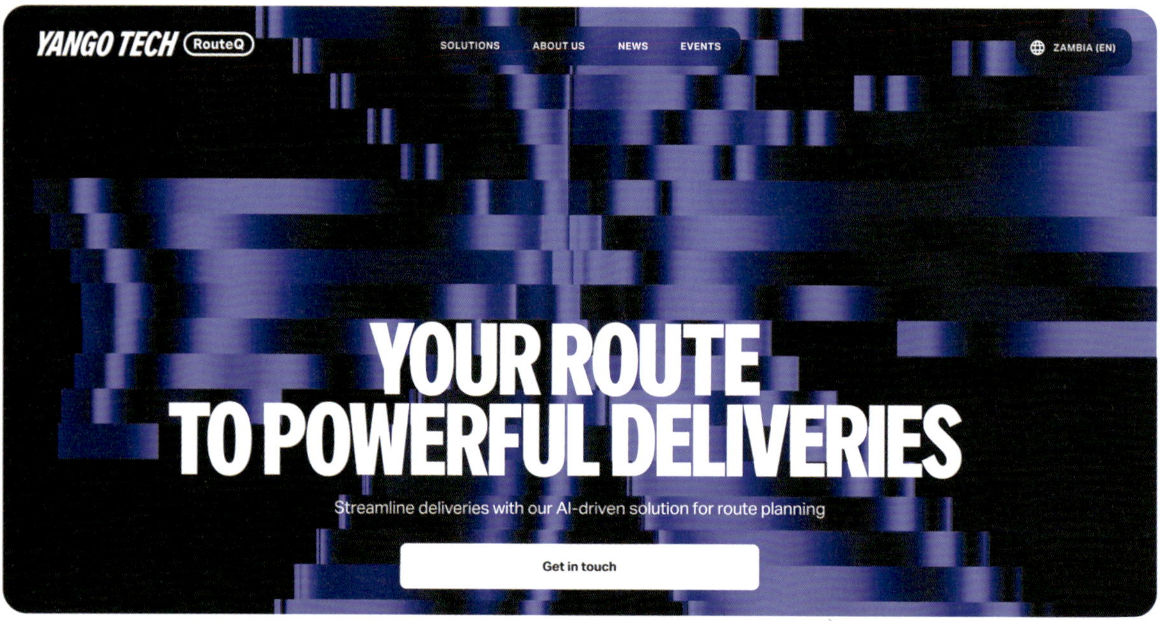
YANGO TECH RouteQ
SOLUTIONS
ABOUT US
NEWS
EVENTS
ZAMBIA (EN)
YOUR ROUTE
TO POWERFUL DELIVERIES
Streamline deliveries with our AI-driven solution for route planning
Get in touch

YANGO TECH
EMPOWER
BUSINESSES WITH GLOBAL
TECHNOLOGIES
Transforming the daily lives of people around the world

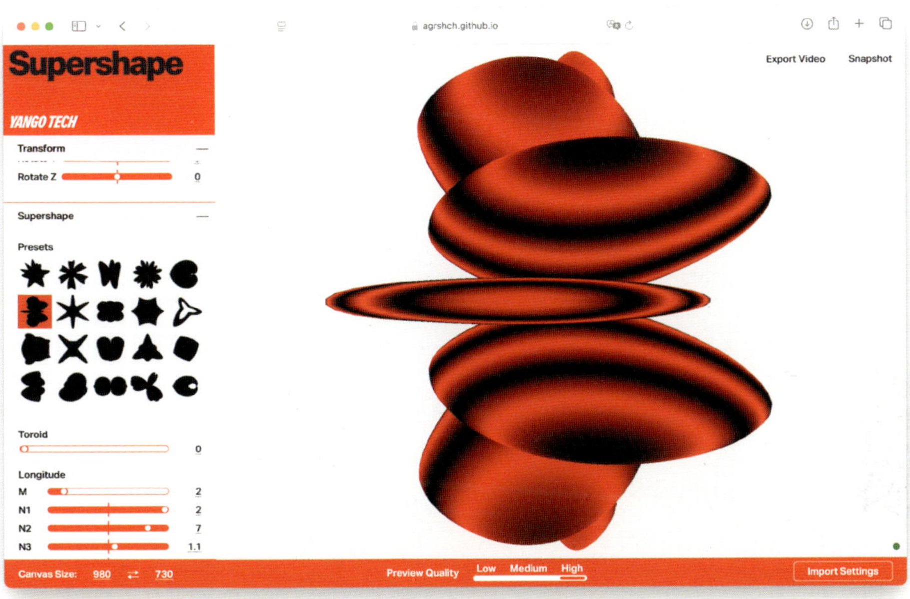

In collaboration with Alexander Zagorsky, Head of Design at Yango, Afterimage developed the visual identity for Yango Tech, a key division providing B2B services. The team created a generative graphics system and a web tool for quick, efficient design creation, with Alexander overseeing the creative direction, typography, and overall design.

Programming Tools/Languages:
JavaScript, p5.js, GLSL Shaders, HTML+CSS

Client:
Yango

GBA (Guilty by Association) is an arts organisation that empowers underrepresented artists and promotes equity in the art world. Cotton's design for GBA highlights individuality, using an artist's signature as the central visual motif. The team developed a web-based logo generator that crafts a distinct logo with each input, reflecting the organisation's commitment to unique creative expression.

Programming Tool/Language:
p5.js

Client:
Guilty by Association

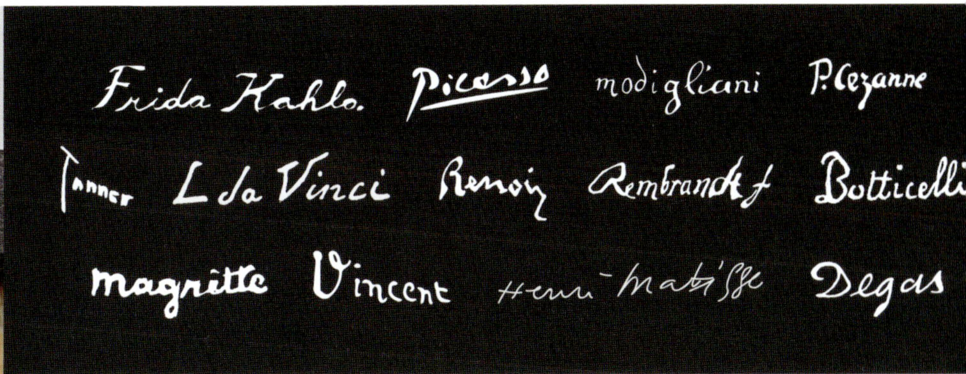
Frida Kahlo. Picasso modigliani P.Cezanne
Tanner L da Vinci Renoir Rembrandt f Botticelli
magritte Vincent Henri-Matisse Degas

Janelle Powers
Gimme Some
Through August 21

GUILTY BY ASSOCIATION
GBA
LAUNCH 1
CAMELLA EHLKE:
HEY WHAT'S UP
MARCH 31 BROOKLYN
CUT-OFF JEANS
GUBI GRACE CHAIRS
GUILTY BY ASSOCIATION
LAUNCH 1
MARCH 31 BROOKLYN

42
JUNE DROP
FLAG BOY
CHARLES:
BEADED
ARTWORKS
On Black Masking Indian Culture
in New Orleans
JUNE 21 BROOKLYN
GBA
GUILTY BY ASSOCIATION
Beaded Artwork 032 (2022)
011-025

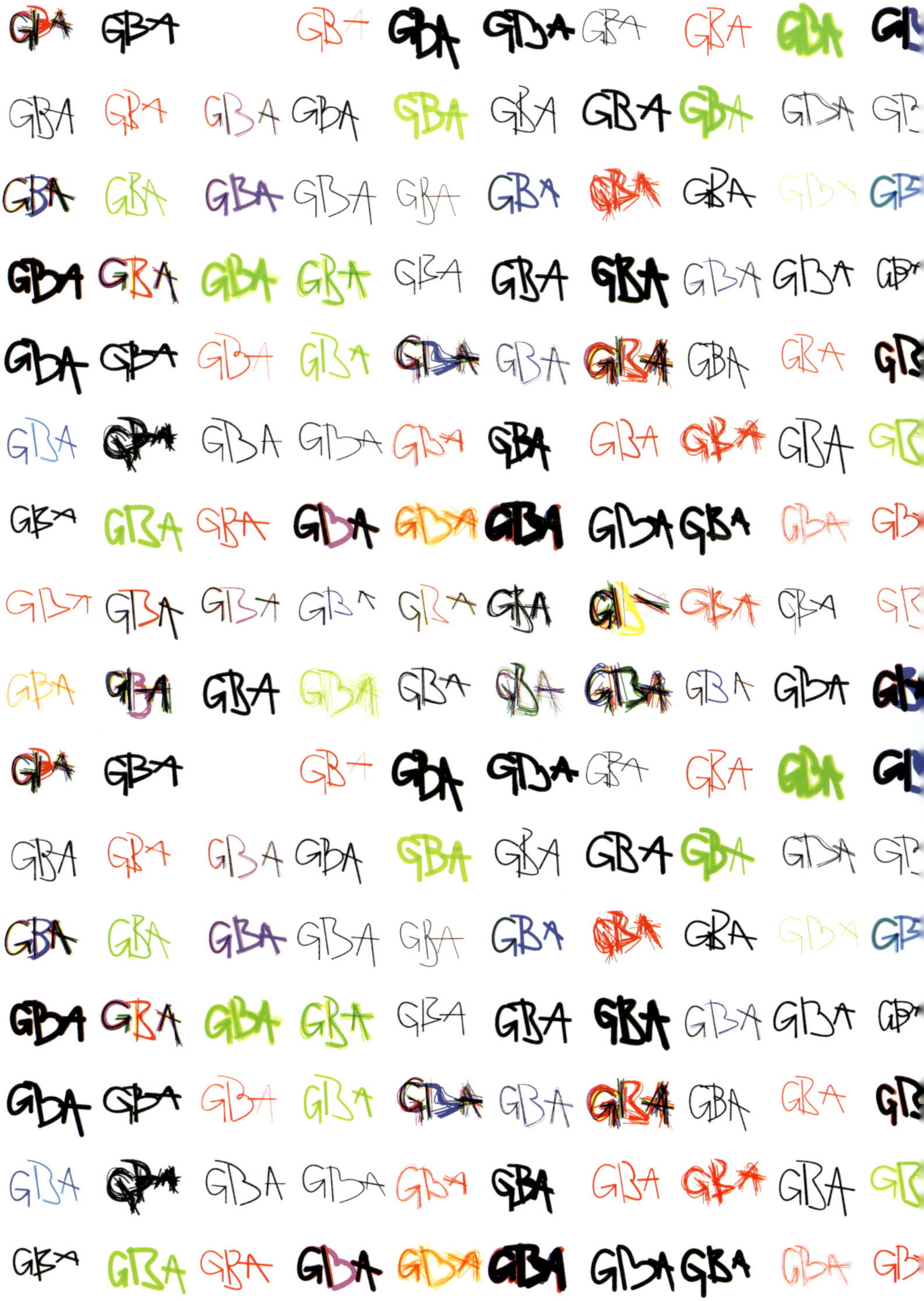

Reimagining Timeless Avant Garde

Vertice, a London-based fashion retailer, merges vintage aesthetics with modern innovation. Its visual identity, generated through a bespoke programme, incorporates a 4D motion system that blends time and space. Through unique video frame manipulation, it explores typography's evolution from 2D to 4D, encapsulating the avant-garde spirit of the brand.

Programming Tool/Language:
Processing

Client:
Vertice

COMMUNS
SPIRIT OF WATER
LIVES IN THE LAKE
ZIGGY CHEN
DECONSTRUCTING UNIFORMS
OUT OF TIME
VERTICE
LONDON

SPIRIT OF WATER
LIVES IN THE LAKE
ZIGGY CHEN
DECONSTRUCTING UNIFORMS
OUT OF TIME
VERTICE

PIXEL ECHO@EXIT

KAUKAU created the key visual for Pixel Echo@EXIT, an audiovisual art live series curated by experimental artists Hong Qile and Mao Wengweng. The design translated digital sound into pixelated visual units, mapping rhythmic reflections through overlapping flashes of light and shadow. This dynamic interplay of elements captured the essence of echoed sound waves in motion.

Programming Tool/Language:
Processing

Client:
PIXEL ECHO

Oracle

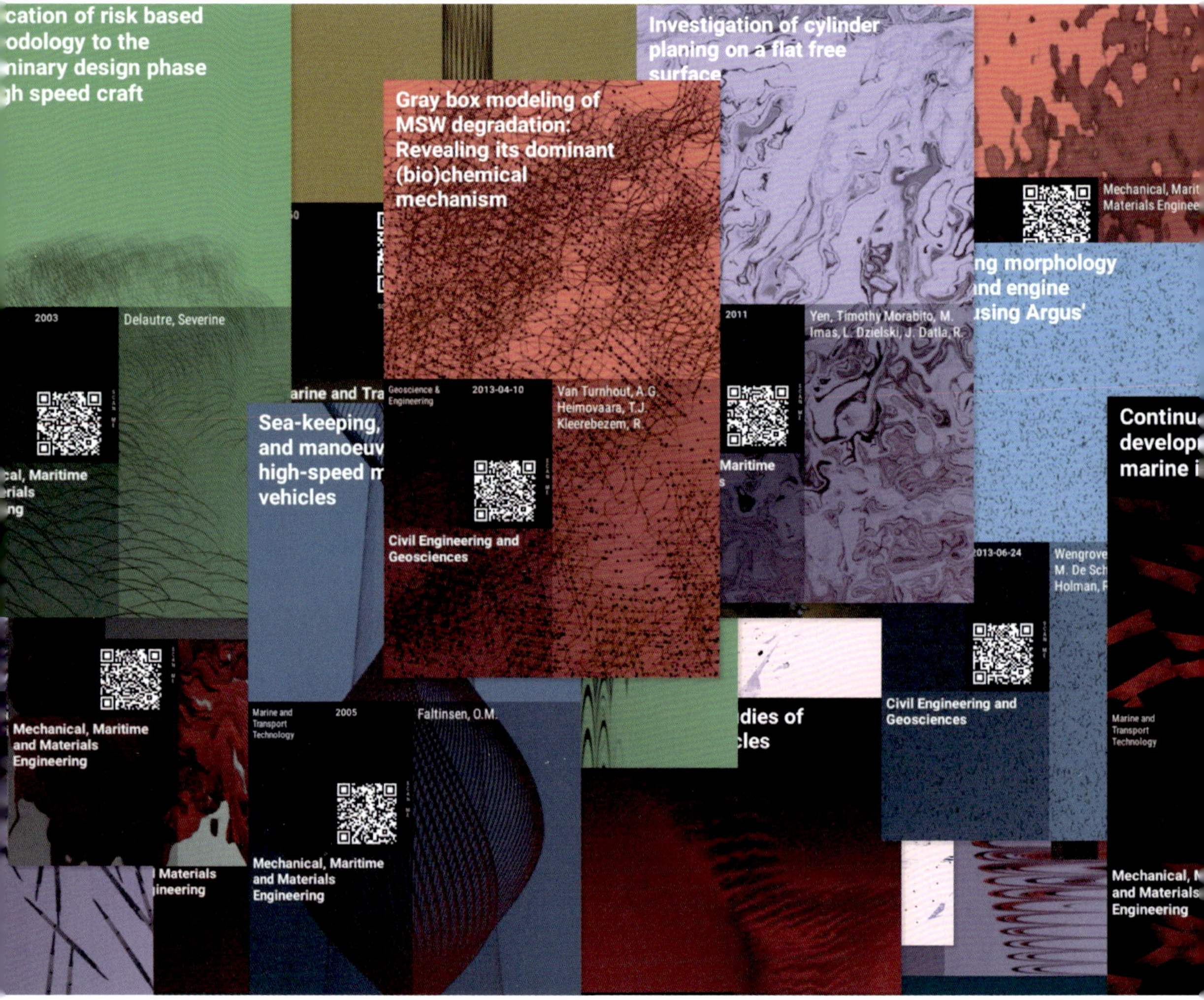

Oracle is a prototype installation and web app developed by TU Delft Library and RNDR, providing access to 150k publications. It generates unique animated covers for each one using a consistent visual system. The project employs machine learning techniques to create multi-dimensional maps from TU Delft's student theses and dissertations, aiming to revolutionise data visualisation in institutional repositories.

Programming Tool/Language:
OPENRNDR

Client:
TU Delft

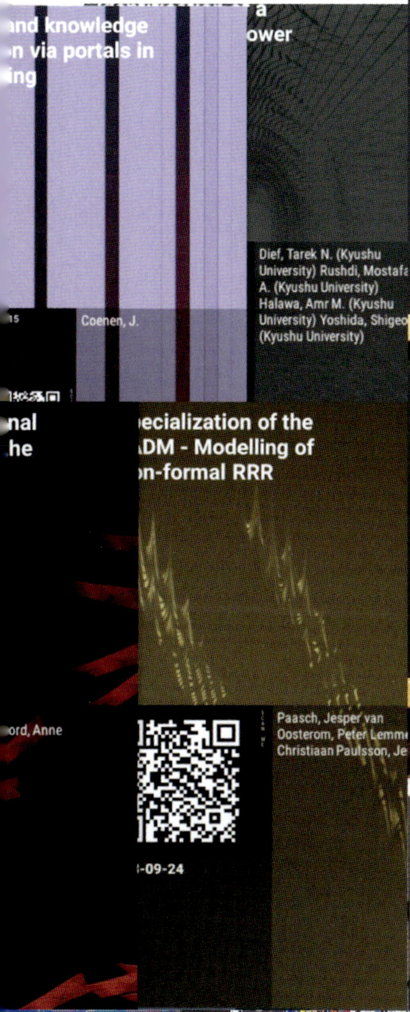
and knowledge
n via portals in
ing
Coenen, J.
Dief, Tarek N. (Kyushu University) Rushdi, Mostafa A. (Kyushu University) Halawa, Amr M. (Kyushu University) Yoshida, Shigeo (Kyushu University)
ecialization of the
DM - Modelling of
n-formal RRR
Paasch, Jesper van Oosterom, Peter Lemme Christiaan Paulsson, Je
-09-24

RELATED
Incompressible, turbulent, turbulence
Mathematische und mikroskopisch-anatomische Studien über Blattstellungen: Nebst ...
1907
Effect of Geometry on the Downstream Flow To...
Master thesis
Tambe, S.
2017
The numerical simulation of three-dimensional flow through or around hydraulic structures
Doctoral thesis
Versteegh, J.
1990
Civil Engineering and Geosciences
Numerical Time Dependent Sheet Cavita...
Doctoral thesis
de Koning Gans, H.J.
1994
Pressure fluctuations in the turbulent boundary layer, advances in diagnostics and con...
2013
Boundary integral equations for the computational modelling of three-dimensional ...
1988
Mathematische und mikroskopisch-anatomische Studien über Blattstellungen: Nebst Betr...
Doctoral thesis
Van Iterson, G.
1907
Explore +50.000 TU Delft theses & dissertations
Scan
Communication

Business

WHAT
REMAINS
FOREVER?

Where
does
injustice
come from?
WHERE DOES INJUSTICE COME FROM?

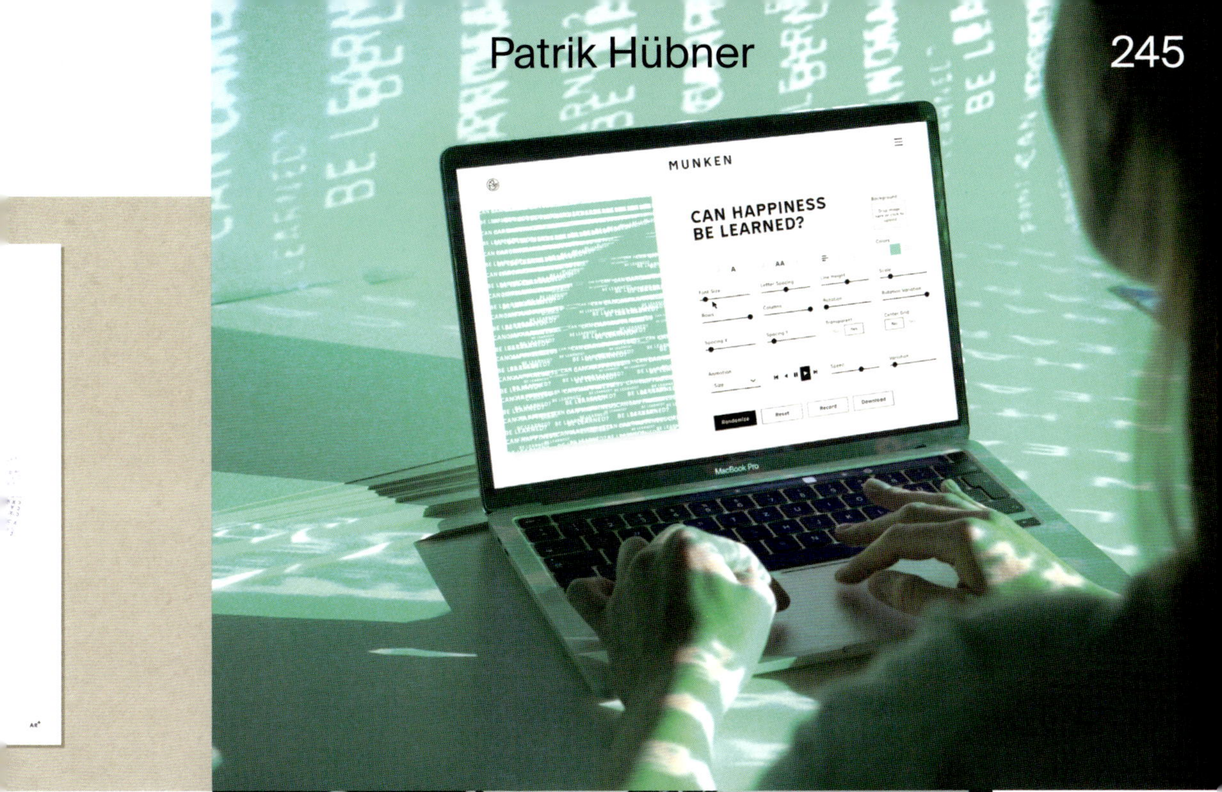

Munken Sans, inspired by the 1960s Tratex typeface, was brought to life through the Munken Creator tool, developed by JUNO Hamburg and Patrik Hübner. This innovative platform combines generative design with typography, allowing users to create static and animated messages. It encourages exploration of storytelling, space, and form, with thousands of unique posters shared and remixed by the community.

Programming Tools/Languages:
JavaScript, Vue.js

Client:
Arctic Paper / Munken Paper

WEL
EL
LC
CO
OM
EL

For Tokyo Dome City, &Form crafted a dynamic identity built around a custom variable font and a unique design algorithm. This innovative approach generated a cohesive visual system across digital and physical media, from videos to promotional items. The proprietary software enabled seamless adaptation for seasonal events, supporting the client's ongoing creative needs.

Programming Tools/Languages:
openFrameworks, Unity, Houdini

Client:
Tokyo Dome Corporation

Super Variable 1.11 | 46
DOME
DOME
DOME
DOME
DOME
DOME
DOME
DOME

DOME

INSTITUTE OF

COLLINS reimagined the Institute of Design's identity to reflect design as a dynamic process that shapes impactful futures. Inspired by László Moholy-Nagy's geometric experiments, they created a flexible visual system that evolves from abstract forms to clear messages. This new identity positions the Institute as a leader in building responsible, transformative design for a better tomorrow.

Programming Tools/Languages:
JavaScript, WebGL, p5.js, Fragment

Client:
Institute of Design

MAKE THE
POSSIBLE
POSITIVE
The
Victor
Morgenstern
Pitch

MASTER
OF DESIGN

Futures in progress.
Class of 2023
Institute of Design

End of Year Show
May 14–24

Empowering ideas
for a better world
Centre for Energy Research
Oslo, Norway
27.01.23
Forskningsrådet

ANTI's project for the Research Council of Norway unifies 38 sub-brands into a dynamic, adaptable visual identity. Inspired by the mathematical Dubins Path, which efficiently connects points, the design reflects the Council's role as a connector of research, funding, and innovation. A custom design generator produces unique variations, ensuring a cohesive, flexible brand presence across all platforms.

Programming Tools/Languages:
Processing, p5.js

Client:
Forskningsrådet
(The Research Council of Norway)

Forskingsdagane
21. september –
2. oktober 2022
Heile Noregs
forskingsfestival

Forskningsdagene
21. september–
2. oktober 2022
Forskningsrådet

CREATIVE HIGHLIGHT

TIM RODENBRÖKER

Tim Rodenbröker (b. 1985, Paderborn) stands at the vibrant crossroads of creativity and technology. Having grown up amidst the rise of computing and the early Internet, he has cultivated a unique perspective that merges his background in graphic design with his specialisation in Creative Coding: an intersection that has not only become a focus in his professional career but also represents a significant emerging trend among today's creatives.

As a dedicated design advocate and creative technologist, Tim's influence extends far and wide. In addition to establishing himself as an expert educator at esteemed institutions such as Elisava in Barcelona, the Glasgow School of Art, and ECAL in Geneva—where he offers a valuable introduction to the world of Creative Coding—he promotes digital literacy through his innovative online school, trcc, which fosters a dedicated community for aspiring coders.

Tim's freelance work continues to garner the attention of notable clients, including The New York Times and IBM. Besides recently co-founding the Coding Systems design studio with Martin Lorenz (TwoPoints.Net) to explore the synergies between flexible visual systems and code, he also plays a key role in the curatorial team of the Design in Motion Festival, further showcasing his passion and commitment to the evolving landscape of design and technology.

The following sections explore his insights on coding, which serve as instrumental starting points for creators looking to expand their skill set using a critical approach. Drawing from his courses, community-building efforts, teaching, and speaking engagements, they aim to inspire and equip a new generation of creative technologists for an exciting future ahead.

FROM CODED AESTHETICS TO TECHNO LITERACY

UNDERSTANDING THE AESTHETIC SHIFT

Hey you! I'm really glad you picked up this book, CODECRAFTED, where over 35 talented and renowned designers, studios, and collectives show in impressive ways how code is used and aesthetically cited in the design of visual identities. From my point of view, a publication like this is an important signal for real progress in design: that the quirkiness; the glitches; the supposed "mistakes"; and the perhaps-somewhat technical-looking interfaces can be shown unchanged and even perceived as beautiful.

When I look back on my studies in communication design between 2008 and 2013, I always feel as though something was missing. On the one hand, new digital technologies were starting to change people's lives at an incredible speed. The smartphone was a brand new invention introduced by Steve Jobs in his legendary keynote speech in 2007, and within a short time later, everyone had one in their pocket. Social media platforms such as Facebook were becoming really powerful tools and the internet had long since taken a turn for the worse, tipping clearly towards commerce and monopolisation.

While all this was happening, the Communication Design department in Münster—under which I was studying—was clearly having trouble catching up. It often even displayed a troubling ignorance towards the emergence of these new technologies. In fact, the department seemed to have regarded itself as a sacred fortress, with new media entering like an uninvited guest. The only official "escape" for those who thought like me was to enrol in the media design programme, which, at the time, served as a catch-all for those who did not fit into the more traditional realms of Communication Design – where "thinking minds" elegantly placed their grand ideas in tightly spaced Helvetica on Munken paper. While I met great professors in the media design field, the students there were typically seen as outsiders: the "freaks" and "nerds"; the ones who wanted to create stop-motion films with dough, played with Lego on weekends, and got teary-eyed at the sight of Luke Skywalker.

In arriving at the conclusion that code could build bridges between the different disciplines, it became clear to me that it was necessary to place coding alongside typography into the foundation of the curriculum, which was unimaginable at the time. There were still so many uncertainties, like how exactly would these two worlds—visual design and coding—be brought together?

Today, as a designer and a design educator, I realise that there is change in the air. The borders of visual design and digital design seem to have dissolved to an extent. More importantly, since the introduction of ChatGPT and Dalle-2 in Europe, something important has become evident: for far too long we have failed to fully consider computation, with all its complexities and effects, as a central issue of our time. After all, as John Maeda once wrote in his brilliant book, How to Speak Machine: *"Computation is made by us, and we are now collectively responsible for its outcomes."*

CODED AESTHETICS: THE TWO METHODS

Visual identities today are typically created in two different ways, which I would like to describe below as "methods". While some of the work cannot be clearly categorised, it is nevertheless important to look at coded aesthetics through the lens of these two categories.

CATEGORY/METHOD 1

A designer has the goal or brief to develop something that looks somewhat technical and/or coded – and utilises ordinary design software to achieve their objective. For the purposes of differentiation, I will refer to the result of this method as an "inauthentic code aesthetic": for example, when they use a "filter" or a no-code tool like Cavalry to create the illusion of technicality as a decorative surface over the object to be designed.

CATEGORY/METHOD 2

A designer develops a (comparatively simple) system or tool with code, which is built in a way that a certain coded aesthetic eventually emerges. This is where (often unexpected) aesthetic features emerge that are negatively labelled as "glitches" or "bugs". However, these "errors" also become elementary communication elements in a visual identity.

There is actually also a third category/method, namely, the one in which both approaches are mixed together. For the sake of clarity, however, I will omit this point and carry on as if there are only the two extremes above.

My goal for the following sections is to try to convince you that there are many good reasons to take the second, more time-consuming route, which requires learning to code. Why? Because I believe that Creative Coding can offer us, as designers and artists, something invaluable at precisely this moment in time. To clarify what I mean, let's take a few slight detours and ask some broader questions, namely, about how we humans currently think and talk about technology.

SURFACE VS. SUBFACE

A long time ago, the computer arts pioneer Frieder Nake argued that computer artworks have one specific characteristic that, from my point of view, distinguishes them from almost all other art forms. They possess both a surface, which is what you see, and a subface, which is the invisible aspect – the algorithm; the underlying system; the "dark matter" that generates the artwork[1] or in this case, the surface.

The subface can be understood as a series of instructions. Let's examine an example of this in the form of the following pseudocode:

1 Frieder Nake - Surface, Subface, Interface - Three Cases of Interaction and One Concept

STEP 1
Create a square canvas

STEP 2
Draw a thin line, where both points have a random positions

STEP 3
Draw a thick line, where both points have a random positions

STEP 4
Draw a circle with a random size and position

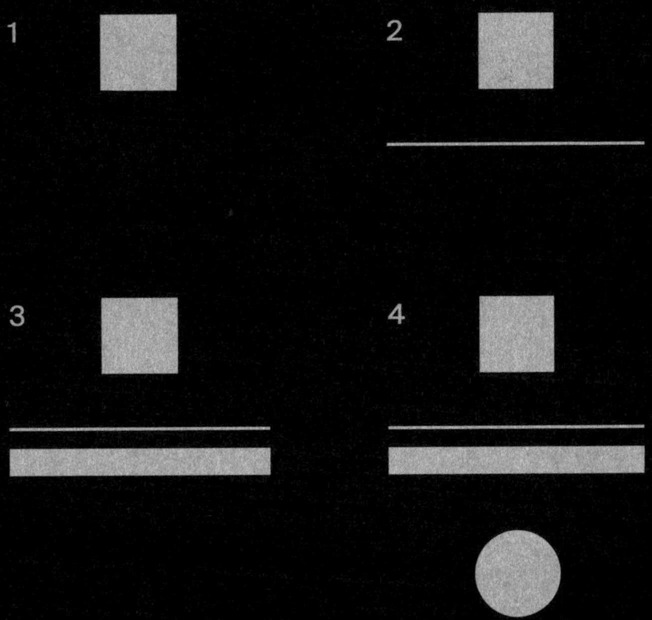

It almost looks like a visual identity, doesn't it?

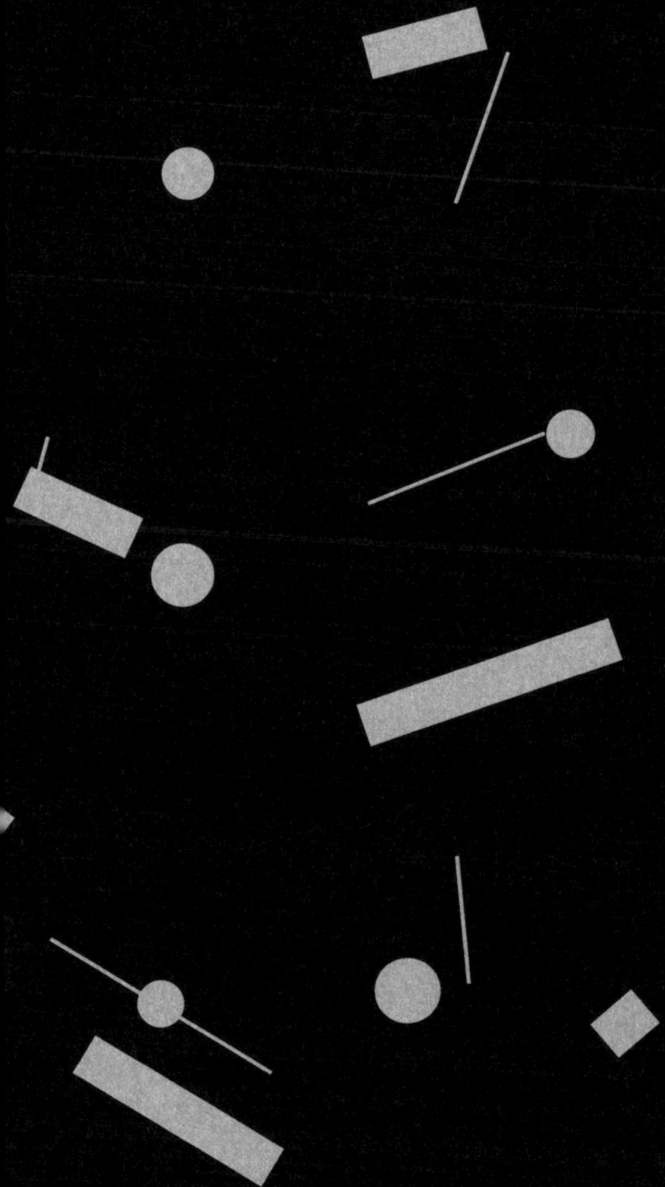

```
let bg, fg;

function setup() {
  createCanvas(900, 900);
  strokeCap(SQUARE);
  bg = color(‘#f1f1f1’);
  fg = color(0);
}

function draw() {
  background(bg);

  // draw the circle
  fill(fg);
  noStroke();
  circle(random(width),
random(height), random(50, 300));

  // draw the line
  stroke(fg);
  strokeWeight(5);
  line(random(width), random(height),
random(width), random(height));

  // draw the rectangle
  strokeWeight(150);
  line(random(width), random(height),
random(width), random(height));
}
```

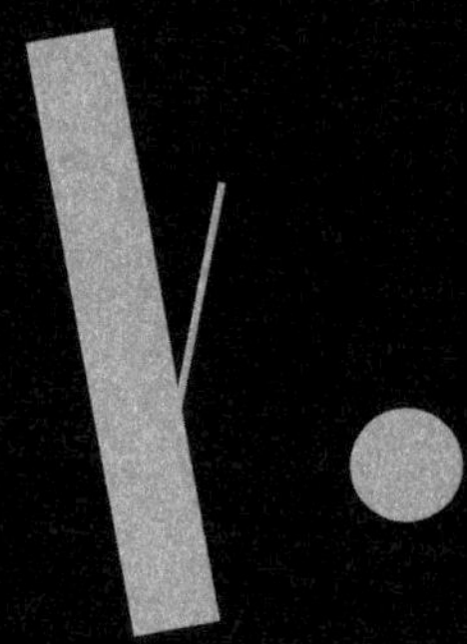

In METHOD 1 (NO-CODE), i.e., when using a commercial and proprietary design tool, the subface is a black box[2]. Although it is possible to enter these instructions via the software's user interface, and it may even be possible to control the parameters at random, the software itself is an enormously complex system with a vast amount of features and functions that we do not understand and, above all, do not need.

In METHOD 2 (CODE), a customised, much leaner and clearer system is developed from scratch. With Creative Coding, which I am promoting here, the system—i.e., the subface—is transparent and clear. It is built in such a way that it is still easy to understand, partly because the developer/designer has thought about the structure in the best interests of clarity. A principle from Permacomputing[3] states that a computer system should only be as complex as a single person can understand. Ideally, aesthetics can take a secondary priority and simply emerge from the system. It is important to note that aesthetic decisions always depend on the design of the subface to ensure its transparency. A transparent system that is maintainable, easy to understand, and "honest" is often called a "white box".[4]

2 A "black box" refers to a system or technology whose internal structure or functionality is disguised or so complex that it cannot be understood. All you can see is the input and the results (output). This means that although it is possible to observe how a black box reacts to certain input, it is not possible to know or understand exactly how the processing works inside. The opposite of the concept of the black box is the "white box" (see also 4), also called the "transparent box".

3 Permacomputing is a community of practice and a set of principles for designing computational systems with limits. It is a call for simplicity, transparency, and sustainability. Learn more at permacomputing.net.

4 A "white box" refers to a system that is easy to understand and maintain. The internal structures are not disguised and completely visible.

THE TIP OF THE ICEBERG: A PARABLE

To illustrate the black and white boxes mentioned in the previous section, imagine that you are standing on a ship and see a large, white iceberg rising from the surface of the water. You are aware that you are not looking at the whole iceberg; most of it lies below the surface of the water and is completely invisible.[5]

Let's suppose the iceberg symbolises a design system. Today, designers focus mostly on the tip of the iceberg. They create surfaces or even just decorate them. With a visual identity that should have a technical aesthetic, this is done super quickly with no-code tools.[6]

5 The iceberg model is a writing technique described by Ernest Hemingway. It has also been presented as a theory of communication by Friedemann Schulz von Thun.

6 A detailed definition of the term "visual identity" can be found in the book The FVS Atlas by Dr Martin Lorenz, also published by Victionary.

Processing is a flexible software etchbook and a language for learning how code. Learn more at https://processing.org.

GUI stands for Graphical User Interface.

A term coined by Dr Martin Lorenz, the thor of the book Flexible Visual Systems.

The tip of the iceberg represents the visible: for example, a key visual or permutation of a visual identity. However, the actual system lies beneath the surface of the water. METHOD 1 only makes it possible to design the tip, whereas in METHOD 2, the underlying system becomes clear. In METHOD 1, the subface is a black box; in METHOD 2, it is a system that can be designed with code: a white box.

Now, one could also argue against this: that the code on page 265 is written in a programming language called "Processing"[7], which, strictly speaking, is also "software" just like Adobe After Effects, for example. However, there are some significant differences. Processing or p5.js, for instance, are white boxes in themselves. Both tools are open source, with their complete source code being 100% accessible. They are also based on a commons leadership,

BEYOND THE ILLUSION: THE CLOUD OF STEEL

In the previous sections, I have narrowed down the argument for learning Creative Coding to the development of flexible visual systems (and identities). What I want to do now is to show you that this way of thinking can be applied to a much larger field that is less technical and more philosophical. This is the part where Creative Coding unfolds its true potential: in the demystification of technology.

When people speak about technology, they often use inappropriate metaphors. A clear example can be found in James Bridle's insightful book, New Dark Age[10]: we use the "cloud" as a symbol for the Internet. A cloud is light, gaseous, floating – innocent. Today, it almost seems as if the Internet is "simply in the air". But of course, that's a myth! The "cloud" consists of buildings full of servers around the world, undersea cables, transmission masts, steel structures, billions of end devices, rare raw materials, supply chains, power politics, and political power, along with landfills full of e-waste. All these substantial elements form the basis of what we now call a "cloud".

Let's consider the Google search engine. You open the page, and the colourful logo smiles at you. Google is your friend, you might think. But just by typing a few letters, you trigger a transcontinental process[11], where powerful algorithms—perhaps at the other end of the world—calculate what you might be looking for based on the vast amount of data Google has gathered about you over the years. The true scale of this process (the subface) is hidden and disguised – and so is the price you pay to use these "free" services.

Our relationship with technology is highly problematic, and we are deceiving ourselves – making our language about technology inadequate and inappropriate. As human beings in the 21st century, we are incredibly dependent on symbols, software, and infrastructures that are harmful both to ourselves and to our environment.

10 James Bridle - New Dark Age

11 Metaphor by Ranga Yogeschwa "Nächste Ausfahrt Zukunft"

While the bad news is that you and I cannot change this—that as individuals, we are all entangled in this problem—we can at least take steps in the right direction and strive to become a little wiser about the situation. To me, this is already occurring and has led to some remarkable new ideas that are paving the way for a better future. However, what do these steps actually entail?

EMBRACING GENERALIST DESIGN

12 Lazlo Moholy-Nagy - Vision in Motion

As I mentioned earlier, I would argue that as designers, we need to change our perspective from the surface to the subface. We must deal courageously with the fundamental structures of software and regard them as an inevitable part of design that must be understood.

To that end, design should move towards "generalism". In the words of Lazlo Moholy Nagy:

> "The idea of design and the profession of the designer has to be transformed from the notion of a specialist function into a generally valid attitude of resourcefulness and inventiveness which allows projects to be seen not in isolation but in relationship with the need of the individual and the community."[12]

This approach also applies to the design of visual identities, to the extent that we should consistently strive to understand and recognise the consequences that the tools we use have for us, our clients, and the systems in which we are embedded.

At a time when software, algorithms, and data are the ubiquitous building materials of our living environment, there is no alternative to a consistent engagement of these materials. We must learn what we are dealing with in order to become responsible designers.

Creative Coding is an effective way to familiarise ourselves with these structures and building materials. This may sound overwhelming to you, but I believe it is easier, more appealing, and more enjoyable than you might think.

JOINING A WORLDWIDE COMMUNITY

To make your journey into Creative Coding less daunting and moremanageable, engaging with other designers and developers is crucial, as it can transform your experiences into inspiring, impactful, and rewarding ones.

For me, the Netherlands is like a utopian Mecca for the entire global design scene. This is where the most radical, yet also the most exciting ideas are born. If I were to point to a spot on the world map where the Creative Coding scene is particularly flourishing, I would intuitively cover this small country with my big index finger!

I am writing this section while sitting in the front row of an event space at the Design Museum in Den Bosch. It is the second day of the ITERATIONS Conference[13], a "Creative Coding Symposium" organised by Vera van de Seyp[14] and Creative Coding Utrecht[15]. Here, designers, artists, and coders come together, driven by a singular desire to share their knowledge and discuss their ideas.

The spectrum of themes being covered is bright and broad: Permacomputing, Friction in Design[16], the aura of digital artefacts, career paths of designers who became creative coders, and even the radical life concepts of a couple who live on a sailboat and create art with software! While the range of topics at ITERATIONS typically revolves around the central theme of Creative Coding, it also touches on fundamentally important social, philosophical, and technological issues.

13 https://iterations.online/

14 https://veravandeseyp.com/

15 https://creativecodingutrecht.nl/en

16 https://designingfriction.com/

The understanding of the term “design” here is different from how it is perceived in the rough design economy, where time is money and ethics are too often reduced to rainbow flags and superficial reactions to trends or sh*tstorms. The people in this room want to learn how to design and cultivate technology in wise ways – and most importantly, they want to do it together. The competitive mentality I have seen in other design contexts is literally absent where people use code. They understand that they need each other – and everyone is aware that the space of code is infinite and that no one can know everything alone.

The ITERATIONS symposium is a great example for the vibe in Creative Coding communities around the world, where people unite to effect change and find better, wiser perspectives on technology.

As I close this section, which further amplifies my plea for coding as a culture, as a tool, and as a way of thinking. I would love to learn what’s on your mind! Feel free to get in touch via feedback@timrodenbroeker.de.

AN INTRODUCTION TO CODING SYSTEMS

THE BRIDGE BETWEEN DESIGN AND PROGRAMMING

In 2023, Dr Martin Lorenz and I began working together, adopting the name Coding Systems as a duo. While it is still unclear what Coding Systems is meant to be, one thing is for sure: it's a match made in design heaven!

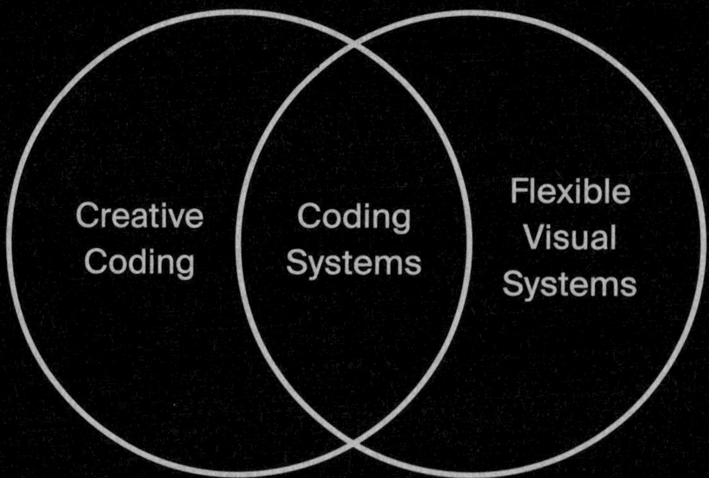

I have been teaching and practising Creative Coding in the field of communication design for many years, and it has always been a huge challenge. I believe the difficulty arises from the perception that graphic design and programming are still seen as two completely separate areas that do not fit or belong together.

Based on my personal experience, when a Creative Coding class is taught in a conventional design faculty, most students have high expectations of the outcomes, but many become frustrated by the steep learning curve. This is largely due to the fact that there is a clear and widely accepted approach missing when it comes to how to teach Creative Coding in the realms of graphic design.

Dr Martin Lorenz's theory of Flexible Visual Systems serves both as a theoretical foundation and a terminological bridge between design and programming. In the eponymous book, which was published by Slanted Publishers in 2022 and is based on the PhD thesis that he wrote at the University of Barcelona, he attempts to categorise flexible visual identities systematically by presenting two categories: form-based flexible visual systems and transformation-based flexible visual systems. Both can also be viewed as methods for analysing and developing flexible visual systems and identities – as covered in the following sections.

FORM-BASED VS TRANSFORMATION-BASED FLEXIBLE VISUAL SYSTEMS

With form-based flexible visual systems, designers define a set of visual components and a set of rules for how these components are used, how the components are laid out, and how the design system reacts to different formats. The system can also include definitions of how the components behave in an animated or interactive context. Components can be geometric shapes, photographs, illustrations, or typographic elements. Altogether, the system can be seen as a generator for “deliverables” or final media artefacts like animations or posters.

Unbeknownst to me, I have always been teaching this approach in my university courses via an exercise called “random compositions” using the following prompt (also covered in the previous Surface vs. Subface section):

Create an application where three different visual components are placed randomly on the screen – a line, a rectangle, and a circle.

In this system, it is always guaranteed that the same components are used. The logic of the programme ensures that all the deliverables look different while remaining within a certain spectrum of possibilities.

17 Dr Martin Lorenz - Flexible Visual Systems, p. 233

The second approach for developing flexible visual systems that Dr Martin presents in his book is the transformation-based flexible visual system. Its goal is to achieve a strong recognition value through transformation, working somewhat like an Adobe Photoshop image filter where an input—an image in this case—is used to generate a modified output.

The simplest example is the conversion of an image into a somehow modified version. The modification itself then is the identity and creates the recognition value.

But, as I understand it, this is just one of countless possibilities. In the Flexible Visual Systems book, Martin points out that this approach is actually about designing a process[17] or a workflow. These processes can also extend dimensionality, so that 2D images become 4D animations or even interactive applications.

In the beginning, I had some difficulty understanding the proper distinction between form-based and transformation-based flexible visual systems. While analysing various visual identities through the lens of the two different approaches, it became evident that, although there are some edge cases, there are also instances that involve both methods. Imagine a photograph, floating through a 3D scene. Does the transformation of the photo make the system transformative? Or is the photo a component in a form-based flexible visual system that allows for three-dimensionality? I think, ultimately, the method is not about making design a science. While a mixture of both approaches can certainly lead to very creative results, the majority of systems can be easily categorised.

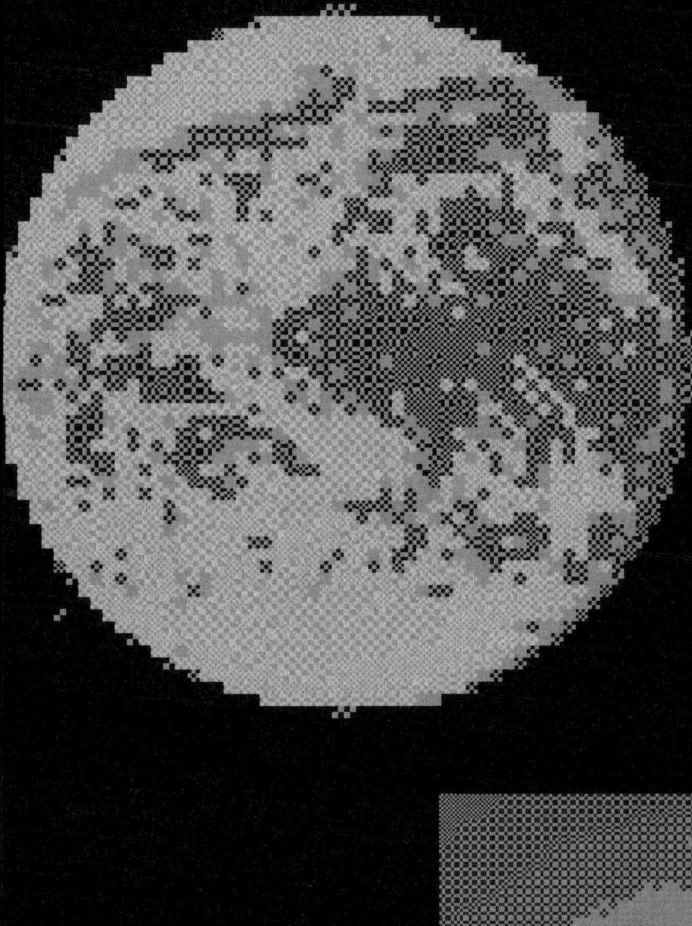

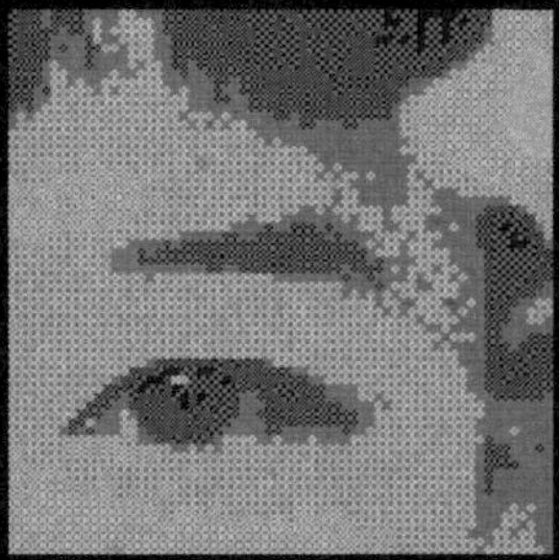

TOOLS AND WORKFLOWS

Code and flexible visual systems are a perfect match, because code is the ideal language to describe system behaviours. Every small programme is already a system in itself: logic structures, loops, and functions describe the behaviour, while variables can embody the status. Ironically, the ambition to develop a flexible visual system exclusively with code can also be limiting. But as you will see, this is more of a benefit than a drawback.

At first glance, you can achieve more in less time with a fully-fledged, commercial software solution such as Adobe Creative Cloud. And of course, this is especially true for those who cannot code. At the same time, having several people working on a visual system can lead to significant inconsistencies. If you want to pass on such a project and make it accessible to others, all you end up with is a vague description of the technical process in a design manual that leaves plenty of room for interpretation. The many possibilities of today's software often lead to rash decorations. Decorative design decisions bloat the system unnecessarily and are especially difficult to repeat. For that reason, the system does not scale well.

A well-made, coded flexible visual system is characterised by its simplicity and determined consistency. These characteristics, coupled with the impression that it is reasonably easy to understand in its technical structure, give it an aura of high quality. The transparency of the system can even become a recognisable feature.

By combining Creative Coding environments (such as Processing or p5.js) with web technologies, entire ecosystems of tools can be developed and made accessible online. HTML, CSS and JavaScript make it possible to create bespoke design software applications, opening up entirely new creative possibilities for design workflows.

Coding Systems represents a proposal for the next evolutionary step in the development of visual identities, in that here, the system itself becomes a bespoke design tool.

ING AT THE BROADER PICTURE

Admittedly, when it comes to practice, there are quite a few pitfalls. The development of custom software applications takes time and requires expertise from various areas. As already mentioned, proprietary software tools are potentially much faster and more convenient to use and work with. Also, the devil is in the details: no Creative Coding environment can compete with a fully featured Adobe Creative Suite.

The intersection of Creative Coding and flexible visual systems is a theory and not entirely compatible with the time-critical, highly optimised, and inflexible workflows in the design industry. However, in times of great confusion, high dependencies on American software companies, and a whirlwind of technological innovation, I believe that the idea behind Coding Systems has something valuable to offer: a sustainable, tool-independent method for building resilient, inspiring, consistent, interactive, independent, and beautiful visual identities.

While “systems thinking” may be a term that is rooted in biology, it is surprisingly applicable to almost every other aspect of life. Everything is a system! System design is not far removed from systems thinking; it follows the same principles. If Creative Coding for flexible visual systems is a formal approach, Coding Systems reaches beyond the formal aspects and delves into the relationships between humans and technology and how we code these systems. Like flashlights in a dark forest, we are continually discovering new aspects that concretise and/or expand the map of systems thinking – and we do so primarily through written conversations that everyone is invited to join in!

Interested in learning more? Check out our website: codingsystems.info.

WHAT IS CREATIVE CODING?

CREATIVITY IN CODE: AN ORIGIN STORY

(Source: timrodenbroeker.de/what-is-creative-coding; master.timrodenbroeker.de/definition.php)

Heinz Nixdorf MuseumsForum (HNF), the world's largest computer museum in the provincial town of Paderborn, sends hundreds of thousands of visitors each year on a dizzying journey through almost 6,000 years of human history. It begins on the second floor with cuneiform writing in Mesopotamia, leads them past Johannes Gutenberg's letterpress printing, shows the transformation of mechanical calculators and typewriters over the centuries, and then focuses their gaze on the short time period of the last 100 years – all on the same floor.

Near a bulky IBM computer from the 1970s, the giggles of teenagers can be heard again and again. Black-and-white photos show people in offices wearing strange smocks, sitting in front of huge machines with tiny tube screens and dully hacking characters into keyboards. At that time, computers could already be found in research facilities and large companies, but nowhere near private homes. There was still no good reason to buy a computer, because the monstrously large machines were not only unimaginably expensive, but also completely useless for private purposes. To make matters worse, anyone who wanted to operate a computer had to programme it – and there were neither modern programming languages that were easy to read, nor anything like the internet, where people could quickly and easily search for the right solution.

As soon as the computer came into the world, the first artists became curious about the new possibilities and perspectives that arose with the large and clunky machines. The computer and computer art have developed almost in parallel, even if only a few artists used to have access to the expensive machines. One of them was Parisian artist Vera Molnar, who became famous for knowing how to tame these early versions of the computer. Towards the end of the 1960s, she was one of the first people in the world to use the promising machine as an artistic tool. Today, she is considered a pioneer of computer art and Creative Coding

DELVING INTO THE DEFINITIONS

What exactly does Creative Coding mean? In my view, most definitions fail because they attempt to explain the term based on a medium. Its entry on Wikipedia is a good example, as—while not wrong—it directly lists examples of use, which strongly narrows the reader's perspective and thus only allows for a very limited understanding the technology itself:

> Creative Coding is a type of computer programming in which the goal is to create something expressive instead of something functional. It is used to create live visuals and for VJing, as well as creating visual art and design, entertainment (e.g. video games), art installations, projections and projection mapping, sound art, advertising, product prototypes, and much more.[18]

To me, it seems more useful to define the term in a more abstract manner, as Mark C. Mitchell and Oliver Bown do:

> [Creative Coding] is a process, based on exploration, iteration, reflection and discovery, where code is used as the primary medium to create a wide range of media artefacts.[19]

This succinct definition also reflects my experience. In Creative Coding, programmers engage in a creative dialogue with the computer. They speak to it in a language it understands (code) and formulate instructions for displaying visual objects on a surface. At first, they have little control over the computer's behaviour – and this is perfectly acceptable, because surprising results always lead to new ideas and perspectives.

The further they venture into the learning process, the more control they gain. Gradually, parallels between human thinking and the logic of the machine become evident. In a sense, Creative Coding is a method that enables programmers to articulate their own thoughts and ideas in a new way. Thus, step by step, an entrance to a new world of design without a previously defined medium opens up to them.

18 https://en.wikipedia.org/wiki/Creative_coding

19 Attributed to Mark Mitchell and Oliver C. Bown (https://ebooks.au.dk/aul/catalog/book/340).

Depending on the programming language used, the spectrum of possible output shifts: some tools are suited for developing interactive web applications, others for rendering moving images, and still others for virtual reality applications. A single programming language can facilitate 3D animation and artwork for print, as well as playful interactions on the web. This is precisely why Creative Coding is so special and yet so elusive at the same time: it is a method that is not tied to a single medium. This is where the enormous potential lies, in that a single method can be used for a wide range of applications.

Accordingly, the (mostly visual) results of Creative Coding are also not directly predictable in advance and are often only vaguely predefined – emerging through experimentation. Compared to conventional programming, Creative Coding is primarily about expression, with functionality taking a back seat. The aim is not merely to write code that is as logical as possible, but also to generate creative results with code.

IVE CODING VS. GENERATIVE DESIGN

Creative Coding is often equated with or confused with Generative Design. While the terms have some overlaps, they each represent something different. Generative Design is a method that involves writing algorithms that can design autonomously. It is about developing a system or set of rules that serves as the basis for generating media in the broadest sense.

Compared to Creative Coding, Generative Design is not theoretically tied to computer programming, but has been used for centuries in design, architecture, and art. Examples include Oriental and Islamic ornaments and patterns based on mathematical principles or the generative photographs of Gottfried Jäger and Karl Martin Gottfried.

THE INPUT-OUTPUT MODEL

A special feature of Creative Coding and Generative Design is that the horizon of these methods far exceeds that of ordinary software tools. Design software is usually created for solving a comparatively narrow range of tasks, leading to clear boundaries. These boundaries dissolve when working with code.

Incidentally, this is also one of the reasons why I do not like to show specific projects or mention a few specific areas of application as examples. There are simply so many ways to use Creative Coding and Generative Design in the most diverse forms that any concrete illustration already limits the parameter of thought and its possibilities. Even the edges of the two terms are not walls, but rather, difficult-to-recognise, subtle boundary lines. To recognise their full potential, you first have to approach them in abstract terms. If you're not sure how, don't worry – I'll get a little more specific in the next few paragraphs.

Generative Design could be described as a method for transforming an existing input in the form of data or interaction into an output in the form of a new medium. In this way, Generative Design makes it possible to convert texts into animations, weather data into 3D particle systems (a great example being BRUTE by Patrik Hübner on PP 080-081), stock prices into sculptures, or even the latest Tweets into interactive installations. The mind-map on PP 024-025 is based on the Input-Process-Output (IPO) model for software development, which I developed together with Patrik Hübner in 2016.

This map already inspires an infinite number of possible project ideas and has often got me dreaming. Imagine a sculpture made up of the structure of a poem. Or a sound installation that transforms the currents in the Atlantic Ocean into music. Imagine a key visual that can translate various film classics into 3D structures – or even an installation that transforms the latest news from The New York Times into a choreography of dancing points of light. Imagine a ballet in which the dancers interact with a generative stage!

While the terms "generative design" and "data visualisation" may seem to have a lot in common, they each mean something different. If you create a bar chart or pie chart with Excel or Google Sheets, this is basically more data visualisation than Generative Design. Data visualisation is primarily to be found in the field of information design. It is about making the data readable or presenting it in an understandable way. Generative Design, as I understand it, is more about expression. The same data can be used to create a diagram or an abstract structure. In Generative Design, it is not necessarily important that the data is readable in the end. However, the data used in a Generative Design system still expresses something. They tell a story, as Patrik Hübner would put it – and is illustrated quite well in the following section.

FORM FOLLOWS MUSIC

The procedure of Generative Design becomes apparent if we were to look at a project I initiated.

In 2011, when I was still a design student in Münster, I devoted myself intensively to learning the piano. The piece I worked my way through back then was the famous Prelude in C by Johann Sebastian Bach. I often went to the public library to practise because there was a grand piano in the basement that you could rent.

A few years later, when I was taking my first steps in Generative Design, I suddenly had an idea: *what would it be like to visualise the iconic piano piece generatively?* This idea excited me enormously. I wanted to know what the prelude looked like – what patterns could be recognised in it.

The challenge was to convert the music into a data format that I could read out with Processing. The sheet music of classical pieces of music can easily be downloaded from the internet today. And in most cases, you can also find their MIDI files: computer-readable versions of the sheet music. Using a converter programme, I was able to convert the MIDI file of Bach's prelude into a JSON format, which I then converted further into an array of numerical values. This makes particular sense for the prelude because it consists of arpeggios, i.e., a sequence of hundreds of individual notes. With the generated numerical values, I was able to convert the prelude into patterns in C, which in turn could have become part of a visual identity for a classical music festival, for example.

IN CONCLUSION

Creative Coding is a method that uses computer programming for artistic expression. In this method, the goal is not predefined, and the process is based on discovery, variation, and exploration of mostly unexpected results.

In contrast, Generative Design is a purpose-driven method in which a process is designed that converts an input in the form of data or algorithms into a medium. While a programming language or a computer can be used as a tool in this process, the fundamental concepts or principles behind this method are not inherently reliant on technology and have been used in art and architecture for thousands of years.

Overall, it is this distinction that highlights the exploratory nature of Creative Coding compared to the structured objectives of Generative Design.

GETTING STARTED WITH CREATIVE CODING

Planning to pick up Creative Coding on your own? In the following section, you'll find a few ideas from me that will hopefully help you kickstart an exciting journey ahead.

CHOOSING THE RIGHT LANGUAGE

First of all, you'll need to choose a language. Personally, I'm partial to Processing as I teach it, and I'm convinced that it is a great language to start with! Many beginners are afraid that they might make the wrong choice at the beginning, and this feeling is greatly intensified by the oversupply of options, which can lead to so-called decision fatigue.

However, at this point, it is important for me to emphasise that the choice of programming language is not as significant at the beginning than you might think.

There are actually criteria that can be used to assess the suitability of a programming language for beginners. Stig Møller Hansen, a friend of mine who has written a doctoral thesis on teaching Creative Coding in graphic design, shares:

"…it can be argued that effective tools (programming languages) must make it easy for novices to get started (low threshold), make it possible for experts to make sophisticated projects (high ceiling), and support and suggest a wide range of explorations (wide walls)."[20]

In the above, Stig is referring to Mitchel Resnick, a famous computer scientist from the MIT Media Lab. Additionally, he also posits that Processing fulfils all the necessary criteria and is therefore a good choice.

20 Stig Møller Hansen: Public Class Graphic_Design Implements Code {//Yes, But How?}: An Investigation towards Bespoke Creative Coding Programming Courses in Graphic Design Education, Aarhus 2019 (p. 31)

It has been a few years since Stig published his illuminating work and while I would put p5.js on a similar level to Processing and argue that those who would rather explore the creative possibilities of web technologies should also take a close look at p5.js. Today, Processing and p5.js are extremely similar in almost all respects. If you can write Processing code, you can write p5.js code, and vice versa.

Keep in mind that, in the long run, it really does not matter which programming language you choose to start with, as nearly every language consists of the same fundamental building blocks. Many new learners worry about making the wrong decision, but there is no need for concern. The language you begin with will teach you principles that apply across all programming languages – there is no lock-in effect.

Processing is an excellent choice for creatives, particularly those who are interested in Creative Coding within the context of visual design. Its ease of exporting image files and videos, especially when compared to p5.js, makes it particularly user-friendly. Ultimately, Processing is fully optimised to meet the needs of artists and designers.

READY TO START?

Learning to code can turn out to be one of those pursuits that are relatively difficult to begin with – much like playing the piano or writing good essays. It simply takes time for you to acquire solid skills. I believe that the best things in life often require effort and challenge us. In the early stages, the code in your sketches—e.g., the small programmes you write with using Processing—may seem quite abstract and illogical. However, the longer you keep experimenting, the clearer the picture becomes – and you will start to recognise patterns. Eventually, there comes a special moment in the learning process when everything begins to make sense relatively quickly. I often like to compare the first weeks and months in the learning process of Creative Coding to climbing a wall. Once you reach the top, you suddenly see a vast landscape with new possibilities stretched before you. With a bit of perseverance, you will soon be able to create interesting and expressive little sketches.

This "climbing the wall" analogy can be broken down into a scientific formula, which Stig Møller Hansen articulates very clearly in his previously-mentioned doctoral thesis. He points out that learning to programme is a so-called threshold concept for graphic designers. This means that, although it may be difficult at first, it ultimately produces a fundamentally new perspective on the interrelationship between design and programming[21]. Anticipating this moment and patiently waiting for it can serve as powerful motivation.

21 Stig Møller Hansen: public class Graphic_Design implements Code {//Yes, but how?}: an investigation towards bespoke Creative Coding programming courses in graphic design education, Aarhus 2019, p. 29

UNDERSTANDING THE FOUR PILLARS

The moment described in the previous section, when you metaphorically climb the wall, is closely tied to recognising an elementary pattern. At a certain point, you will be able to discern which parts of your code actually originate from Processing (or call functions from Processing, to be precise), and which parts of your code are purely Java (or JavaScript, in the case of p5.js). You may also notice that the main pillars of a Processing application are functions, conditional statements, loops, and variables. Mastering these four basic elements means that you have essentially conquered the hardest part.

Loops

Of all four pillars, this one is perhaps the most fascinating and offers the biggest "aha" moment. Put simply, a for-loop is an instruction in a computer programme to execute a specific block of code multiple times. A computer has superpowers and can execute certain sections repeatedly at the same time. For that, you need the for-loop. In Creative Coding, you will often use the for-loop to distribute elements – linearly, circularly or in a grid format[22].

```
for (int i = 0; i < 100; i++) {
// do something
}
```

22 Check out www.timrodenbroeker.de/coures/for to learn more

Conditional Statements

A conditional statement is a construct that controls specific lines of code based on whether a specified condition is true or false. Think of a traffic light: If it is green, you drive; if it is red, you wait.

```
if (trafficLight == "green") {
println("go!");
}
```

Functions

Functions are a crucial part of programming and are designed to perform a specific task. They take input parameters, carry out operations on that input, and then provide an output. Functions help programmers break down complex programmes into smaller, more manageable parts, making the code easier to read, debug, and maintain.

In fact, they work a bit like a recipe:

```
cookASoup("onions","potatoes","salt","pepper");
```

Variables

A variable is a small piece of information that can be reused and modified. Imagine wanting to use a particular colour in your sketch. Wouldn't it be incredibly time-consuming to repeat the colour value at every place where it is needed? The principle of variables comes into play here, allowing you to define a colour once and easily change it if necessary. The colour value is then automatically applied wherever it is needed.

There are various variable types for almost every kind of information: an int is a whole number, a float is a decimal number, a string is a piece of text, a char is a character or a symbol, and a color is a colour value – among others.

```
int age = 40;
```

SHORTCUTS ARE NOT YOUR FRIEND!

This may hurt a little, I know – but it is very important that you understand. You are surrounded by temptations: ChatGPT is just a click away and you might think it can handle all your coding tasks. While it is true that Chat GPT and other AI systems are pretty proficient at coding, think twice below relying on them and don't get trapped!

If you truly want to learn Creative Coding and work creatively with technology, the best approach is still to DIY: write the code yourself. Only then will you achieve the goal of seeing the bigger picture. In other words, you cannot climb the wall with artificial intelligence!

CONNECT WITH A COMMUNITY

Last but not least, make sure you connect with other human beings who are on the same journey – nothing is more motivating and empowering. There are plenty of meetups and events around the topic in many cities around the world. If face-to-face interactions are not your thing, you can join an online community where people will be just as eager to help you with any questions you may have.

I speak from my own experience here, as I run such a community – and you are more than welcome to visit the timrodenbroeker.de community to learn more!

MAY THE SOURCE BE WITH YOU

These are just a few of the many tips I could share with you. I hope I was able to ignite a spark of courage and curiosity that inspires you to embark on your own journey of learning to code. For me, Creative Coding remains an incredible adventure, and I am profoundly grateful to have discovered this world that fuels my creative work.

In my quest to share this passion to others, I developed an online learning platform dedicated to Creative Coding for designers over many years. It consists of 18 online courses packed with hundreds of engaging video lessons. Just as the fields of design and technology continue to evolve, the platform is constantly growing – with new content being added regularly.

Whether you are starting from scratch or looking to deepen your skills, I invite you to explore the courses for a step-by-step guide through the exciting realms of Creative Coding – and look forward to having you join us!

PRINCIPLES FOR CODING DESIGNERS

VERSION 0.1

Designers and coders carry a great responsibility today, because the products they develop are often used by millions of people. This is a set of principles for coding designers, which primarily serves to consider the wider implications and responsibilities of code as a tool for building software. To broaden the context, I include coded visual identities in the concept of "software".

1 EVERYTHING IS A SYSTEM

As designers who code, we don't simply create end products – we design the underlying systems from which those products emerge. This systems-oriented perspective allows us to explore design more deeply, gaining a bird's-eye view that helps us see the bigger picture.

2 WE MASTER THE BASICS

Success in coding begins with understanding that all programming languages share core principles. Mastering these principles enables us to leverage specific frameworks and libraries effectively. In Creative Coding, Dr Martin and I use tools developed and maintained by the Processing Foundation, such as:

- Processing for rendering images and animations, allowing for rich visual experiences
- p5.js for building web-based applications that engage users interactively

We complement these frameworks by learning the core languages of the web: HTML, JavaScript, and CSS. This foundational knowledge allows us to embed applications seamlessly and create intuitive interfaces for user interaction.

3 WE KEEP IT RADICALLY SMALL

Low complexity is not only beautiful; it is essential for resilience. The fewer components a system has, the more maintainable and durable it becomes. We design custom systems that are simple enough for a single person to fully understand and manage.

4 WE FULLY EMBRACE OPEN SOURCE

We critically question the use of proprietary software. Instead of relying on feature-bloated, expensive tools, we embrace Free and Open Source Software (FOSS) and hardware. If there is an acceptable free alternative, we choose it – even if it requires extra effort. That way, we also shield ourselves from the ideology of frictionless design and the temptations of no-code solutions, which limit our creativity.

5 WE EMBRACE LIMITATIONS

"It is boundaries that unleash our potential", as Kate Raworth once said. We perceive boundaries as beautiful and regard them as features and benefits. The challenges they present encourage growth and strengthen our communities through collaboration and collective problem-solving.

6 WE EMBRACE IMPERFECTION

We celebrate the quirks that arise from our principles and constraints, drawing inspiration from the Japanese philosophy of Wabi Sabi. These imperfections are not flaws; rather, they become integral to the identity of our products, adding character and uniqueness.

7 WE WRITE TO ENSURE OUR WORK IS UNDERSTOOD

Writing is an essential tool for coding designers. It ensures that our work is comprehensible, especially when collaborating with others. Clear documentation bridges gaps in understanding and fosters mutual comprehension among team members to enable smoother workflows.

8 WE TAKE RESPONSIBILITY

Coded design systems often carry implicit values, such as transparency, sustainability, and ecological responsibility. However, they can also be exploited for purposes like greenwashing. As coding designers, we continuously question the incentives behind our projects to ensure they align with our values. We uphold ethical standards and reject work that conflicts with our principles and beliefs.

9 WE ARE A COMMUNITY

Coding designers thrive through collaboration. While traditional design is often seen as an individual pursuit, coding relies heavily on sharing and collective problem-solving. We share our expertise/knowledge, build networks, and draw strength from our interconnected community to foster an environment of mutual support and innovation.

Please note that this is a draft proposal that is open for discussion. I welcome your feedback and ideas via email at feedback@timrodenbroeker.de. Thank you for engaging in this important conversation!

PP 052-053

Vilnius TechFusion Brand Identity
Creative Coding: Mindaugas Dudėnas

PP 054-057

Cohere
Special Credits: Myungsik Jang, Yurii Khomovskyi, Angelica Yiacoupis, Daniel Kozma, Elif Gurbuz, Fernanda Ruiz, Lou Hisbergue, Amy Joycey, João Miranda, Zuleika Sedgley, Harry Boyd, Adam Heslop, Arnaud Le Roux, Fabio Catapano, Jake Greenwood, Julius Steinhauser, Mat Hill, Matthew Curtis, NaN, Zosia Swidlicka

PP 058-059

Artery
Creative Coding: Mindaugas Dudėnas
CGI: Rokas Mežetis
Photography: Kernius Pauliukonis

PP 060-061

Inion Brand Identity
Creative Coding: Mindaugas Dudėnas

PP 062-065

Mo Museum Brand Identity
Creative Coding: Mindaugas Dudėnas
Photography: Audrius Solominas, Robertas Daškevičius

PP 072-075

Isomorphic Labs
Special Credits: Jamie Rickett, Myungsik Jang, Yurii Khomovskyi, Michael Mason, Variable.io

PP 076-077

Finiam
Illustration: Rita Laranja

PP 082-085

Lobe
Design & Creative Coding: FAY
Interior Photography: Asterios Moutsokapas

PP 086-087

Komma
Collaboration: Komma

PP 094-097

Inform Architecture
Creative Coding: Yun Kuo

PP 098-099

OneFootball
Research Partner: CrowdDNA
Interaction Agency: Artificial Rome

PP 102-103

DeNites
Collaboration: Filipa G. Ribeiro

PP 106-109

Intrinsic
Special Credits: Katee Hui, Felix Faire

PP 110-111

Motion Visual Identity for Studio VEH
Concept, Creative Direction: Studio VEH

PP 112-113

MovingLayers
Brand Strategy, Identity Design: Studio VEH

PP 116-117

Enjoei
Type: Blackletra
Creative Direction: Tátil

PP 136-139

OSESP - Orquestra Sinfônica de São Paulo
Creative Direction: Lais Ikoma, Ralph Mayer
Research: Stella Bonici
Motion Design: Ronaldo Arthur Vidal, Rônatan Bica
Creative Coding: Ariel Tonglet
Case Design: Lais Ikoma, Ralph Mayer, Satsuki Arakaki
Brand Strategy: ACE

PP 144-145

OVO Energy Forecast
Commissioned by: Saatchi & Saatchi

PP 148-151

Freeform
Type Foundry: Monotype
Photography: Mari Juliano

PP 158-159

Vietnam Festival of Creativity & Design 2023
Organisers: RMIT University Vietnam, UNESCO, VICAS
Media Partner: Hanoi Grapevine
Installation Back-end Developer: CODY
Installation Support: VFCD Team, Hanoi Grapevine
Event Photography: VFCD Team

PP 164-165

Ubisoft+
Collaboration: Mata
Type: Monotype

PP 166-167

HARD Imagination
Collaboration: Dark Matter Labs, Hard Art

PP 168-169

I know…
General idea: Bill T. Jones
Digital Creation: Ruben van Leer
Web Design: Martijn de Heer
Web Development: Amir Houieh
Sound Design: Henry Vega

PP 174-177

Paris Electronic Week 2023
Photography : Lucas Matichard

PP 186-187

TBWA Type System
Type: Plau Design
Creative Direction: TBWA

PP 188-189

b•••coming
Web-Interactive Programming: Jeonghyo Lee

PP 190-193

Digital Culture Index
Data Index: Synthesis Consulting Group
Web Design: Neat Digital

PP 212-215

AMBIENT KYOTO
Graphic Design: Takuto Okamoto
Motion Design: Toshiki Okamoto

PP 216-217

Cumulus Conference
Social Media Design: Ekaterina Altukhova
Case Study Art Direction: Stefan Lashko
Case Study Design: Katya Molchanova

PP 222-223

Minding the Digital
Collaboration: Ben West

PP 224-227

FEEEEL MACAU 2023 Generative Art
Technical Support: TREX INFORMATION TECHNOLOGY LIMITED
Photography: Bob Wong, Anthony Chong

PP 230-231

LAB#01: Medios Sintientes
Creative Coding, Generative Design: Federico Guardabrazo

PP 232-233

Yango Tech
Creative Direction: Alexander Zagorsky
Identity Design: Alexander Zagorsky, Vladimir Auev
Photography: Yana Davidova

PP 242-243

Oracle
Project Lead TU Delft: Vincent Cellucci

PP 246-249

Tokyo Dome City
Master Design Architecture: Hoshino Architects
System Development: aircord
Type Design: Toshi Omagari
Motion Designer: Hironori Sugie
Sound Design: Yosi Horikawa
Sound Design (Signage): Marihiko Hara

PP 254-256

Connections Enabling Change
3D: CATK
Illustration: Camilo Huinca
Photography: Anne Valeur
Mathematician: Øystein Andersson Klemetsdal
Development: Try Apt, Knowit

&Form PP 246-249

&Form is a visual communication design studio dedicated to creating timeless, high-quality design solutions. Their branding approach ensures seamless translations across digital, print, and spatial forms, maintaining beauty and consistency. They also run Form, a non-profit initiative exploring design's impact and creative philosophies, sharing insights to inspire and shape the future of design.

Accept & Proceed PP 166-167, 178-179

Accept & Proceed partners with visionaries, people who hunger for radical ideas, and those don't flinch at solving world problems. They work with brands on beauty and change, and design with both analytics and aesthetics in mind. They also actively embed themselves into culture and don't wait to create.

Adam Ho, I.S.P. PP 090-093, 160-161

Adam Ho, I.S.P. is the independent studio of Queens-based designer Adam Ho. His practice explores fluid, generative brand identities, blending graphic design with intuitive interaction design. With a focus on adaptability and experimentation, he crafts dynamic visual systems that evolve, pushing the boundaries of branding and digital experiences.

Afterimage PP 110-113, 216-217, 232-233

Afterimage is a Berlin-based studio specialising in creative technology and computational design. Using generative methods and custom tools, it enhances human creativity and modernises design processes. Founded by graphic designer and creative technologist Anatoly Grashchenko, the studio collaborates with in-house teams while Grashchenko also teaches creative coding, advocating for its integration into contemporary design.

André Burnier PP 116-117, 186-187

André Burnier is a Brazilian graphic designer and creative coder with over 15 years' experience. Based in São Paulo, he holds a Master's in Graphic Design from AKV | St. Joost (2016). His work explores generative design, algorithmic art, and custom tools, blending programming with visual communication to push contemporary design's boundaries.

Andstudio PP 190-193

Andstudio is a passionate collective that redefines design, blending strategy, aesthetics, and functionality to create business-aligned solutions. From revitalising legacy brands to shaping identities for space tech startups, they embrace new challenges, pushing the boundaries of brand and digital innovation.

ANTI INC PP 254-256

ANTI is a creative studio driven by storytelling, crafting brands, adverts, digital experiences, and content for TV and podcasts. Their name reflects their philosophy — A New Type of Interference — challenging conventions and redefining narratives. Partnering with visionary clients, they uncover unique stories and present them in bold, unexpected ways, creating a distinct competitive advantage.

Behalf Studio PP 158-159

Behalf is a design studio offering creative solutions across branding, graphic, and digital design. Their work is concept-driven, research-led, and fuelled by intuition and experimentation. With no set formula for innovation, each project poses unique questions. Through collaboration and honest partnerships, they craft engaging brands, refine publications, and create designs that resonate with audiences.

COLLINS PP 148-151, 250-253

COLLINS is an independent strategy, design and communications company that combines creativity, craft and technology into ideas and experiences that improve people's lives. By putting insight and imagination at the centre of everything they do, COLLINS makes brands that can't be ignored. COLLINS accelerates growth and builds better futures at scale.

Cotton Design PP 066-071, 154-157, 234-237

Cotton, founded in 2023, is a creative agency known for integrating design, technology, and data. Led by Talia Cotton, a designer, coder, and former Pentagram leader, the agency pioneers algorithmic design as a core creative process. Recognised by Fast Company and D&AD, Talia speaks globally on coding's role in expanding design possibilities.

DesignStudio PP 098-099, 164-165

DesignStudio is a global design agency that shapes brands and experiences through radical collaboration. With studios in London, New York, and Sydney, its 100-strong team partners with organisations worldwide to define ambitions, build brands, and drive change. Clients include Airbnb, Premier League, Panasonic, British Airways, Logitech, AT&T, and Riot Games.

DIA PP 118-135

DIA is a branding and graphic design studio specialising in kinetic identities and typographic systems. Based in New York and Chamonix, the studio redefines identity design by making motion a core element. Their approach integrates generative tools and autonomous design systems, ensuring internal teams can easily create, adapt, and manage dynamic branding while maintaining creative consistency.

DIGRAPH PP 184-185

DIGRAPH is a creative studio that merges the analytical precision of computational design with the artistry of craftsmanship. As digital expression evolves, they celebrate the unique beauty of both digital and physical forms. By bridging these often polarised approaches, they strive to craft captivating experiences that enrich our understanding and appreciation of creativity in all its manifestations.

Dimitris Lelakis (Lelism),
Maria Tsilomitrou (Studio Chill) PP 094-097

Dimitris Lelakis (Lelism) and Maria Tsilomitrou (Studio Chill) are cross-disciplinary designers merging visual communication, architecture, and motion. Dimitris crafts structured narratives, while Maria builds vibrant, memory-infused visual worlds. Their collaborative, research-driven practice explores type and form, seamlessly blending analogue and digital mediums to create immersive, dynamic visual scenarios.

Diplomatie Studio PP 172-177

Founded in 2019, Diplomatie Studio blends visual identity design with experimental approaches across print and digital media. Embracing controlled errors and dissonance, the studio explores rhythm, turbulence, and frequencies through a multidimensional creative process. By merging image, technology, and technique, they push the boundaries of visual communication through continuous experimentation.

FAY PP 082-085

FAY is a graphic design and creative technology studio crafting future-forward brands and interactive experiences. Blending design with emerging technology, they create dynamic identities, immersive installations, and generative tools. Their innovative approach ensures brands evolve seamlessly, while close client collaboration fosters bold, experimental solutions that redefine consumer engagement in a rapidly changing world.

FIELD.IO PP 104-105, 144-145, 162-163

FIELD.IO is a global creative, design, and innovation studio that fuels imagination and moves minds. Blending creativity and technology, they craft future-focused brand solutions, immersive experiences, and storytelling. Collaborating with top brands and cultural institutions, they unite diverse talent to create multi-sensory designs. Founded in 2009, FIELD.IO operates from London, Berlin, and across Europe.

formless twins PP 188-189

formless twins is a graphic design duo, Sangah Shin and Jaejin Ee, whose practice moves fluidly between Seoul, New York, and Amsterdam. Their name embodies a philosophy of contradiction and adaptability. Exploring marginalised aesthetics - vernacular design, kitsch, and cuteness - they challenge creative hierarchies with irony and playfulness, fostering unexpected connections and new cultural dialogues.

Gadel Mukhametshin PP 114-115

Gadel Mukhametshin is an Art Director and Graphic Designer based in Almaty. Holding a Bachelor's in Graphic Design from Kazan State University of Architecture and Engineering, he has over seven years of experience and 60+ completed projects. He believes great design evokes emotion, striving to understand users' needs and reflect them in his work.

Hajime Tsunoda PP 218-221

Hajime Tsunoda is a Tokyo-based designer who works across graphic, motion, and audiovisual design, alongside experimental software engineering. By synchronising movement with sound and transforming static graphics into interactive experiences, he explores new modes of expression that emerge from the intersection of graphic design and digital interfaces.

KAUKAU PP 170-171, 240-241

KAUKAU is an interdisciplinary design community comprising designers, artists, writers, programmers, and engineers. They specialise in visual solutions, including art direction, brand visuals, publications, photography, installations, and interface design. Driven by innovative mediums, they use cutting-edge technologies and diverse visual languages to build connections through unique visual thinking.

Koln Studio PP 230-231

Koln Studio is a Madrid-based graphic design studio specialising in branding, visual campaigns, editorial design, and creative direction. It combines strategy and design to craft impactful identities for organisations. The studio collaborates with international creatives and teaches a Master's programme at IED Madrid. Focused on clarity and cultural relevance, Koln Studio bridges aesthetics and functionality across its projects.

Lava PP 196-211

Lava is an Amsterdam-based branding and design studio that believes brands should be alive to adapt and engage with the future. They create living identities and bespoke tools by merging strategy, design, and technology. Focused on people, the studio values direct communication and long-term relationships, working collaboratively to future-proof brands in a rapidly changing world.

LEÓN ROMERO PP 180-181

LEÓN ROMERO is a Barcelona-based studio founded by Jorge León and Mikel Romero. They emphasize collaboration to create bold, functional solutions in visual identity and graphic design. Alongside client projects, they host workshops that celebrate the diversity of visual expression, engaging communities in creative exploration.

LOKSOPHY DESIGN PP 224-227

LOKSOPHY DESIGN is a creative studio based in Macau with a global perspective. They deliver precise, strategic design solutions for both commercial and cultural sectors, driven by a commitment to generating business value.

Mike van der Sanden PP 086-087, 182-183, 228-229

Mike van der Sanden is a multidisciplinary designer fascinated by the tension between control and chaos. Using creative coding, he explores the boundaries of visual comfort, finding beauty in friction. His work blends structure with disruption, creating a dynamic dialogue where the unexpected and intentional coexist harmoniously.

Onda Studio PP 076-079, 102-103

Onda Studio transforms ideas into meaningful brand experiences by blending strategy, creativity, and functionality. Focused on purpose-driven narratives, the studio aims to inspire growth, collaboration, and positive impact through design.

Patrik Hübner
PP 010-032, 080-081, 100-101, 140-143, 244-245

Patrik Hübner, a programming designer and creative director, has worked at the intersection of design and technology for over 15 years. Since discovering generative design in 2014, he has integrated data-driven storytelling into branding systems globally. As a consultant, he collaborates with brands, agencies, and institutions while also lecturing and leading workshops on generative design.

Pentagram Design PP 054-057, 072-075, 106-109

Brothers Luke Powell and Jody Hudson-Powell aredesigners from Somerset, England. Founding Hudson-Powell, they created music videos for PJ Harvey and Gorillaz before joining Pentagram as partners. Their practice merges design and technology, inventing systems that bring conceptual depth to commercial and cultural projects for unique, technically driven, and playful visual identities.

Polar, Ltda. PP 136-139

Polar is a studio that designs for today's needs while anticipating tomorrow's perspectives. Specialising in visual identity, packaging, digital, typography, animation, and editorial projects, it offers diverse solutions across virtual, print, spatial, and audiovisual media. The studio brings together professionals from various cultural backgrounds, working with partners, brands, and companies to create purposeful collaborations.

RNDR PP 168-169, 242-243

RNDR is a design studio focused on interactive media, creating 'tools' that evolve through their use. They develop processes, visualisations, code, and interactions, producing diverse outcomes from installations to generative identities and real-time prints. Motivated by how technology transforms society, they also lead OPENRNDR, an award-winning open-source framework for creative coding.

Seri Tanaka PP 212-215

Seri Tanaka is a Tokyo-based art director and graphic designer. Balancing universality with flexibility, she works on corporate identities, visual identities, and art direction across art, music, and publishing. Her notable projects include branding for Sake Senkin, Komi Art Museum, and AMBIENT KYOTO. Her work has also been recognised with the JAGDA New Designer Award as well as at Cannes and NY ADC.

Skala Design PP 152-153

Skala is a Zurich based graphic design and branding studio that creates distinctive work for institutions, brands and people within culture, education and business. Clear visual gestures and systematic typography, applied into multilayered means of expression, form the foundation of their practice.

Sons & Daughters ID PP 052-053, 058-065

Sons & Daughters ID is a branding agency that combines strategy, design, and technology to create distinctive and impactful brand identities.

Studio Dumbar/DEPT® PP 034-051

Studio Dumbar/DEPT® is an international agency with Dutch roots, specialising in visual branding and motion. Known for attracting global talent, its diverse portfolio spans industries, from business and government to culture and non-profits. Notable projects include Dutch Railways' identity, Adidas Futurenatural, the Van Gogh Museum refresh, and DEMO, the world's largest design-in-motion festival.

Thonik PP 146-147, 194-195, 222-223

Thonik, an Amsterdam-based design collective led by Nikki Gonnissen and Thomas Widdershoven, blends creativity with social and political impact. Committed to a digital-first approach, the studio prioritises moving images as the foundation for campaigns, visual identities, and motion design. Collaborating with long-term partners, it seeks to enhance visual culture while shaping a more meaningful future.

Tim Rodenbröker PP 258-296

Tim Rodenbröker blends his graphic design background with expertise in creative coding, a growing trend among modern creatives. As an educator at institutions like Elisava and ECAL, as well as through his online school, trcc, he champions digital literacy and inspires aspiring coders worldwide. Co-founder of the Coding Systems studio and part of the Design in Motion Festival team, he continues to shape the future of design and technology through his teaching, community-building, and collaborations with notable clients like The New York Times and IBM.

W.H.Y. Brand Consultancy PP 238-239

William is the Founder of W.H.Y. Brand Consultancy, based in London with over 15 years of experience in brand design. His diverse portfolio spans digital, print, and environmental design across Europe and Asia, with clients like the UK Parliament, Vodafone, BBC, TED, and LVMH. His award-winning work blends strategic innovation with emotional impact.

ACKNOWLEDGEMENTS

We would like to thank all the designers, studios, and companies who were involved in the production of this book for their significant contribution to its compilation. We would also like to express our gratitude to all the producers involved for their invaluable opinions and assistance, as well as the professionals in the creative industry who were generous with their insights and feedback throughout the entire production process. Last but not least, to those who made specific input behind the scenes but were not credited in this book, we acknowledge and appreciate all your effort and continuous support.

FUTURE EDITIONS

If you wish to participate in viction:ary's future projects and publications, please send your website or portfolio to we@victionary.com